"I like the conversational, friendly tone. It makes the material seem accessible to the reader. It's as if the author is seated next to the reader at the mixing console and is pointing out things to watch for."

– Bruce Bartlett, audio engineer and author of
Practical Recording Techniques

"I really like Brad's heart for the local church. I think he approaches the subject in a genuine and honest manner that is encouraging."

– Mike Sessler, ChurchTech Arts

"I'm very excited about having this book available for my church, and for churches where I assist in ministry."

– David Scott, Worship Leader and Associate director
of Georgia Festival Chorus

"What a great book! Brad has taken his years of audio/visual training and personal experience and produced an excellent resource for every Worship Leader and every Audio Visual Tech. From the most basic sound, lighting and video systems to fairly complex systems, Brad has put together an encyclopedia of knowledge that builds on the basics to provide an easy transition to larger and more sophisticated systems. Not only does he address the 'how to,' but the 'why we should and why we should not's' associated with this important area of our ministry. Brad has a heart for excellence in Worship that resounds throughout the book. Whether you are a beginner or a seasoned veteran, I heartily recommend this book to you. I believe that you, like I, will count it one of your most valuable tools in ministry."

– Dennis J. Brown, Associate Pastor Worship Arts,
First Baptist Church

"Finally! Thank you, Brad Herring and Focal Press, for bringing us a terrific overview of Technical Production for Houses of Worship. Your experience, skill, and artistry are evident throughout. I especially appreciate your attitude of humility and step-by-step suggestions for dealing with 'choir complaints.' This immediately is required reading for my production volunteers."

– John Weygandt, Scenic and Lighting Designer,
Willow Creek Community Church

Sound, Lighting and Video: A Resource for Worship

Brad Herring

ELSEVIER

AMSTERDAM • BOSTON • HEIDELBERG • LONDON
NEW YORK • OXFORD • PARIS • SAN DIEGO
SAN FRANCISCO • SINGAPORE • SYDNEY • TOKYO

Focal Press is an imprint of Elsevier

Focal
Press

Focal Press is an imprint of Elsevier
30 Corporate Drive, Suite 400, Burlington, MA 01803, USA
Linacre House, Jordan Hill, Oxford OX2 8DP, UK

Library of Congress Cataloging-in-Publication Data
Application submitted

British Library Cataloguing-in-Publication Data
A catalogue record for this book is available from the British Library.

ISBN: 978-0-240-81108-6

For information on all Focal Press publications
visit our website at www.elsevierdirect.com

09 10 11 12   5 4 3 2 1

Transferred to Digital Print 2011
Printed and bound in the United Kingdom

Working together to grow
libraries in developing countries

www.elsevier.com | www.bookaid.org | www.sabre.org

ELSEVIER   BOOK AID   Sabre Foundation
            International

Contents

PART 1 • Sound Systems for Worship

PART 2 • Lighting Systems for Worship

PART 3 • Video Systems for Worship

CONTENTS

CONCLUSION

APPENDIXES

FROM THE HEART OF BRAD

When I first undertook this project, it was with some in trepidation. There is simply so much material to cover, it seemed like too much information to discuss in one book. Perhaps this is why to date, such a comprehensive book has not been written.

After some research and many outlines and drafts we came up with the layout of this book. We all believe this will be a tremendous help to ministries world-wide. The introduction section is critical for vision casting and overall analysis of media systems in the Worship environment. The rest of the book places emphasis on systems and interconnections with helpful advice on using these systems.

There are many people who have contributed years of knowledge, and timeless help to make sure this book is accurate and helpful. Without them, this project would not be nearly as comprehensive as it has become.

I'd like to especially thank David Scott, Rob Dillard, Mike Meads, John Curtis, Mike Sessler, David Hepburn, Osabuohien P. Amienyi and Bruce Bartlett for their technical expertise and of course, my parents and Becky (my loving and supportive wife) – without your support and patience this would have been impossible.

God is doing incredible things and Media and Creative Arts Ministries are playing a huge role! Churches are able to connect with people in ways never before possible. With the emergence of video, dramatic arts, contemporary worship, and new delivery formats we are able to reach more people and speak to them more specifically than ever before.

These are exciting times! My one piece of advice to any church reading this book – don't simply change because the church down the street or across town is changing – do what God has called you to do – and do it with fervor. There is a specific thing that God has called you and your ministry to do – make sure you know what that is and pursue it full force. If everyone went to contemporary or blended worship, who would be relevant to the people who desperately desire traditional worship? What would become of those people? Likewise, if everyone catered to the 30/40 year olds, who would be there for the young singles? We all have our spot in ministry that God has called us to! Sometimes it's an entire church calling, other times it's a departmental calling – regardless God has a calling on YOUR life. Seek it out and go full speed ahead!

Foreword

In every instance, media and creative arts can help you communicate to the masses – the trick is learning how to apply it appropriately so that the message is received and the teaching reinforced in a way that makes it easy for the people to apply it.

Don't simply change because the church down the street or across town is changing – do what God has called you to do – and do it with fervor.

So, pray. Then pray some more. And when you get done with that – pray again. Make SURE you hear from God and know the direction He has for you and your ministry. Love your people – both your flock, the volunteers and paid staff that put in countless hours preparing for and supporting services.

I believe if we look at Scripture and analyze the life of Christ we will quickly see that He was about people. He spent almost all of His time cultivating the one on one relationship. I believe if Jesus were to come today instead of 2000+ years ago He would not embrace media, but instead He would choose 12 people. What we do – it's ultimately about loving people and we need to be careful to not lose sight of that.

In fairness, I do believe that those 12 people and likewise those that they raise up would most definitely use media and every other tool available to them to further the Gospel and reach people with the life changing message of Jesus! That being said, I encourage you to do the same! Whatever it takes – reach the lost, disciple the believer, and raise up leaders. I firmly believe that Media and Creative Arts Ministry can assist you in doing this. I believe this book will prove to be a vital resource that will help cast vision and provide quick reference for years to come.

God bless. Be strong. Think outside of the box. Reach a lost and dieing world.

Special Acknowledgments & Thanks

The help of the following people and companies truly made this book possible.
Thank you!

Becky Herring (for all of your tireless proof-readings and image finding!)
Barbizon Atlanta
Technical Elements
Dave Wagner
Josh Leblanc
Michael Ramps
Winfrey Shields
John Curtis
William Meads
Bill Hawes
John MacCullen
Mike Sessler
David Scott
Rob Dillard
David Hepburn
Osabuohien P. Amienyi
Bruce Bartlett

The entire team at Focal Press, and especially
Cara Anderson
Danielle Monroe
Kara Race-Moore

I could not have done this without you all.

A HISTORY OF MEDIA AND MEDIA DELIVERY

To understand how the world of audio/visual affects our worship today, I believe we need to first look at the history of media and the delivery process of both Worship and the Gospel message.

Many people will make the argument that the church does not need sound, lighting, video systems and drama. They will argue this principle on many grounds. But I believe we can look back in history and learn how worship (including Biblical teaching practices) have evolved and see clearly how media is a key component for the church of today.

Although this book is not about drama, it is interesting to note that drama has been vastly used as a vehicle for religious expression – people were looking for ways to communicate the Gospel truth and began to caravan and put on stage shows. This concept was not different than many of our churches today – they wanted to be relevant to the people of their generation. They wanted to speak to them in ways that communicated clearly God's love, and what better way to do that than drama? So, when you look at the purist form of the work, we see it being something that glorified God.

This takes us back to our primary discussion – Media in Worship.

In the days of Jesus, Paul, John, and the other Biblical heroes that we read and study, they were blessed with a world of architecture that assisted in the reproduction of the human voice. As you might recall from your history books, electrical power had not yet been discovered and obviously, loudspeaker technology was centuries away. A solution must be found – and that solution was to build places of theater and worship that allowed the voice to be heard very clearly over long distances.

When Jesus taught, scholars believe he often found natural places that easily amplified the voice making it possible for him to teach to the multitudes.

Today, however, we live in a very different world. Today we have technology that reproduces the human voice and projects it to literally tens of thousands of people at once. So architects and many church builders find themselves more worried about the aesthetic component of construction versus the acoustic qualities and function of the worship center.

While this makes for a visually appealing room, it creates many challenges for sound systems, lighting systems, and video systems. It also destroys the concept of "Jesus didn't use things like this" – He didn't have to, we however, are often forced to.

The modern day House of Worship is typically a rectangle or fan design. All too often, rectangular designs come with short ceilings. This is not ideal for sound, video, or lighting. Likewise, fan shaped Worship areas offer challenges with sight lines, consistent seat to seat audio coverage, and in facilities without catwalks – properly lighting the alter or stage area.

The History of Early A/V Systems

Early Audio/Visual systems incorporated basic flood lighting or in some cases track lighting. Sound systems usually consisted of column speakers that eventually moved to center cluster arrays. Often, these arrays were stadium horns with mid-range cabinets added to the mix. The idea was localization of the spoken word. (By localization I mean the ability for the ear to ascertain where the source of the sound is coming from). It made sense as the majority of the service was spoken and much of the music was acoustic in nature. Video systems were rarely used, and if they were used it was normally more of a portable system utilizing PowerPoint™ at best.

As music becomes more of the forefront in worship, we see a trend towards left/right stereo systems. Likewise, lighting systems upgrade to more theatrical styles (but still usually a basic PAR CAN or similar point and shoot light sources). Video systems become more popular, but still primarily rely on PowerPoint™.

Quickly it was realized that the left/right speaker system had its drawbacks. While it sounded pretty good for music, it lost its localization for voice. It was also difficult to achieve consistent coverage patterns in true stereo throughout the auditorium.

The recognition of these problems led to the creation of a Left/Center/Right system design. With this system, the voice was typically channeled in the center cluster while musical instruments were placed in the stereo feed. This was the best of both worlds, but required a lot of equipment and additional training on mixing techniques.

As speaker technology evolved, we see line array technology emerge on the worship scene. While not applicable for every situation, line-array systems present the ability to evenly cover an auditorium while reproducing an excellent sound. We still see line-arrays combined with center clusters (to take into consideration localization issues), but often the arrays are closer together than a left/right system, thus minimizing the localization problem. We also see center line-arrays as well.

The Modern Day House of Worship

Today, lighting systems are very theatrical based in many modern Houses of Worship. It's not uncommon to see moving lights as well as ellipsoidal instruments and PAR Cans. Video systems are quickly becoming hi-definition with wide-format 16:9 screens, IMAG (Image Magnification) is common, and dynamic video content is quickly becoming more common. Houses of Worship are moving from PowerPoint™ to dynamic worship presentation software like Easy Worship, Media Shout, Sunday Plus, and Pro-Presenter. The modern day church is utilizing systems that rival any theater you would visit. The result is a dynamic presentation of the Gospel that captures the attention of the congregant and speaks to them in a relevant media savvy method.

Lets review our earlier comment and stated belief that if Jesus came today that He would still choose 12 people. Think about how Jesus taught. Can you imagine him on a stage while 30 moving lights swept around Him? Does His teaching method strike you as someone who would have produced fancy video productions? While no one has the definitive answers obviously, I'd like to say that I think not. The Gospel is strong and it stands on it's own.

> The result of modern hi-tech delivery methods is a dynamic presentation of the Gospel that captures the attention of the congregant and speaks to them in a relevant media savvy method.

That's huge.

No video. No fancy sound system or screaming worship concert. Twelve sold out people, and He Himself sold out. Dedicated to God and determined to save a lost and dying world.

Media systems are not a necessity. Regardless of our generation – the Gospel message on it's own is relevant. The truth does proceed from it. God's Word will not return void – that's a promise. However, media systems can strengthen our message, improve retention, and speak to people in ways that traditional communicators just can't.

Now, once again – balance. Like stated earlier, I believe that some of those 12 people would most definitely use media if the timetable of history were today versus 2000+ years ago. But here's the key – everything we do with media must ultimately be PEOPLE oriented. Because that's what this is all about. Reaching people with the saving Gospel message and helping to usher people to the throne of Worship as a corporate body.

> Here's the key – everything we do with media must ultimately be PEOPLE oriented.

We simply must be able to overcome today's construction obstacles and present people with a clear and concise message of Hope and provide them with barrier free environments that encourage un-encumbered worship. That's what media ultimately does in church worship. We must also understand that people today are inundated with media content – it's everywhere we turn. Television, radio, internet, sporting events – we simply can't escape modern media pushes. Almost every young person you look at today has iPod earpieces crammed in their ears or are walking in a daze as their fingers quickly tap out cryptic text messages. Podcasts are the rage and it's virtually impossible to visit a website without a pop-up.

INTRODUCTION

Ask yourself – where is God in all these pushes? It's a fair question. Think about your last few Internet surf sessions. Consider all the pop ups you encountered. How many of them pointed you to the Gospel or offered eternal hope?

Tell me the last time you saw something on Television that grabbed your attention and spoke to you and allowed the Holy Spirit to convict you and grow you? Okay – it does happen some, but again – it's not the norm. As believers – as people with the most amazing news in the world – we poorly use this and all other media outlets to spread our message of hope and salvation. Christian films are by and large terrible. The production values are so low that they come across cheesy and as a result, are often irrelevant to the viewer. The acting is often so terrible that the message is lost because it's so obviously trite. I'm not saying every Christian work is this way that's not the case, but I am saying the vast majority lacks the credibility for a lost audience to stay captured and catch the message.

It's a shame. Such an opportunity just squandered away.

Then there is the argument of the modern House of Worship being a theater that is merely spectacle with no substance. And to an extent, I'd agree that this argument can be true. However, in some instances, there is a proven effectiveness in using high-tech solutions to capture the seeker or the non-believer. As a church we must be careful, if you get people in the building and don't communicate clearly God's love and His plan for their lives, then disciple them in truth, and help develop their personal relationship with Christ – what's the point? If your goal is not to do this, go tour with a rock band and stop wasting the church's resources and time. We should be about bringing people closer to God and developing relationships. Media in worship should be pointed at achieving these goals.

A pastor's primary tool is the Word of God – Scripture itself. A minister of music's primary tool is the score written on paper (or in today's world, a fancy flat-panel display). A youth minister's tool is often activities and being free to be goofy around kids. A small group leader or Sunday School teacher's tool is curriculum. YOUR TOOL IS MEDIA. It's your opportunity to create something that will speak directly into someone's life and change it forever! Or, you could just choose to be a button pusher and barely squeak by every Sunday. The choice is really yours. But isn't it exciting to realize that you – someone who is normally considered a 'behind-the-scenes' person has the opportunity with every meeting, to present something that speaks directly to the people in attendance? What a great concept!

As people who are interested in using media and creative arts in worship we simply MUST BE ABOUT CHANGING LIVES.

Paul asks the question in the book of Romans, "How will people know if they don't hear". Sure, Paul's talking about the role of evangelism and sharing verbally the saving grace of Jesus Christ, but in today's society, a pastor without a sound system or a recording facility or even good video projection is

OFTEN NOT HEARD. This is a serious conundrum. You, as a person passionate about media, or entrusted in the role of media support, are not a button pusher – YOU ARE AN INTEGRAL PART OF WORSHIP.

If you don't understand this, you need to stop right now and reconsider your reason for being involved in media ministry. Because this is key! This is everything. Without you, the Word is not heard, the Word is not seen, the Word is not taken to the masses. Without you, the people don't hear, and that, my friend, is what is all about.

As time continues, acoustically perfect environments become harder and harder to find. Furthermore, we begin to realize that IMAG (Image Magnification) helps larger groups relate to the primary communicator, and ultimately we go full circle to our early beginnings and realize that we can, once again, present the Gospel with dramatic arts. However, now with technologies that didn't exist back then, we can use media to emphasize the message. Media has become integral to worship – obviously not the act of worship itself, but definitely the process and the effectiveness of unobstructed corporate worship and clear concise teaching.

Systems Integration

It's important to think of Sound, Lighting, and Video as three in one. One of the most common mistakes churches make is thinking of sound, video and lighting as three independent systems. Most churches today struggle with the most fundamental success in audio reproduction. Many of these churches want to incorporate video – often they are pressured to do so from many sources. The church becomes so driven to add video, they skip over lighting. A poorly implemented lighting system will often times allow light spillage onto the video screens, thus washing out the image. The end result is a mediocre video projection system that looks bad and combined with a poor audio system, sounds bad as well.

Given the example above, when you think about sound, lighting, and video as one large media system you have one poorly performing media system versus three individual systems operating at various efficiencies.

When you think about this way, it doesn't make any sense to implement one system without properly implementing the others as well.

I firmly believe that audio is the base of your media ministry. I visit and work with a lot of different churches. It never fails – when I attend a service that is well mixed with a good sound system the congregants are involved in worship. The majority of people are participating in singing and responsive readings. Likewise, a poorly mixed system or a poorly designed sound system yields the opposite results – very few people outwardly participating.

A well mixed service on a quality sound system instills confidence in the people. They can clearly hear the worship leader and more easily engage. Likewise, a poor sound system can actually deter ministry growth. I've worked with churches that are seeing steady decline in choir, orchestra, and praise team activity. On the surface, it appears to be a staffing problem – often blamed on the minister of music or the worship pastor. However, many times, the problem is really poor technology. The people simply can't work with the existing system – and remember, these people are not technically savvy – many times they don't know how to communicate with us. They simply grow frustrated and move on to other ministry areas.

I am reminded of an example of this. I was called out to a church once to sort out a problem. The pastor was frustrated because the choir was complaining weekly about the sound quality. They kept saying they couldn't hear. The sound engineer was frustrated because he felt like he was cranking the system and didn't understand how they couldn't hear. I showed up, and sure enough – the people were frustrated. So, I made my way to the sound booth to speak with the engineer. He was clearly on edge. He looked at me and said "Brad, watch this." He proceeded to bring up the stage monitor system without the front of house speakers. From 120 feet away, we were measuring 80 db at the front of house position from ONLY the stage monitors. The sound engineer looked at me and queried, "How can they not hear that?" I had to admit, I was perplexed. I was quickly understanding his frustration.

I made my way back to stage, thinking the whole time, "What is going on here?". As I made my way to the choir I began to pray. As I approached the choir, God laid on my heart a simple question to ask the choir. I looked at the group of singers and asked them "WHAT can you not hear?". Their response (almost in unison) was "EACH OTHER!! We can't hear anything but those speakers – they are too loud!".

I think I heard the sound engineers head hit the sound console as it dropped in ultimate despair! But the lesson here was realizing that all to often, non-technical people don't know how to communicate with technical people. We have to know how to ask the right questions to solve the problem. So, many times, poorly designed media systems can actually deter ministry team growth and in some cases actually decline in participation. We need to be savvy enough to realize this and fix the problem.

Video projection systems are VERY dependent on lighting – both stage lighting and ambient lighting. Without addressing the lighting in your facility it is foolhardy to plunge full speed ahead with video projection. Likewise, dynamic video content is really driven home with good audio. Often, video projects include subject matter like "man on the street interviews" or testimonies. If the sounds system can't handle the task, the video is for naught.

Instead, these three systems should be thought of as one big integrated system. First, sit down and determine your immediate needs as well as your long-term goals and needs. Then design your system to meet these goals.

I recommend starting with your sound system. I believe it is the key to unencumbered worship. Your sound needs to be tight. Spend money on training your media teams. Go to conferences, invest in one-on-one training, and purchase video- and book-based training products. Your investment in training will pay off many times over. Your people will be more confident and less frustrated. They will perform their tasks better and worship will be facilitated.

Next, focus on your lighting and ambient lighting. If your goals include extensive video and creative arts development, you simply have to control ambient light. You have to be able to dim your house lights, and you need at least basic stage lighting control. In a more advanced contemporary service you need moving lights and haze along with more detailed traditional lighting plots.

Finally, once your sound and lighting systems are in place, add the video. Now, you can buy adequate projectors versus wasting money on super high lumen projectors simple to overcome bad lighting. You can also make educated decisions on things like screen gain, rear projection vs. front projection, and other equipment related needs.

If you follow this line of thinking in systems integration you will have a more efficient system that will perform optimally. It's simply good use of ministry dollars.

I can't stress this enough. Media systems should be well thought out as a whole. Most of all – get the basics right. If you continually find yourself with the wrong words on the screen, experiencing feedback, late microphone cues, improperly lit stage areas, unplugged microphones, and other such problems your media ministry will never grow like it should – it will never have the positive effect that you are working so hard to get. Once you get the basics down, and properly integrate systems, you will begin to see lives changed.

Our job as media ministry people is to support those called to preach, teach, and lead in worship. We have a huge roll in ministry. We are the support staff that enable the anointed ones to see their calling to fruition.

PART 1
SOUND

CHAPTER 1

Anatomy of a Sound System

THE HEART OF EACH SOUND SYSTEM IS THE SAME

A modern-day House of Worship sound system can be as complicated as the day is long. Many systems today have integrated digital signal processing (DSP), digital mixing consoles, automixers, complicated matrix systems, complex delay systems, and more! However, when you get down to it, every sound system is ultimately the same.

Think of a professional sound system as if it were an automobile. You have your basic entry-level vehicle – it often has no air conditioning and is simply a motor, a transmission, a steering wheel, four tires, and a few seats. Getting to 60 miles per hour takes forever and is celebrated when it happens. But this vehicle gets you from point A to point B and doesn't cost much.

Conversely, you have the high-end luxury car. Leather interior, biometric recognition systems, integrated GPS, super sound-dampening materials for an enjoyable ride, a motor, a transmission, a steering wheel, four tires, and a few seats. This car gets to 60 miles per hour in the blink of an eye – often exceeding 100 miles per hour without the driver knowing it. It cruises down the road – its occupants in complete comfort – and gets from point A to point B – however, at a premium price.

One vehicle definitely performs better than the other – there is no question. But, at the heart – both vehicles ultimately work the same. There is a motor, a transmission, four tires, and a few seats. If you can drive one, you can drive the other. Perhaps you don't know how to work some of the high-end features such as the integrated GPS, right off the bat, but you can crank the car, put it in drive, and get from point A to point B. Likewise, if you commonly drive the high-end vehicle, you can get in the entry-level car, crank it, and get where you are going (although you might have to rely on some old-school methods such as reading a map).

A sound system is no different. Despite their size and design, ultimately they are all operated the same way. If you can operate one sound system, you can operate any of them. Perhaps you won't be able to use all the extra equipment tethered to it, but you will be able to fire up a microphone or CD player and get sound out of the speakers. You will be able to perform a rudimentary mix and get through the event.

A GOOD SOUND ENGINEER MAKES OR BREAKS THE SOUND SYSTEM — NOT THE OTHER WAY AROUND

A sound system is only as good as its operator. I'd say that at least 75 percent of the churches I visit could get much more effectiveness out of their sound system if only the operator knew the fundamentals of sound and mixed accordingly. Most of the problems we encounter in church sound systems are not the direct result of a poorly designed sound system, but the result of poorly trained operators. Solid and consistent training of the basics of sound is absolutely critical to the success of the modern-day House of Worship. A bad sound system design can still achieve quite a bit in the hands of a qualified and well-trained operator.

SOUND

4

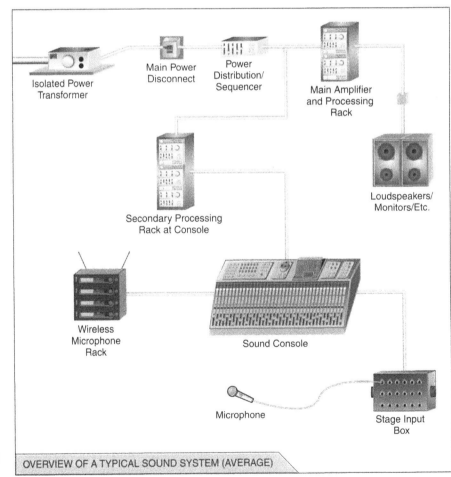

OVERVIEW OF A TYPICAL SOUND SYSTEM (AVERAGE)

FIGURE 1.1
Overview of an average sound system layout.

You Do Get What You Pay For

While training is important so that your sound engineer can perform optimally it's obvious that a well-designed sound system will allow that person to truly excel. Going back to the car analogy, it might be possible for a highly skilled driver to perform well at the races with an old clunker, but a finely tuned sports car, in the same hands, will far exceed the results of the clunker. Keep in mind, when planning a sound system, that you get what you pay for. But, perhaps more importantly, your sound system is only as good as the weakest link.

> **TIP**
> A preamp is an amplifier that boosts the sound signal prior to it entering the signal path in the console. A cheaper preamp will often alter the true sound and can adversely alter the reproduction of the sound.

You can spend all the money in the world on speakers and amplifiers but cheap out on the console (sound mixing board) and your system will not perform as it should. The console will prevent the signal from being the best it can be. Usually, due to cheap preamps, the signal coming into the board will suffer, because as it passes through the signal path it will continue to pick up excess noise, and this noise floor will be present in the system. The result will be a less–than-adequate reproduction of sound.

Time after time churches upgrade their old analog console for a new digital console – and they are blown away. They have better gain control, the signal is cleaner, and the system is performing better than ever. Often, they are astonished. This is true in all aspects of your sound system – not just the sound console. So pay close attention to every piece of equipment (and cable) that you choose.

In all your media systems, don't go cheap on the components that are difficult or impossible to change once the system is installed. Make sure to spend the money where it counts (cables, patch panels, connectors, power, etc.). These are the things that can't easily be changed down the road. Other items, such as consoles, microphones, and stage monitors are a little easier to upgrade later on and might be bargaining chips for your "value" engineer if need be. But I urge you – STAND STRONG. Nothing is worse than not having the tools you need to do ministry because you lost (or worse yet, didn't fight) at the "value" engineering meetings.

Are You Grounded?

Often overlooked, and rarely understood, it's important for a sound system to be on its own circuits with its own isolated ground. Done properly, the power for the sound system will run back to an isolated transformer specifically for the sound system.

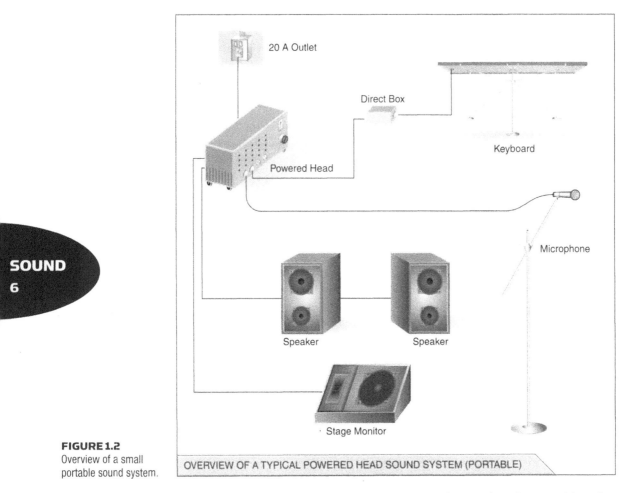

20 A Outlet

Direct Box

Keyboard

Powered Head

Microphone

Speaker   Speaker

Stage Monitor

OVERVIEW OF A TYPICAL POWERED HEAD SOUND SYSTEM (PORTABLE)

FIGURE 1.2
Overview of a small
portable sound system.

This is the single most important thing you can do to reduce hum and interference noises.

Once you get this isolated ground – protect it! Don't plug a moving light, orchestra light, or other non-sound-related device into the sound power. These devices can add noise through the power line that can cause operational problems and poor sound quality. Likewise, don't go plugging your guitar amps or other sound devices into building power. The second you do, you defeat the whole process.

COMPONENTS OF A BASIC SOUND SYSTEM

The Mixing Console

At the heart of every sound system is the mixing console. This is the centerpiece of any sound system. Most likely, when someone says "sound system" you think of the large console on the floor of an arena with a confident-looking person (often dressed in black) standing behind it. The mixing console is the central heart of any sound system.

Realizing that at the time of this writing, over 80 percent of churches in America are comprised of 100 people or less, most of the sound systems encountered are very rudimentary. Often the mixing console will be a powered mixer (in other words the primary mix controls, system equalization, effects processing and amplification will all be built together as one unit). However, larger congregations will have need for a larger mixing console. Many of these congregations will turn to digital mixers and many will also use submixers.

When you first approach any typical mixing console, it's common to be a little intimidated. At first glance, all you see are rows upon rows of different-color knobs and controls. It looks like a beast – and that's when you stand behind a small mixer! When you find yourself in front of a 48- or 52-channel console, or, heaven forbid, a large-format digital mixer, you might just want to dive for cover!

Relax. That's a standard feeling. But here's the secret: if you learn about 16 button/knob functions you can run almost any console out there! That's right – all those buttons and knobs and controls that look so intimidating are really duplicating the same function per channel. And regardless of the type or size of the console, just like with the automobile example, they all work pretty much the same. With the knowledge of a handful of controls you can operate almost any console out there!

So, take a breath, grab a cup of coffee, and let's explore the typical mixing console.

Lets start off by taking a typical console and breaking it into two primary sections – the input section and the output section.

FIGURE 1.3
A typical mixing console for an average-sized church. Mackie 1604VLZ shown here. Photo courtesy of Mackie Designs Inc. All rights reserved.

The input section is where you manipulate your various input sources (microphones, playback devices, effects returns, etc.). The output section is where you route the various signals to the different outboard components of the sound system (processing, amplification, powered speakers, stage monitors, etc.).

Input Section

Let's look first at the input section. Often, this is where the first wave of intimidation comes for newer users. Don't despair. The input section is easy. Each channel will consist of an intermediate volume control

SOUND

8

(usually a fader, but in some cases it will be a knob). This control is almost always located at the bottom of the channel strip. Above this strip will be a section of knobs that control the equalization of the channel's inputs, and another section of knobs that control the auxiliary sends for the channel. Finally, at the very top of the channel you will usually find a GAIN control (sometimes called TRIM). This is the master volume control for the channel.

The controls on one channel duplicate across the entire input section! So, if you look at Figure 1.5a of a typical channel strip, you will see the volume fader, auxiliary, equalization, and gain controls. Now, when you look at the channel in more detail, you'll notice the Auxiliary knobs all do the same job and the equalization knobs work like you'd expect. See – this is already getting simpler. Let's take a look at each control and discuss how it works.

GAIN CONTROL

As mentioned earlier, the Gain (sometimes referred to as Trim) is almost always going to be located at the top of the channel strip. For practical purposes, you can think of this as the master volume control on the channel. This is the knob that the old saying is very true of: "A little bit will do you." The Gain control is actually affecting the gain of the preamp.

I like to explain volume structure for a sound system much like a water supply system. When you visualize how water works – you have different control stations. Think about the main water cut-off to the house. If you turn it a little bit, water gushes out. Likewise, if you turn the faucet to the kitchen sink on the same amount, water trickles in comparison.

Now, think of that example when you consider your Gain control. The Gain control acts like the main water cut-off – turn it a little bit, and you get a lot of volume proportionally. Your fader or volume control on the channel acts more like your kitchen faucet – move it the same amount as the Gain control and you get much less volume proportionally.

Another function (usually located near the Gain control) is the PAD control. This is a great feature for certain input devices (such as CD players). Some signals come into the console at a higher db level – you know you are experiencing this when the GAIN is all the way down and you can barely touch the fader without blasting yourself through the back wall! If you engage the PAD it will reduce the signal and allow you to build proper gain structure. One key benefit to using the PAD with higher signals is that it will allow you more manipulation of the signal with the fader – you can now use the fader to make small, minute changes to the signal, whereas without the pad you could not. This gives you more ability to craft your mix.

THE FADER

If the GAIN is your big volume control, the fader is your small volume control. This allows you more finite control of the signal and is the primary control you use for your mix. While your mix is ultimately a concert of all these functions, the fader is your primary control for fine-tuning the mix. This will be explained in more detail later in the "Gain Structure" section.

SOUND

9

Also near the fader (usually just above it) is the MUTE button. This button allows you to quickly mute the channel without changing a bunch of settings or moving the fader. Check your specific console manual to see if the MUTE button also mutes your auxiliary outputs as well as the main outputs and subgroups – some consoles differ in this regard.

AUXILIARY CONTROLS

Usually, the next bank of controls is the Auxiliary knobs. It's not uncommon for people to not realize what this group of knobs do.

It's helpful to think of them as simple signal splitters. The auxiliary section will usually contain between 2 and 16 knobs, depending on your console and its purpose. Each Auxiliary control will usually have a master Auxiliary control (although not always) and will have its own output jack on the back of the board.

Imagine that channel one has a keyboard input. The channel, without Auxiliary controls, will take the sound of that keyboard, route it to the subgroups (if the console has them), and then to the main outputs. That's great – except you need that sound in other places too! You might need it to go to the stage monitors, a CD recording or video feed, a hearing-assist feed, or any other output source other than the main speakers.

The Auxiliary controls allow you to do just that. The more Auxiliary controls you have, the more places you can route the signal. This is why many consoles designated for mixing stage monitors have so many Auxiliary controls – they want to be able to send each signal to many places. Auxiliary controls give you a great deal of flexibility and are very useful for live and recording mixing.

Auxiliary controls also allow you to send the signal to outboard effects units such as vocal reverb units, delay units, equalizers, feedback, and many other processing sources.

EQUALIZER CONTROLS

The equalizer controls act much like your car or home stereo – however, they usually have more frequency bands. A typical small console will have a high, mid, and low control. A higher-end console will often have a high-mid and a low-mid control in place of the mid control. Most consoles will also have center frequency adjustment points for each frequency band control. The number of these center frequency controls tends to increase as the price of the console increases.

Good equalization techniques often elude beginning audio engineers. Your volume can be spot-on, but bad equalization will destroy your mix.

SOUND

10

The best way to learn how to equalize is to get a couple of buddies (ideally male and female) and spend some time in your church. Give them a microphone (one at a time) and ask them to read a book. As they read aloud, dramatically adjust each equalizer control independently. Start at the high frequency and work your way down, resetting each control to center before moving to the next one.

As you do this, listen to the dramatic change of tonal quality in the voice. You should hear a substantial difference as you pan through the various frequencies.

While each console is different, typically the high-band equalizer will act more like a shelf. This means it will affect a certain frequency (usually around 10 to 12 KHz) and boost or cut the frequencies above this set frequency. The mid range will affect the middle range of frequencies. On many consoles the mid is centered somewhere between 1 and 3 KHz. Again, on many consoles you have the opportunity to use the center frequency control to alter what frequency the mid control is centered at. It is not uncommon to be able to sweep between 100 Hz and 8 KHz. Whichever frequency you select will be the center frequency. When you boost or cut the mid range, the frequencies on either side of this center frequency will be adjusted in a typical bell shape, as you would expect to see from a Parametric Equalizer. Obviously, this gives you a wide range of control. Finally, the low frequency control once again acts like a shelf, usually affecting frequencies 80 Hz and below (although this will be different from console to console).

You will also often find a "roll off" button – this will automatically reduce frequencies below its set point (often 80 Hz). This is helpful when you are trying to eliminate low-end noise, microphone stand movement, footsteps, and other low-end nuisances. However, if you are sending content to a subwoofer you'll want to make sure the roll off button isn't accidentally engaged on channels that include low frequency information (such as playback devices, kick drums, bass guitar, etc.).

NOT HEARING A LOT OF DIFFERENCE AS YOU CHANGE THE EQUALIZATION?

One important note: if you don't hear a lot of difference when you make subtle changes to the equalizer control, your system is most likely poorly configured and needs to be adjusted. A properly set up sound system with good room equalization will be very responsive to even the slightest amount of equalization change (assuming you are affecting a frequency that is being utilized in the material you are adjusting for). A lack of equalization response could be due to poor room equalization (acoustics) or poor system design. Consult a trained and trusted audio professional for advice and systems adjustment.

SOUND

11

Equalization is key to good sound. While it can be used as an effect, it is primarily used in modern-day Houses of Worship to achieve good tonal control of individual inputs and to reduce feedback potential (otherwise known as increasing your gain before feedback).

NOTCHING FEEDBACK

One very useful tactic for equalization is to reduce the feedback. Often referred to as "ringing out the microphones," equalization can help you increase your gain before feedback (or in layman's terms – you can get more volume before your sound system starts squealing like a stuck pig) – and everyone knows that this is a helpful thing.

When ringing out your microphone, it's best to use a Parametric Equalizer. This will allow you to choose a very specific frequency and dial in the amount of Q (the bandwidth) that the change will affect. We'll discuss this more in the Outboard Equipment – Equalization section. When using equalization to reduce feedback it is helpful to use as small of a Q as you can – the larger the Q the more frequencies you are affecting. The Q will tell the parametric how far to extend past your center frequency when

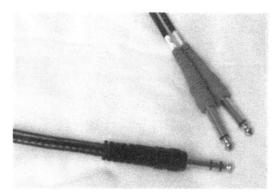

FIGURE 1.6
Typical insert cable.
Photo by Brad Herring.

it boosts or cuts the signal. So, the more Q the more frequencies that will be altered and the more your sound will be affected. When notching for feedback, you want to reduce the offending frequencies that are creating the feedback loop but not alter the tonality of the sound.

The Parametric Equalizer would usually be patched into the console via an insert cable and the insert jack. An insert cable resembles a "Y" cable. On the single connector side is a male Tip-Ring-Sleeve ¼-inch connector and on the other side of the cable are two individual Tip-Sleeve ¼-inch connectors. The single Tip-Ring-Sleeve connector plugs into the INSERT jack on the console, while one of the Tip-Sleeve connectors becomes the SEND and the other becomes the RETURN. It will depend on your console as to whether the TIP is the SEND or the RETURN and vice-versa.

The actual process is rather simple.

1. Choose a microphone channel (obviously with the microphone plugged into it and placed where it will really be used). You can do this with the microphone placed in a stand, but it's better if someone is holding the microphone and walking around the stage with it.
2. Bring the gain all the way down.
3. Increase the fader until it reaches unity (usually shaded a different color on the fader surface) or until the microphone begins to produce feedback.
4. Assuming you reach unity prior to feedback, begin SLOWLY increasing the gain until you reach the point of feedback.
5. Identify the frequency that is ringing – dial it into the EQ and slowly reduce the gain on the EQ until the ringing stops. NOTE: Give the system time to respond. Sometimes you might have to mute the channel or reduce the gain to make the feedback loop stop – then slowly reintroduce the gain. Once you have properly equalized the frequency you should be able to take the gain higher than before.
6. Continue increasing the gain until feedback occurs again – then repeat the process.

NOTE: Anytime you alter the EQ regardless of how minute you also alter the tonal quality of the sound. Ringing out a microphone should be done with

FEEDBACK

Feedback is the result of projected sound from the PA system being picked up by the microphone and reintroducing it to the system slightly out of phase (due to time delay). This loop increases in intensity until the frequencies excite to the point of feedback. Feedback can happen at any frequency, but is most often heard at higher and lower tones.

very conservative taste – you should monitor the channel with the talent's voice so you make sure you are not removing frequencies that will alter the sound beyond what you are willing to accept.

You'll never get to a point where you will not get feedback – it's just an inevitable part of live sound mixing. The point is to try to get to a point where you can get the volume you need (plus a safety margin) without feedback.

TYPICAL EQUALIZATION PITFALLS

- *Man in the Hole* Have you ever stood in a tunnel or a big open room and listened to someone speak? The voice is hollow and has a weak resonance to it that makes the voice difficult to understand. In our world of sound systems, this is most commonly a result of too much mid-range EQ and sometimes too much low-frequency EQ. Dial them back a little bit and see if the tonal quality doesn't improve.
- *Tin Can Effect* This is the old AM radio sound – or like your head is in a bucket. This is the result of too much high frequency and sometimes the lack of mid and low frequencies.
- *My Ears Are About to Explode From the High Pitch* This is perhaps the worst. When the volume is extremely loud, and the high frequency is excited, this creates a very uncomfortable sound for your audience. Adjust accordingly.

TIP
Remember: As sound pressure (volume) increases or decreases equalization changes! A good sound engineer is constantly making minute adjustments to the equalizer and constantly listening for changes.

SUBGROUP ASSIGNMENTS

These buttons are usually (but not always) located near the fader. Not all consoles will have subgroups, but most of your mid to larger size consoles will utilize them.

Subgroups are a sound engineer's best friend. Subgroups allow you to take complicated mixes and combine similar channels into groups. An example of this would be choir microphones. If your church has nine choir microphones, you can assign all of them to the same subgroup. Now,

TIP
Make sure when using subgroups that you have assigned the SUBGROUP faders to their appropriate outputs (normally the MAIN output) – otherwise your signal will go nowhere!

mix the nine individual microphones to taste. Once you get the mix set, you can increase or decrease the SUBGROUP fader to control the overall volume of that entire group of microphones in the main mix. This allows you to alter the overall volume of a group without individual changes and trying to maintain the mix.

PFL

Pre-Fader Listen (PFL), also sometimes called SOLO, will allow you to listen to that specific channel in the headsets. This is a great tool for isolating problems or simply listening to channels to identify what signal is coming through it. PFL is also used for identifying a sound in a mix. For instance, if you are mixing an orchestra and you find yourself having trouble identifying the bassoon, you can PFL the bassoon channel, hear it, and disengage the PFL, and your ear will tend to hear the bassoon in the mix. This will allow you to identify the sound and determine if you need more or less of it in the mix.

SOUND

14

You want to make sure you know how this feature works prior to using it in a service! Most consoles offer PFL and SOLO features that allow that individual channel only in the headphones (as described above) but some consoles do what's called a "destructive solo." This means that they mute all audio sources other than the channel selected and only that channel is heard in the house sound system! That would be a very unpleasant surprise, so make sure you understand how your particular console functions!

Equalizer

Out-board equalizers play an important role in the success of your sound system. First, they control the tonal quality of your sound system. The equalizer (combined with acoustic treatment) is your only way to overcome the natural sound of the room.

Sound is actually a series of sound waves. As these waves are projected from their source, they proceed until they hit something. If these waves hit something reflective (like a solid wall or glass), they bounce back and cause a phenomenon known as reflections. If these waves hit a dense curtain, carpet, the human body, or other such dense materials they tend to be absorbed.

As these sound waves bounce around your room they cause different effects in the room. Often, they interact with each other to cancel out certain frequencies in the room or to emphasize certain frequencies.

In an effort to control the room, equalization is used to increase or decrease the affected frequencies in the room. Normally, a qualified systems integrator will utilize a series of test microphones, measuring equipment, and other tools to identify the problem areas in a room and equalize to overcome them. Now, obviously, these waves interact at many different points in the room – thus affecting each seat differently. The systems integrator (or engineer) will average his finds to make the overall room balanced.

When combined with proper acoustical treatment you can get a very nice-sounding room. The more advanced planning that goes into the design of the room the better your result will be.

TYPES OF EQUALIZATION

As alluded to earlier, there are two primary types of equalization – Graphic and Parametric. The specific use will dictate which one is ideal for your application.

A Graphic Equalizer comes in preset octaves (such as full octave or one third octave). So, for instance, if you affect 1 KHz, you are affecting a preset range of octaves on either side of that frequency. A Parametric Equalizer on the other hand allows you to select the frequency, then select the bandwidth (basically the octave range) on either side that you wish to select. With a Parametric Equalizer, you can choose to affect a very broad range or an extremely narrow range.

A Parametric Equalizer is normally made with very few bands of control (usually between two and four), while a Graphic Equalizer typically has 15 or 31 bands to cover the entire audible spectrum.

If you are looking for very specific frequency control and want to make sure to not affect a broad range of frequencies, then a Parametric Equalizer is your best bet. If you are looking for broad tonal control and basic room adjustment a Graphic Equalizer is more often employed for the task.

TIP
When you increase or decrease the gain of a frequency or frequencies with an equalizer, you are increasing or decreasing the overall system gain as well – be careful or you'll find yourself clipping and/or feeding back!

GRAPHIC EQUALIZER

A Graphic Equalizer is fairly easy to operate. By selecting the appropriate fader to the frequency range you wish to affect, you simply boost (increase) or cut

(decrease) the level as it's centered around 0 db. If you are unsure which frequency you are hearing, it's easy to dramatically cut a frequency to the fullest extent of the control and listen to the change – it should be dramatic. You should then be able to quickly decide if that's the correct frequency or not.

Usually on the side of the Graphic Equalizer you will have a series of selection buttons. One will be a db selector. This button determines how much range each fader has. Since the unit is limited in physical space, each fader can only be so long. By selecting your db range you can effectively make the fader cover more range or less range. So, if you are trying to have more fine control you would select the lower db setting, but if you find yourself needing more dramatic control you'd select the higher db setting.

You'll also notice a bypass button. Sometimes this will be labeled as ENGAGE or ON as well. Either way, it does the same thing – it allows you to activate the EQ or bypass it completely. This is helpful. You'll sometimes find that as you adjust the equalizer you will do more harm that good. It's easy to "over eq." When you think you might be beyond a point of doing good, you can quickly bypass the equalizer. If it sounds better with the EQ bypassed then you've "over eq'ed" the system. Start working backward to undo what you've done or reset the equalizer and start over.

PARAMETRIC EQUALIZER

The Parametric Equalizer is going to have a series of controls on it. First, you will normally have Frequency, Q, and Gain controls.

The Frequency control allows you to select the frequency you wish to center on. The Q (sometimes called bandwidth) will allow you to select how many frequencies on either side of the center frequency you wish to affect. This is very helpful for improving gain before feedback, reducing ringing nodes or similar fine-tune adjustments. A larger Q on the other hand is more typical for controlling tonality.

As mentioned earlier, a Parametric Equalizer is more limited in actual bands that it can affect, but is more flexible in providing the user the option of affecting more or less bands overall with a single central frequency.

The Role of Equalization

Equalization plays a vital role in modern-day sound systems. Not only does it help us balance the room but it also permits us to control the overall tonal quality of the mix – both as a final mix and on an individual channel basis. Equalization allows the engineer to "color" the mix.

Equalization for a typical sound system will usually begin at 20 Hz and top out at 20 KHz. This is the best case sonic range that we humans can hear.

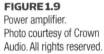

Amplifiers

Amplifiers are used (as you might imagine) to amplify the signal. They take a line level input and process the signal – ultimately converting it to power. This powered signal can now pulse the components of a speaker and allow it to reproduce sound.

SOUND

17

Amplifiers are rated at different power levels (measured in watts) and different impedances (measured as ohms). It's important that you match the correct amplifier with the correct speaker. Underpowering and overpowering alike are bad for a speaker and will shorten its lifespan. While buying the correct amplifier might seem like a budget challenge, it's the right path in the long term – as you will be a better steward of your ministry dollar.

As a general rule of thumb, when choosing the correct amplifier for your needs, the amplifier's continuous power should be equal to one and a half or two times the speaker's continuous power handling (at the same impedance). If you are wiring two similar speakers in parallel, the amplifier's continuous power should equal four times one speaker's continuous power handling.

TIP
Most people know that OVERPOWERING a speaker is bad, but many overlook the fact that UNDERPOWERING a speaker can do just as much damage and shorten the service life of the speaker.

Amplifiers are also available in various impedances. In the typical House of Worship, you will most commonly work with 70 volts, 25 volts (commonly used in low-voltage feeds with many speakers – such as nursery rooms, hallways, bathrooms, etc.) and 8-ohm, 4-ohm, and occasionally 2-ohm amplifiers (most commonly used in distributing power to the primary speaker components of a sound system and stage monitor system).

Amplifiers, as with all electronics, vary in price. You do indeed get what you pay for. A higher priced amplifier will likely have cleaner circuits, operate more efficiently, and long work better in the long term.

FIGURE 1.10
Typical loudspeaker.
Photo courtesy of
Electro Voice.

When considering ohms, realize that a speaker's rating is cut in half every time you plug another speaker into the same circuit. For instance, if you have a stage monitor amplifier that feeds four stage jacks and your stage monitors are 8 ohms each, when you plug in the first speaker, it's running 8 ohms. When you plug in the second, they are both now running at 4 ohms. Add a third, and you are running 2 ohms. If your amplifier is rated at 8 ohms, you are really putting a strain on the amplifier and will significantly shorten its lifespan – not to mention the possibility of overheating the amplifier, tripping circuits, or, worst case, causing a fire. Fire is bad.

Also, realize that for every foot of cable you run to the speaker, you increase resistance. This reduces the efficiency of the amplifier and makes it work at less than specified wattages. Likewise, the use of under-sized cable will increase your resistance – causing the cable to heat up (again presenting a possible fire hazard) and reducing the overall workload of the system.

Speakers

Next to a person standing behind a console, the loudspeakers are probably one of the other primary things people think about when they hear the term "sound system." They are the main component that is usually seen by the audience and of course that's where much of the sound actually comes from!

When considering speakers, there is a lot to think about. The first choice is, are you looking at a distributed system or an array system? This will narrow your search.

A distributed system is a system that uses many speakers spread over a wide area. They are time-aligned digitally and work together to cover a large area of sound by focusing on a small area per speaker. The speakers are then adjusted so that they blend together and create a uniform coverage area.

This is more of an old-school approach, and while it can work very well in certain cases I tend to steer people away from this concept. It requires a lot of setup and a lot of equipment, and can very easily be altered by room environments such as temperature and humidity.

An arrayed system uses clusters of speakers to cover large areas. You have most likely seen a center speaker array in older churches. This is a combination of speakers that work together to provide an even coverage area throughout the entire audio spectrum (ideally). More recently designers began working with Left/Center/Right systems to combine good vocal reproduction with hi-fidelity music reproduction. This system design works well in most rooms, but requires a lot of equipment and a fair amount of training to get it all performing well.

Finally, most recent (as of the writing of this book) is line-array technology. This technology uses a series of small boxes – one on top of the other – to purposefully phase in and out with the other cabinets around it to create even coverage.

> **TIP**
>
> **A Note About Line Arrays** Simply stacking a small group of speakers together vertically does not make a true line array. A true line array is any number of driver elements that are spaced no more than a quarter of a wavelength apart. The speaker cabinets in a line array are designed to sum and subtract from each other as a whole. This allows them to work in tandem with each other and evenly cover an area. Many smaller systems of vertically stacked speakers work well – but they are simply vertical arrays. Make sure to know what you are getting before signing on the dotted line.

Once you determine which system you want in your House of Worship, you can begin to look at the individual specifics of each manufacturer's design.

There are some systems out there that might not sound the BEST, but they work – even if dropped off a truck, kicked around storage, and just generally abused. Other systems might not be so road-worthy, but produce a much higher-fidelity sound. Both of these categories of speakers have their place in ministry.

HOW SPEAKERS ARE MEASURED

Most loudspeakers are measured by the same standards.

- *First – Size.* You will commonly see a speaker referred to as a 10, 12, or 15. This refers to the size of its woofer component. So, if a speaker has a 12-inch woofer it's a 12-inch cabinet – or sometimes simply called a 12.
- *Second – Number of Components.* For instance, a two-way speaker will have a low and a high range component. A three-way speaker will have a low, mid, and high range component.
- *Third – Driver Type.* Some speakers are horn loaded and some are ribbon speakers, while others are coaxial designed. Each driver type has its own characteristics. For instance, a horn tends to be more in your face but can really help you push vocals through a mix. A coaxial design will tend to sound more like a hi-fi system and will lean toward sounding more like your high-end home stereo system. Ribbon speakers are often loved by audiophiles but are commonly limited by weather restraints and can suffer from directional control problems.

- *Fourth – Power Handling.* Speakers are rated in wattage. Usually, a higher wattage cabinet will produce a louder signal, and many times this signal will be of higher fidelity (this is especially true with subwoofers). As a broad statement, more watts will typically give you more sound – and generally a tighter sound. The speaker is also rated in continuous power and peak power. As you might expect, the continuous rating is what the speaker is designed to operate at over a sustained amount of time – the peak rating is its maximum rating for short bursts of signal. Operating for long periods of time at the peak power rating will ultimately damage the loudspeaker.
- *Fifth – Frequency Response.* The human ear can typically hear from 20 Hz to 20 KHz (depending on age, history of exposure to loud sounds, and other, similar factors). But the human body can FEEL much lower that that and sometimes reacts to sounds much higher. For instance, sometimes sounds above 20 KHz can make a person's hair stand up on their neck. Sounds lower than 20 Hz are often felt instead of being heard since the longer sound wave creates air pressure that pushes on the body or thumps the seat. These lower frequencies can go far in creating atmospheres and environments where people get excited about the music they are hearing. So you can see how all of these frequencies work together. Commonly a speaker will translate from around 30 Hz to 16 KHz, but this varies from speaker to speaker.
- *Sixth – Directional Design.* A professional loudspeaker usually has a published coverage pattern. This is the average coverage predictability of the loudspeaker. You will notice when you look at the specifications that it varies from frequency to frequency, but the overall average is specified. Typically, this will be 100° × 100°, 60° × 40°, 40° × 20°, etc. This refers to the angle from the center of the horn or tweeter that the sound will cover horizontally and vertically. Many loudspeakers have a rotatable horn, which will allow you to swap horizontal and vertical coverage as needed for your purpose. Remember, this is not a perfect measurement (for instance, if you walk to 34° of one side of a 60° pattern you are still going to hear sound – but the majority of the high and mid frequency sound energy will be encapsulated within that pattern).

TIP
One thing to remember in regard to loudspeaker placement – ideally your main speakers for the audience will be on top of or slightly in front of the most downstage microphone (the microphone closest to the audience). This will help reduce feedback in your mix. Any microphone that is in front of a loudspeaker it is mixed into will have a greater tendency to feedback quicker than if it were located behind the loudspeaker.

Input Devices

All of the previous components do little good if there is no signal going through the system to amplify. Input devices range from microphones to musical instruments with direct connections to CD players, minidiscs, computers, iPods and more!

The input device is really the main reason for a sound system in the first place – that is, to take a signal and amplify it so it can be heard by the masses. With that in mind, it's critical that you seriously consider how you connect devices to your system.

MORE ADVANCED SYSTEM COMPONENTS

As systems get more complex, there are more components utilized. Unfortunately, many Houses of Worship get stuck on the very basic components that we have already discussed and they stop there. The reason that's unfortunate is because the very basic components merely make the system work in a fundamental way – the audio gets louder and can be heard by the people.

But that audio is usually dull and uninteresting. It doesn't do much for dissolving walls during worship and helping to usher people into the Throne room. Often times, it creates walls by the mix being inefficient, poorly balanced, and prone to feedback.

With proper training, the church can utilize many of the more advanced system components and really begin to craft their mix.

I often tell people that there is no difference between media team and worship team. In reality, we are all on the same team – it's just that the guys on the "media team" play a different type of instrument. As a House of Worship sound engineer, the mixing console is your "instrument." With it, you can craft a mix and really make it stand out. You can take a soloist and, by the manipulation on the raw signal that you impose, make the hair stand up on people's necks (not because the system is screaming with feedback, but because you build in a dynamic that stirs the soul).

Beyond the Basics

We'll look at many of these components later in the book, but I believe it's important that we mention them here so we realize that they are slightly more advanced than the basic components and that you start to ponder how you can begin to use these tools in your mix.

PREAMPS

One of the first "upgrades" many people make is in the area of preamps. As defined earlier, a preamp is an amplifier that boosts the sound signal prior to it entering the signal path in the console. Most entry-level or cost-conscious mixers skimp on their preamps. A preamp sits behind the microphone input of the console and boosts the low-level "mic" signal to a line-level signal that can be more easily manipulated and processed.

The preamp really determines how the original sound source will sound. A cheaper preamp will tend to make the source sound really thin and thus reduce a lot of the original dynamics. A real bad preamp will add a lot of noise to the system, thus increasing your noise floor and reducing your gain before feedback. In a nutshell, this means the system is going to potentially start screaming with feedback much earlier than if the signal were cleaner.

One simple solution is to purchase rack-mounted preamps from a reputable manufacturer that specializes in this very thing. Another option is to purchase a more expensive soundboard with nicer preamps built in.

ELECTRONIC PROCESSING

Electronic processing includes advanced equalizers, crossovers, compressors, limiters, gates, DSPs, effects processors, feedback suppressors, and more. Electronic processing allows you to truly impact the sound after it reaches the mixer. Some components help you to limit spikes, others help you eliminate feedback, some help you alter the tonality of the sound, and some simply help you get a clearer mix.

Electronic processing is a vital part of a quality sound system.

SUBWOOFERS

The subwoofer is a critical loudspeaker component that should never be foregone, but especially in Houses of Worship that are contemporary in nature. One of the primary ways to build excitement and energy in a room is to "pump up the bass." In a contemporary service, the subwoofer can be used to really drive kick drums and bass guitars. In a traditional service the subwoofer is invaluable in rounding off the full spectrum of sound for instruments like the keyboard and upright bass while also helping to punch the bass in a quartet or other musical group.

Subwoofers create a huge dynamic in any sound system. Regardless of if you use it as a big thumper or simply to create a full-range sound, the subwoofer is a critical part of any sound system.

Generally speaking, when it comes to subwoofers, the more power they take and the heavier they are to lift the bigger the punch will be. Subwoofers are often cut because it's difficult to find room to put them, but the effort is well worth it in the end. Another reason subwoofers are foregone is cost. There are companies that make a lot of bang for relatively little buck, and there are also companies that produce outstanding subwoofer designs along with a price to go with it. Both have their place in ministry. The choice of quality and punch in a subwoofer is up to you, but going without one should never be a consideration if you can help it.

Excitement is built through a quality sound mix. In contemporary services, a significant enabler of excitement in a mix is a quality subwoofer that is properly crossed over at the right frequency and powered correctly. As with anything, a subwoofer used with poor discretion can create more problems than good, but used with taste the subwoofer can be your best friend in energizing the mix.

POWER CONDITIONERS

Another important feature on your sound system is a power conditioner. A power conditioner will protect the system from power spikes, which can do serious damage to the electronics that make up your sound system.

Power conditioners come in different types and different strengths. Your most basic power conditioner is a rack-mounted multistrip power conditioner. Often these come with lighting built into them, which can be helpful in illuminating the components within the rack that are underneath it.

More advanced protection is located before the rack and is substantially more expensive, albeit it offers more protection as well as sometimes providing a little bit of AC cleanup.

UNINTERRUPTIBLE POWER SUPPLY BACKUPS

Uninterruptible Power Supply (UPS) backups are another great addition to your sound system. They are especially critical if you are using a digital console. Many digital consoles can take several minutes to reboot after a power failure. Having them on a UPS will keep the console up and running during a short blackout.

If your system is mission critical you can connect it to a backup generator that automatically kicks on with building power failure. It is not uncommon to see this type of generator system for large commercial buildings. The average House of Worship will be well served with a simple UPS solution similar to what you might use on a high-end computer desktop.

Now that you have an idea of the various components that can make up a sound system, let's take a look at the typical connections you will run into when interconnecting these components.

CHAPTER 2

Connections in a Sound System

By and large most connections for a sound system are fairly standardized. The wiring for these connections is very standardized.

For each purpose, there is a proper connection. When it comes to sound systems, the fewer connection points you have, the better off you are. With every connection point comes an opportunity for noise and failure. So, by minimizing the number of connections you have in a sound system you increase your odds of good performance. You also simplify troubleshooting when something does go wrong.

Sound systems have two primary groups of connections: Signal Level (Mic Level and Line Level) and Powered Level (Speaker Level).

Signal Level connections are high- or low-impedance connections, while Powered Level connections are post-amplifier connections (such as those found on the back of a speaker).

XLR MICROPHONE CONNECTION

XLR microphone connections are a professional quality balanced input for mic level (low-impedance connections). You will notice that the ground pin is slightly longer than the other two pins. This ensures the ground will always connect first when mated.

> **TIP**
> A balanced input consists of two conductors of the same type that each have equal impedance to ground. Conversely, an unbalanced line has two conductors that have an unequal impedance to ground.

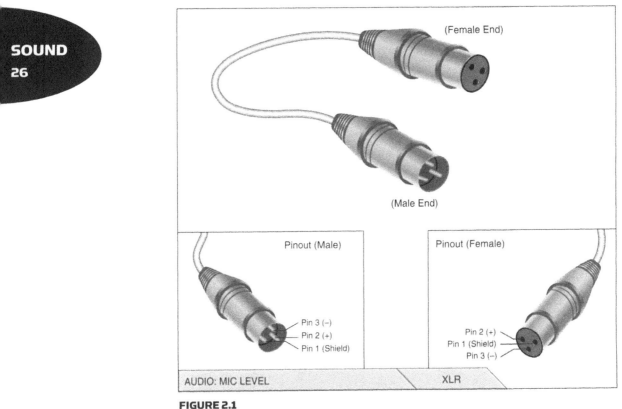

(Female End)

(Male End)

Pinout (Male)

Pin 3 (−)
Pin 2 (+)
Pin 1 (Shield)

Pinout (Female)

Pin 2 (+)
Pin 1 (Shield)
Pin 3 (−)

AUDIO: MIC LEVEL   XLR

FIGURE 2.1
Wiring pinout of XLR connection.

¼-INCH TIP-SLEEVE CONNECTION (TS)

A Tip-Sleeve connection is always an unbalanced mono signal. When being used for a signal it is considered a high-impedance connection. When being used for power (such as for speaker connections) it is a Powered-Level connection. Obviously the Powered-Level connection requires larger gauge wire and often-times the actual connection is made in a more sturdy fashion. A Tip-Sleeve connection is recognizable due to the single band on the sleeve of the connection.

A Tip-Sleeve connection is typically used for applications such as connecting a guitar to an amp or direct box, while a speaker cable utilizing a Tip-Sleeve connection would connect an amplifier to a speaker.

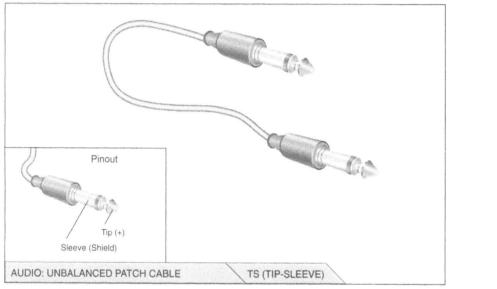

Pinout

Tip (+)

Sleeve (Shield)

AUDIO: UNBALANCED PATCH CABLE   TS (TIP-SLEEVE)

FIGURE 2.2
Wiring pinout of TS connection.

¼-INCH TIP-RING-SLEEVE CONNECTION (TRS)

A Tip-Ring-Sleeve connection, depending on its application, is a stereo connection or a balanced connection. If it's being utilized for low power output (such as a headphone output), it allows for a stereo connection. When being utilized for signal, it allows for a balanced connection. A Tip-Ring-Sleeve connection is recognizable because of the two individual bands on the sleeve.

You will also commonly see a Tip-Ring-Sleeve connection used on an insert cable, with one conductor being the send and the other acting as the return (while the opposite end of the cable will have two Tip-Sleeve connections to plug into the outboard equipment).

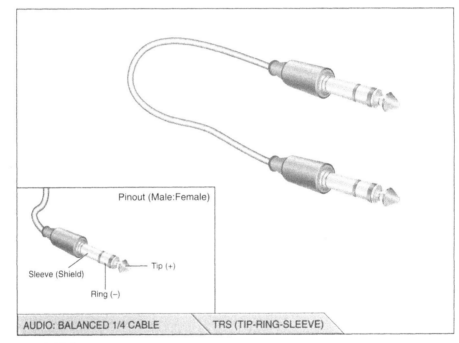

Pinout (Male:Female)

Tip (+)

Sleeve (Shield)

Ring (−)

AUDIO: BALANCED 1/4 CABLE   TRS (TIP-RING-SLEEVE)

FIGURE 2.3
Wiring pinout of TRS connection.

⅛-INCH MINI-PLUG CONNECTION (MONO AND STEREO)

The ⅛-inch mini-plug connection is used for smaller electronics (such as an MP3 player) as well as headphone outputs. The signal can be mono (single band on the sleeve) or stereo (dual band on the sleeve). It wires just like its big brother the ¼-inch connector, but is much smaller in size. The ⅛-inch mini-plug is typically used for low-wattage powered connections (such as headphones), although in many applications it carries line-level loads.

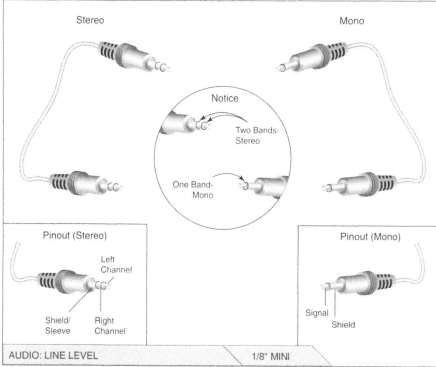

FIGURE 2.4
Wiring pinout of ⅛-inch mini-plug stereo and mono connection.

RCA OR PHONO CONNECTION

The RCA (or PHONO) connection is most commonly seen in consumer electronics and other pro-sumer components. Often used for audio (and composite video), the RCA connection is a rather common connection for sound systems.

The RCA connection is an unbalanced high-impedance line-level connection.

TIP
It is also important to not confuse an RCA output with a coaxial digital connection. Always take the time to read what you are connecting to!

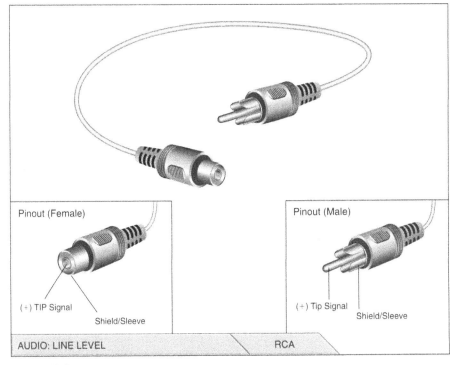

Pinout (Female)

(+) TIP Signal

Shield/Sleeve

Pinout (Male)

(+) Tip Signal

Shield/Sleeve

AUDIO: LINE LEVEL   RCA

FIGURE 2.5
Wiring pinout of RCA connection.

PUNCH BLOCK CONNECTION

Originally brought over from the phone and network industry, punch blocks have become an acceptable way of interconnecting line and mic level connections. Punch blocks can accept a large number of connections in a relatively small area. However, you do lose your shielding in the process, so it can be a component susceptible to noise.

TIP
Placing your punch block in a grounded metal enclosure will help you get some level of shielding back.

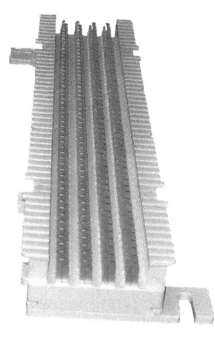

FIGURE 2.6
Photo of a punch block connection.

BARRIER STRIP CONNECTION

Barrier strip connections are most commonly used for speaker-level powered connections. They are simply a set of screw terminals that have a conductor connecting one side to the other. By utilizing a spade connector on the end of the wire, you can screw the wire down and then connect it to the wire on the other side simply by making a tight connection at each screw.

Barrier strips can be joined together so that one screw on one side will connect to multiple screw heads on the other, thus allowing you to split the signal. Again, impedances should always be considered when doing this. For instance, many output impedances are low, thus allowing you to be able to connect several devices together without much worry; but many input impedances are high, so connecting multiple inputs could cause problems such as distortion and low-frequency loss.

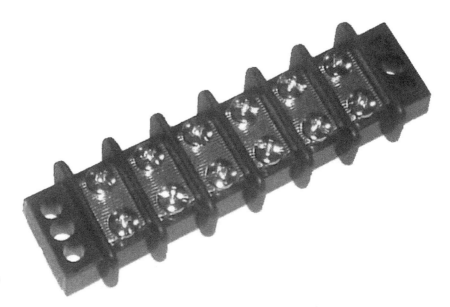

FIGURE 2.7
Photo of a barrier strip connection.

BANANA PLUG SPEAKER CONNECTION

Banana plug connections are power-level connections that typically connect to the back of an amplifier or speaker. A banana plug allows for quick and easy speaker line connection. They can also be piggybacked into one another to stack out of an amplifier (line impedances should always be considered when doing this).

Banana plugs come in all kinds of colors, so the most important thing to remember when wiring them up is to stay consistent – otherwise your speakers will be out of phase by reversed connections. You will often find one side of the banana post to be ribbed – traditionally this would be used on the ground (black) side of the amplifier's binding post.

SOUND

33

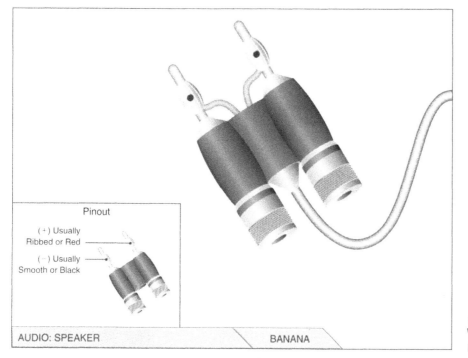

Pinout

(+) Usually
Ribbed or Red

(−) Usually
Smooth or Black

AUDIO: SPEAKER   BANANA

FIGURE 2.8
Wiring pinout of banana
plug connection.

SPEAKON SPEAKER CONNECTION

Neutrik introduced the NL series speaker connection that is now standard for any high-end professional sound system. These connections twist and lock into place, thus eliminating an easy accidental unplugging as was so often the case with the ¼-inch connector. Likewise, these connections are rated for more power and are a lot easier to wire (since you can get them in set-screw or solder models).

The NL2 is a two conductor, the NL4 is a four conductor. They make other configurations of this cable as well. You can use the NL4 connection and only wire pins 1+ and 1− for a normal passive speaker. Bi-amped connections can use the 2+ and 2− pins as well and carry all four conductors to the speaker at once.

SOUND
34

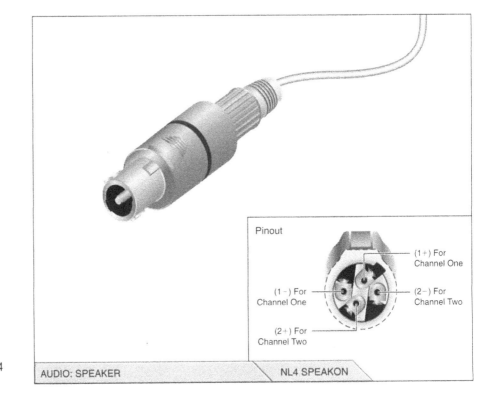

FIGURE 2.9
Wiring pinout of NL4
connection.

Pinout

(1+) For Channel One

(1−) For Channel One

(2−) For Channel Two

(2+) For Channel Two

AUDIO: SPEAKER   NL4 SPEAKON

SNAKES

While a sound system can be connected directly via a microphone cable, it is far more common to see most interconnections via a stage snake. A snake typically has a large number of stage connections on one end and a fan-out of connections on the other side.

A permanent snake might be hardwired into the wall, running with several different wires back to the console where it will enter a patch panel or connect directly to the console, while a temporary snake will most likely have a stage box that will contain all of the stage connections and a fan-out on the other side that connects to the console.

TIP
A fan-out is the end of the snake with several individual connectors. This end would normally be connected at the sound console.

There are two types of snakes – analog and digital.

Analog Snakes

Until recently, the only option for an audio snake was an analog snake.

SOUND

35

FIGURE 2.10
Analog Whirlwind snake.
Photo courtesy of Whirlwind. All rights reserved.

Analog snakes contain all of the channels inside one multi-conductor wire that runs the distance between the stage box and the fan-out. The more connections, the larger in diameter this multi-conductor wire will be. Large channel snakes that reach longer distances can be quite large (and quite heavy).

If you want to break out to a monitor console, recording mix, or other output, a transformer-based splitter is recommended. Trying to split signals without using a transformer-based splitter is possible, but it will hurt your overall quality. A transformer-based splitter will make sure the signal stays pure and isolated from noise and impedance mismatches. Transformer splits are often very expensive.

Analog snakes are susceptible to interference and noise, and take up a lot of room. Until recently, there was no choice: If you wanted to pass large channels of audio from the stage to the mixing console you had to use a snake of some sort.

There is nothing special about a snake. The connections inside are wired exactly the same. Most commonly, the ones on the stage side are panel mounted (flush mounted to the surface — in this case, the surface of a box). However, both sides of the snake can be what's called a "fan-out." This is where each individual channel is mounted on the cable itself – just like with a regular microphone cable.

Some snakes offer multi-pin connectors so you can tie them in directly to a box or attach a fan-out.

FIGURE 2.11
Mass connector.

The wire that runs the distance of the snake is a multi-conductor wire. Simply put, this one large bundle of wire contains all the wiring needed for each connector in each connection. This simply saves you from having to run each individual wire separately (which would be a huge pain and take forever). Oddly enough, it would also tend to be more expensive as each cable would be a fully finished cable. Inside the multi-cable all the cables are regular wiring with one big rubber exterior wrap for protection and extra shielding.

TIP

It's important to not run power down a regular microphone snake. The wiring inside is not heavy duty enough to handle the current, plus the fact that the wire is shielded will increase its likelihood to maintain heat from the added resistance – this can start a fire. If you need another reason to not do this, the combination of line level, mic level, and speakerlevel signals can create crosstalk in your system.

Digital snake

Fairly recently, digital snakes have emerged in the marketplace. As a quick summary – if you can utilize a digital snake, do it.

Digital snakes offer huge flexibility in running the signal and splitting the signal. Plus, they usually have excellent preamps and amazingly low signal to noise ratios. This means more headroom in your mix and a much better sound.

Early on latency was a huge issue for digital snakes.

Today, however, that problem has been solved by most manufacturers. Digital snakes can run on regular Ethernet cables or Fiber cables. The Fiber cable is usually preferable due to the increase in bandwidth and distance; however, it

TIP

Latency is the delay created by the analog to digital and digital to analog processing,

is usually much more expensive and tends to be more fragile as well.

Most Houses of Worship will be well served with a standard Ethernet digital snake solution. It is important to choose a snake with redundancy. After all, you are now relying on one single cable to transmit all of your signal information. Should that cable meet some unfortunate and unforeseen fate, you want another cable there to seamlessly pick up the signal and keep the show audio going.

We talk more about digital snakes in the Going Digital portion at the end of the Sound for Worship section of this book. But it's important to realize that you have a choice, and as digital technology continues to take over the world of pro-audio, it is definitely the way of the future.

FIGURE 2.12
Roland digital snake.
Photo courtesy of
Roland. All rights
reserved.

CHAPTER 3

More on Microphones

MICROPHONES AND LINE-LEVEL SOURCES

Overview of Microphones

Microphones come in a variety of flavors. They are referenced primarily by their "pickup pattern." Much like a loudspeaker has a coverage pattern, so does a microphone. There are five basic patterns categories for microphones, and these are referred to as "polar patterns." You will seem them listed as Omnidirectional, Cardioid, Super-Cardioid, Hyper-Cardioid, and Bidirectional.

Like reading a speaker coverage pattern, polar patterns can be intimidating until you realize what you are looking at. Often times, a manufacturer will give you readings at various frequencies. For most of your work you will suffice knowing the basics. As you advance, you can really gain from knowing the individual frequency response of your specific microphone as it pertains to vocalists of different ranges, monitor placement, and more! The illustrations in this section are meant as a reference. I find it helpful to imagine the pickup pattern of a microphone as if it were a flashlight. Wherever the field of vision would be illuminated is where the sound will be picked up. With a flashlight, if the beam does not illuminate something, it's not seen. Likewise, with a microphone pickup pattern, if the sound is not within that pattern, it's most likely not heard. Knowing where a microphone *does not* pick up sound is often just as important (sometimes more so) than knowing where it *does* pick up sound.

The illustrations here will provide you a good visual of what the polar pattern is trying to tell you. They are not intended as an accurate depiction of any specific polar pattern, but rather to help you understand the general direction in which sound will be picked up and rejected. Notice, they are slightly exaggerated to help you visualize the reception and rejection areas for each major class of microphone. The areas with the black-and-white gradation are where sound is most likely picked up from that type of microphone. Each manufacture will supply a polar pattern with their microphone, showing how it specifically performs. You will notice that the actual area of reception and rejection varies from microphone to microphone, but the same similar characteristics follow.

- *Omnidirectional* – An Omnidirectional microphone picks up sounds equally from all directions. There are some cases in which an Omni-directional microphone can be helpful, such as a lavaliere microphone for the pastor or teacher. As the person turns his or her head one way or another, the microphone tends to pick up the voice fairly evenly. However, it is important to realize the tradeoff. An Omnidirectional microphone is picking up sound from everywhere – this means your stage monitors, loudspeakers, and anything else in proximity to that microphone. This can cause a feedback nightmare. It can also make it hard to get a good, tight mix since it will pick up other instruments nearby. (See 3-to-1 Rule later in this section, Figure 3.1).
- *Cardioid* – A Cardioid microphone picks up a tighter area of sound in front of it and rejects most sound behind it (including the areas 45 degrees off the rear axis of the microphone and the area directly behind it) (See Figure 3.2).
- *Super-Cardioid* – A Super-Cardioid microphone has a narrower reception area (helping to reduce sounds coming from off-axis angles). However, as you can see in the illustration, it also starts to pick up sounds from directly behind the microphone as well (See Figure 3.3).
- *Hyper-Cardioid* – A Hyper-Cardioid microphone has an even narrower reception area in front of the microphone, but as you can see, it also has a significantly larger reception area directly behind the microphone. The microphones are very sensitive to directionality. It is important that the microphone be pointed directly at the sound source you are wishing to capture (See Figure 3.4).
- *Bidirectional* – A Bidirectional microphone receives sound from opposite sides of the microphone equally. This is similar to a figure-8 pattern. Such a microphone could be very useful for an interview where two people are sitting opposite each other, or any other situation where you would like to pick up sound from both sides of the microphone fairly equally (See Figure 3.5).

FIGURE 3.1
Omnidirectional microphone.

Omni-Directional Pattern
(Illustrated)

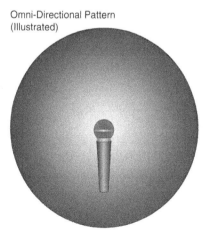

Cardioid Pattern
(Illustrated)

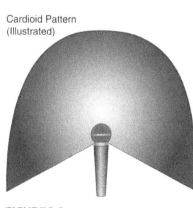

FIGURE 3.2
Cardioid microphone.

Super-Cardioid Pattern
(Illustrated)

Hyper-Cardioid Pattern
(Illustrated)

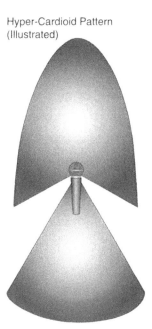

Bidirectional Pattern
(Illustrated)

SOUND

41

FIGURE 3.3
Super-Cardioid microphone.

FIGURE 3.4
Hyper-Cardioid microphone.

FIGURE 3.5
Bidirectional microphone.

TIP

Why should you care about the areas
where a microphone REJECTS sound? Because
these are the areas in which you would want to position
stage monitors, loud instruments, and other unwanted sound
sources. For instance, placing a stage monitor directly in front
of a performer using a Hyper-Cardioid microphone would be
foolish as it has such a huge reception area directly off the rear
axis of the microphone. You would pick up stage monitor sound
as well as the primary voice. You would get a lot of unwanted
clutter in your mix – not to mention the feedback issues
you would most likely face. Likewise, if a performer were
using a Super-Cardioid microphone you would most
likely want to place a trumpet player 45 degrees
behind the vocalist. This would reduce as much
of that sound as possible from this
microphone.

Boundary Microphones

Often referred to as "boundary microphones," there is a special breed of microphones that work by picking up sounds reflected on the area they sit upon. Boundary microphones are often used in boardrooms and theatrical sets. They have a very small profile and pick up sound from a broad area. These microphones usually pick up sound in either 90- or 180- degree patterns.

Boundary microphones are often used on the front lip of a stage with 90-degree coverage. This allows them to pick up the sound of the performers but reject the sound of the audience behind it. Other times, a 180-degree boundary microphone will be used (such as on a wall or set piece) (See examples of boundary microphones Figure 3.6 & Figure 3.7).

Care should be taken to avoid areas like bookshelves or other cavernous areas, as you will tend to pick up unwanted echoes. Also, if placed on a hollow floor, exaggerated footsteps and other loud impact noises can be a problem.

SOUND

42

Phantom Power

In a nutshell, phantom power is a 9–48v DC power source that powers condenser microphones. Condenser microphones must have power to operate. They receive this power via battery, an external power supply, or through the Phantom Power feed from the main console.

Phantom power was designed to eliminate the need for batteries or external power supplies. Almost all modern consoles have phantom power. Basically, the console sends voltage down pins 2 and 3 with respect to pin 1. Pin 1 is connected to the cable shield, the ground wire inside the cable, or sometimes to both.

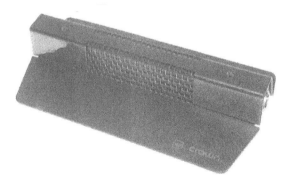

FIGURE 3.6
Crown PCC-160 microphone.
Photo courtesy of Crown Audio.
All rights reserved.

FIGURE 3.7
Crown PZM-30D microphone.
Photo courtesy of Crown Audio.
All rights reserved.

The big thing to remember as a sound engineer in the House of Worship is that Condenser microphones require phantom power in order to operate, and Dynamic microphones do not. So, if your choir microphones are not working, more than likely they are condenser microphones. Check to see if you are sending phantom power.

TIP
Condenser microphones require phantom power; dynamic microphones do not.

3-to-1 Rule

The 3-to-1 Rule is perhaps one of the most important to know concepts in sound engineering. While not a steadfast scientific number, the 3-to-1 Rule will keep you out of trouble.

Many people think that the more microphones you place in front of something the better off you are. In reality, just the opposite is usually true.

SOUND

43

Sound is a relatively slow medium. At sea level, sound is measured at 340.29 meters per second. While this seems fast compared to the family sedan, in reality it's quite slow. Also, the speed of sound is variable depending on many factors such as altitude, humidity, temperature, and more.

As sound leaves the source, it begins to travel toward the listener. Imagine you have two microphones placed in its path, side by side. Certain frequencies will actually reach one of the microphones before it reaches the other. As these frequencies are carried through your sound system and amplified out the main speakers, this delay can actually cancel the frequencies out. The result – less sound.

Imagine this example. Find a small pool of perfectly calm water. Toss a pebble in the center and watch the waves ripple out from the source of entry. Now, toss another pebble off to the side of where the first one landed. What you will observe is the waves will interfere with each other and some of the waves will diminish or dissipate all together.

The same is true with sound. As sound moves through a room it can be negated or summed depending on the size of the sound wave and the distance it travels. This effect is often referred to as a "comb-filter" effect.

After much mathematical study, it was realized that an average of 9db or more in reduction was needed to keep a microphone from canceling out the sound of a nearby source. A rule of thumb for sound engineers has become the 3-to-1 Rule.

FIGURE 3.8
3-to-1 Rule illustration.

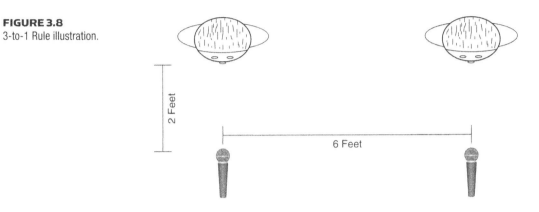

THE 3-TO-1 RULE IN PRACTICE

Basically, the 3-to-1 Rule simply states that for every 1 foot a microphone is from the primary source, the nearest neighboring microphone should be 3 feet away from it. So, using a common example, if your hanging choir microphone is 4 feet away from the primary source it is aiming at, the microphone beside it should be approximately 12 feet away.

Now, I bet if you are having troubles getting a loud-sounding choir (and we are assuming they are singing out), if you look at your microphones, they are very likely much closer to each other than this rule states. If you decide to move them further away, your stomach will turn when you see the mathematical distance play out. Nonetheless, in every situation where I have moved the microphones, in accordance to this rule, the sound always gets better and louder. The math simply works.

Choosing Vocal and Instrument Microphones

Many church sound engineers don't understand the basics of microphone technique. The subject of choosing the correct microphone and placement is a topic for a book unto itself, but we will take a brief moment and discuss the most common microphone applications for the House of Worship and see some typical ways to properly mic these situations.

Every sound system should have a basic workhorse vocal microphone and an instrument microphone. Perhaps most common to the industry is the Shure SM58 vocal microphone and the Shure SM57 instrument microphone. Pretty much anywhere you look, you will find these microphones being utilized. Many other manufacturers make similar microphones. They are usually in the $100 budget (give or take) and work fairly well. Some manufacturers will offer different warranties, some will have better feedback rejection, some will have proximity effect (this is where more bass is added to the voice as the vocalist gets closer to the microphone), and others won't. Regardless of which microphone you choose, it should be rugged, offer the desired frequency range and provide a good signal-to-noise ratio.

In 95 percent of most churches, a Shure SM58 and an SM57 (or equivalent) will get you through the day.

However, as you begin to seek a better sound, you will start to look at higher end vocal microphones from companies such as Shure, DPA, Sennheiser, Neumann, and more. You will see that these microphones provide a better frequency response curve and a nicer tone, and certain microphones compliment certain vocal ranges better than others. As the quality of microphone goes up, so does the cost. Like the old saying goes, you get what you pay for.

TIP
Your sound system is only as good as its weakest component. If you choose a $1200 vocal microphone but project it from a $200 pair of speakers, odds are you won't hear much difference than you would with a $150 microphone. Your system will always peak at the lowest common denominator in the chain.

Again, when you consider that over 80 percent of churches in America are meeting with congregations smaller than 100 people, the majority of church budgets are going to be small. So, with that in mind, spending your money on the basics will get you through most cases. I personally recommend having a good number of Shure SM58's, Shure SM57's, and a few Shure SM81's on hand at all times. If you have an orchestra, you might want to have a few Shure SM98's or Beta 98's as well.

For the average church, there are few applications where you would use a SM98 or Beta 98 that an SM81 couldn't handle, but the 98 just can't be beat for convenience and ability to travel with the sound source (since it's clipped on).

I recommend Shure because they are the industry standard, but there are other microphone companies that offer very similar basic microphones. For instance, I commonly use the EV 267a vocal microphone. It's similar in characteristic to the SM58, but I've found it tends to have better feedback rejection and less proximity effect (the voice getting more bass tone as it gets closer to the microphone). The extra feedback rejection can be a huge help to struggling church sound engineers who are trying to get everything figured out.

Likewise, Audix and several other manufacturers offer several entry-level microphones that compete with the SM58, 57, and 81 as well. The choice is yours, but make sure that you have a number of quality microphones that can handle vocals as well as instruments.

MICROPHONE TECHNIQUES

So, what if you want to get better instrument sounds and tighter mixes? Listed below are some typical microphones and placement for typical church instruments. These suggestions are primarily for live reinforcement on your stage during worship. While many of these solutions could be used for recording, they are intended for live reinforcement on stage.

Drums

There are several ways to mic a drum set. The cheap and easy way is two condenser microphones on boom stands over the drum – one on the left and one on the right. The typical microphone for this is the Shure SM81 or other high-quality condenser microphone kit, or a high-quality stereo microphone of choice mounted in the middle.

Ideally each individual drum would get its own microphone, usually mounted with a drum-rim mount if possible or on a boom stand if it's your only choice. The old workhorse, the Shure SM57, is a possible microphone for each drum, or you can go with more specialty microphones for each one. For instance, common choices for the snare drum would be microphones such as the Shure PG56, the Audix i5, the Sennheiser e905, and other similar choices.

Toms are often miked with Audix D4's, Sennheiser e904's, Shure PG56's, and other similar microphones.

In general, on the toms and snare you want to place the microphone within an inch or two of the drumhead itself, but out of the way of the player and his or her sticks.

The high-hat can be miked with a variety of microphones – the Shure SM81, Neumann U 87, AKG 451, or other similar choices.

The kick drum would be miked either directly in front of the head or, if the head is cut, the microphone should be boomed inside the kick drum for maximum effect. It should not be resting on any insulation inside the drum. Several microphones are good for this purpose – such as the EV RE20, Shure PG52, Audix D6, or AKG D 112, just to name a few. Ultimately, you want to experiment to get the best sound for your system and taste.

Shure, Audio Technica, Audix, and other manufacturers also make Drum Microphone Kits that are sold in packages that include the mounts. These are often wise choices for the House of Worship.

Piano

The piano can be miked several different ways. Some people will place a PZM microphone directly on the soundboard of the piano. If you do this, it's important to place the microphone directly on the soundboard surface (and not attempt to rest it on cloth or foam, etc.) so it can pick up the vibrations of the sound.

If you are running short of microphones, it is possible to place a Cardioid microphone such as a Shure SM57 or equivalent directly underneath the piano. It is better, if possible, to mic the piano directly over the hammers of the strings. Again, the Shure SM57 can be used if you have nothing else around. If you mic the piano this way, you should use a boom stand and place one microphone over the high-frequency strings and another microphone over the low-frequency strings.

A higher-end solution is to use a pair of AKG 414's over the strings themselves in the piano. Normally, if you don't have a good mount, you can use gaffers tape and tape the microphones laterally over the strings – again, one more over the high strings and the other over the lower strings. The larger condenser microphone will pick up a very rich and warm sound that will be reproduced well.

DPA also makes a subminiature microphone, the SMK 4061, which works really well and simply mounts to the soundboard via a magnetic base. They are low profile and their wires are very small in diameter as well, allowing you to close the piano lid.

SOUND

47

Guitar (acoustic)

When miking an acoustic guitar, it's common to aim the microphone at the sound hole of the instrument. Once again, the SM57 is a typical choice here. Other good choices would include the Shure SM81 or other condenser microphone. Other engineers will choose to move the microphone 3 or 4 inches down the neck and point it back toward the sound hole to reduce the boominess of the sound.

> **TIP**
> If you place the microphone near the sound hole, be aware of the boomy sound (due to the sound hole's resonance). You will need to turn down low-frequency EQ to get a more natural sound.

Guitar (amplified)

Obviously, you can take a feed directly out of the instrument and into a direct box. However, most musicians like to use an amplifier to modify the sound to their taste for each song. Ideally, you will want to mic the amplifier. In a House of Worship setting, a Shure SM57 sitting with the element about 2 inches from the cabinet's speaker will work great.

Horns and Woodwinds

Again, a Shure SM57 or SM81 pointed at the bell of the instrument from directly in front of it will give you a good sound. Given my preferences, I'd rather use a Shure Beta 98 with a horn clip where applicable. This way the microphone moves with the player as he or she shifts the horn around during play. Flutes and clarinets can be miked with an overhead configuration with a condenser microphone of choice.

Strings

Strings are usually boomed just slightly over the strings. A good condenser microphone should be used whenever possible. Your standard Shure SM81 would work well here. A Shure SM57 would work if nothing else were available.

Vocals

Vocal microphones almost always get gypped in Houses of Worship. Typically a Shure SM58, EV 267a, or other similar microphone is used – one microphone for all people. While this will get you by, when you want the vocal to truly excel, you should step up the microphone. Higher-quality microphones will increase the sound quality of the voice. There are also some microphones that are naturally equalized for the female voice as opposed to the male voice.

One step up would be to go to the Shure Beta line over the SM line. The Beta 58 will give you a much better sound than the standard SM58.

SOUND

48

Audix, AKG, Crown, Neumann, and Sennheiser all make quality vocal microphones for a high-end performance. The hard fact is that if your vocalists are just average at best, a general microphone will be quite fine. However, as your vocalists get better, your choice of microphone will have a much greater impact on your sound quality.

Using CD Players, Minidiscs, and Other Playback Devices

We've discussed microphones, but the other major source of input comes from playback devices. The market is flooded with various makes and models, ranging from $25 consumer units to $6000 and up commercial units. Again, you get what you pay for.

A common issue with playback devices is a very hot signal coming into the console. As with any input on your console, always start with a conservative volume level and ease the volume up until you reach the desired decibel level.

Many churches use consumer CD players and have troubles raising the fader more than a hair – even when the gain is all the way down! This is a result of the hot signal coming into the console. Most consoles have a PAD function. A PAD will effectively reduce the signal volume, allowing you a little more range on the fader.

Obviously, if you can barely move the volume fader before the volume is knocking off wigs on the back row, you have a gain structure issue (we talk more about gain structure in the next section). A PAD is really your primary way to improve this situation. If a PAD does not work, then you need to examine the entire gain structure of your system and consider backing off the amplifiers or DSP send levels so you can bring the overall system gain down, thus allowing you to increase the gain on these devices, and then lower the gain on other inputs to balance the system performance. Again, we'll talk more about this in the next section.

Most consoles give you a stereo input channel or a RCA connection input for playback devices. The idea is that you can play "preshow" music prior to your event. It has been my experience that these inputs are often useless unless you have a dedicated unit that is for nothing other than your audience zone. More often than not, they run directly to the Main Output bus. There is no way to channel them to the stage monitors, backstage speakers, or other areas where people other then the audience can hear them. This dramatically limits their usability.

TIP
Since the CD Player and other playback units are line-level devices, they should always be plugged into a line-level input.

CONNECTING PLAYBACK DEVICES TO YOUR CONSOLE

Many people are intimidated when they look at the back of a mixing console. Don't be. The inputs and outputs of a console are simply a few connections that repeat across the back. Pay attention to the labels and plug your devices in accordingly.

If your CD player is a consumer unit, it will most likely have RCA (sometimes referred to as PHONO) connections. If this is the case, I recommend using a MONO RCA to ¼-inch MONO adapter.

You can now use the standard RCA cable and connect it to your CD player. On the other end, place your ¼-inch adapters on the cable and plug the cable into a LINE input on your console. If you are in a situation where you must plug a line level device into a direct box and then use the mic input, you want to turn off the phantom power to that channel if the mixer allows you to do that. But it is always advisable to plug these devices into a line-level input.

Unless your CD player utilizes XLR balanced connections, it is a line-level device, unbalanced device. This means you should keep the run as short as possible. I would not exceed 12 feet on an unbalanced connection and would prefer to keep it to 3 or 6 feet when possible. The longer the run, the more interference and noise you will likely encounter.

Another option, if your CD player does not have XLR outputs on it, is to use a direct box. The direct box will change an unbalanced high-impedance signal into a balanced low-impedance signal. You can now run the device a much further distance – you can even place it on the stage if you wish and run it to the console via your stage connections.

Remember that your best component in a sound system is only as strong as your weakest one. Don't cheap out with cheap cables, and minimize adapters as much as possible. **One rule of thumb with pro-audio: Every connection allows for noise.** Avoid the temptation to use numerous barrel connections to lengthen a cable – just get a cable the correct length. Avoid multiple adapters (such as going from ¼-inch to ⅛-inch to RCA). Get the right cable, with the right connections. Doing so will save you headaches down the road.

SOUND
49

Computers, MP3 Players, and Other Similar Units

Computers and MP3 players offer us a great opportunity for playback. However, with these devices often come hard drives. Many consumer products

will not provide a clean input for your sound system. What might sound fantastic on a pair of $25 computer speakers might not sound as good when reproduced on a high-end professional sound system.

Often you will hear the whining of the internal hard drive and other noisy electronics emanating

SOUND

50

> **TIP**
> A great benefit to using a good direct box is that most of them have a PAD feature on them! You can select a low selection on the direct box and reduce the signal going into the console; this will help your overall gain structure (especially if your console does not have a PAD feature).

from your computer through the sound system. One key to success here is to use a high-quality sound card. Another useful tip is to turn the volume of the computer and the playback software to full. This tends to help overcome the noise floor on most electronic devices.

I've also encountered this problem while using a non-hard drive MP3 player while it was connected to the computer for charging. Disconnecting the device from the computer and running it off the battery greatly reduced the noise floor.

Line Level vs. Mic Level

There are two primary levels on a modern day mixing console – line level and mic level.

In a nutshell, mic level is (as you might expect) a non-amplified level of a microphone signal. This is a balanced low-impedance signal that's capable of traveling longer distances without hum pickup or high-frequency loss than an unbalanced high-impedance signal. This connection is typically coming from a professional grade microphone, although some high-end processing equipment, playback devices, and other similar electronics will use mic-level inputs and outputs. A mic level is normally referred to as −60 dBu.

A line level has been amplified at the source and is usually (although not always) unbalanced. Line-level signals will provide you a louder input signal than a mic level input. A line-level input will have a nominal level of around 1 volt and is usually notated as +4 dBu.

Conversely, most consumer sources (such as low-end CD players) are lower than line level and are usually noted as −10 dBu.

If you have a line-level signal coming into an input that is expecting to see a mic level, your sound will be distorted and mostly unintelligible. If you bring a mic level sound into a line-level connection, the volume will be very low and sometimes inaudible. It is important that you match your line and mic levels appropriately.

So, that's the theory. In the real world, however, things aren't that cut and dry. Manufacturers began offering a line of "pro-sumer" equipment that tries to match the needs of the professional world with the price of a high-end consumer product. Different equipment manufacturers will handle output in different ways. Some manufacturers might put preamp-like circuits in the design to boost the signal, while others might not. Some have less clean power circuits, while others are top notch.

The end result is that anything can happen. It's always a good idea to test new inputs – regardless of their function. You can test your input by bringing the gain all the way down on the channel, bringing the fader all the way down, and muting the channel. Then, plug in the device and power it on. Insert your media and press the play button. Once you know the content is playing, un-mute the channel. SLOWLY, bring up the volume fader – either until you reach the desired volume or you reach infinity on the channel. If you get to infinity and have not yet reached your desired volume, slowly increase the gain until the desired volume is achieved.

TIP
It's always a good idea to test new inputs – regardless of their function!

If the gain is all the way down and you can barely raise the fader, you have a mismatch for your circuits. At that time, change devices, PAD the channel, or utilize a direct box with a PAD feature to resolve the problem.

Utilizing Direct Boxes (DI's)

We've discussed direct boxes, but what are they really? A direct box is basically an impedance matching device that will convert an unbalanced high-impedance line-level or instrument-level signal into a balanced low-impedance mic-level signal.

The use of a direct box will allow you to achieve a couple of things. First, it allows you to make a low-impedance balanced connection that can travel hundreds of

SOUND

52

feet without hum pickup or high-frequency loss. Second, most direct boxes will offer a PAD for the signal. This will help you maintain a good gain structure for your system.

Direct boxes come in a couple of flavors – passive or active. An active direct box will have some sort of power supply (often a battery) or will run off phantom power. The idea is that a very high impedance will not load down the source and will result in a better sound. A passive direct box utilizes a transformer to change the impedance from high to low. In both cases, the quality of the direct box will determine the quality of your sound.

Generally, a cheaper active direct box will give a better sound than a low-end passive box. However, an active box will start distorting when it gets low on power, so more maintenance and care is needed. When choosing which one to use, it ultimately comes down to your specific situation.

CHAPTER 4

Gain Structure

Perhaps the single most important concept to grasp in sound engineering is the concept of gain structure. Your gain structure will determine the overall signal-to-noise ratio and distortion level of your sound system.

If the channel gain is too low, you are likely to not get optimum performance. You will have to push your fader volume so loud to get any volume out of the system that your noise floor will be tremendously high.

If the channel gain is too high, you will not have the ability to get your input and output channels at useful operating points/within unity range. This will effectively leave you without the ability to get a good mix. It will also cause you to find feedback quicker than you can say, "Oops."

The performance of your sound system centers on gain structure. Good gain structure is the cornerstone of achieving a balanced mix with a good signal-to-noise ratio and minimum feedback problems. If your system has proper gain, your amplifiers should be getting a nominal-level signal, but not so high as to cause clipping, which can damage loud speakers. Your system's master faders should be in the design center/unity area that is designated on your console, and all of your input channel faders should be in the general area of unity. Unity for most consoles is about three-quarters of the way up on the fader. It's also noteworthy to consider that the more faders you have in use, the lower the average fader should be to avoid overloading the mix bus.

NOTE: Many a technical person has taken this idea of "design center/unity mixing" to the extreme. The unity gain portion of fader travel results in the cleanest signal-to-noise ratio in the circuit. This will give you the most bang for your buck. But the bottom line is that the mix needs to sound good! Simply making sure that all the faders are lined up at design center/unity all the time does not make a good mix.

The idea is to set your gain to a setting that will allow you to keep your input faders near the unity area. They will not stay locked there. A mix is dynamic and therefore is always changing. The faders will move around (that's why they slide in the first place). The goal is to keep the integrity of your gain structure as much as possible.

If the system has a correct gain structure, then everything will ride fairly evenly. If it does not, you'll find yourself with the master faders barely up and your input faders barely up or slammed full – this is not what you want to see. You want to try to avoid pushing your faders much past unity. The signal-to-noise ratio quickly degrades after this point and you will find yourself more prone to bad noise and feedback. Instead, back off the fader a touch and increase the gain. This is what it means to balance your gain structure.

It's important to remember that every item in the signal flow will in one way or another impact your overall gain structure. For instance, if you boost 800 Hz on an equalizer, you've just increased the gain in that frequency area. Likewise, if you cut 1.2 kHz, you have decreased the gain in that frequency area. Adding effects units into the mix will increase the gain of that channel (think about it: It's taking the original signal and then summing the effects on the return).

As you start to complicate your mix by using equalization, subgroups, and outboard processing, the gain structure changes. If a sound engineer does not stay on top of the mix, he or she will quickly find the gain structure completely out of whack. This will result in poor mix quality and feedback, and consistency issues.

GAIN AS A WHOLE-SYSTEM APPROACH

Proper gain structure is not a property of just one component; it's a property of the entire sound system. As mentioned earlier, your amplifiers have gain, your processing equipment has gain, your digital signal processors have gain (and usually in multiple places), your inputs and your outputs of your main console have gains, and even your line level can have an amount of gain (if using a direct box or an instrument with volume controls such as a keyboard or guitar).

That's a whole lot of gain to keep track of.

When it comes to amplifiers, different people feel differently about the subject. First, you want to make sure your amplifiers are matched in both wattage and impedance to the speaker(s) they are powering. An amplifier can hurt a speaker component by underdriving it (too little power) just as much as it can by overdriving it (too much power). So, it's important that you power your speakers properly.

Some people advocate turning the amplifier gain input sensitivity controls to full blast and setting the system from there. Personally, I've never liked this approach. It depends on the amplifier and the manufacturers recommendation, but generally speaking, I prefer to set my amplifiers at about 85 percent of their capacity. This gives me a little headroom in the amplifier and keeps me from overdriving the speakers. I also believe with many brands of amplifiers this reduces my overall noise in the line going to the speakers, which will reduce the amount of hiss in the system.

A standard professional practice is to set up the mixing console so that it is peaking at 0 on the mixer's main output bus meter, then adjust the amplifier until the desired volume is achieved. If you find yourself cranking the amplifier all the way, you most likely need a larger amplifier, a larger speaker, or more speakers.

Once you have the gain level of your amplifiers and DSP (Digital Signal Processing) set, turn your attention to the console. Start with a CD, and play it. Set the input and output gain accordingly. Now, turn to your live mix. You're trying to get to the volume you want, while balancing the overall system gain.

If your console has very little movement on the controls, and your master volume is way down, you're going to want to examine your DSP and amplifier gains. You will want to slowly back off these gains (again, not in any one area, but as an overall group) while you slowly increase the fader settings at the console. If you find your system way out of balance, it is best to start over and set the gain structure from scratch as described above. Set the mixer to produce 0 levels on the master meter (with your input channels operating near design center/unity), then turn the DSP and amplifiers up until you reach the desired volume.

SOUND

55

TIP

When setting your gain structure, you want to make sure to leave yourself some headroom. Don't max the system out at the console level – always have a little more gain on the console so you can get louder than normal when you want or need to.

Ideally, your individual channels will have at least 30 to 40 percent more gain available to them once your system is set. This way, it's always possible for you to increase the volume of the system without having to affect your amplifiers and DSP's. Generally speaking, once you get your main system components (DSP, amplifiers, room equalization, etc.) set, you want to leave them alone.

Using the Meter Bridge to Set the Gain

Some consoles have individual channel meters, while others allow you to solo the channel; and that channel's input will then become visual on the main system meters. Some engineers will use this to set their gain. They will solo the channel (or watch the signal meter on the channel) and set the gain until it's approaching 0 dB. Generally speaking, when you solo the channel and look at the meter on the main meters, you will get more resolution and therefore more accuracy. If your system is set up properly, this can work well. It's simply another tool in the arsenal and is up to the individual sound engineer as to how he or she does it.

CLIPPING

Signal clipping is not always a bad thing – let me clarify. Almost every console has a clip light on the input channel and a clip area on the meters. Most amplifiers have a clip light or meter bank, and many pieces of outboard equipment have clip indicators. Universally this is indicated by the color red. It's either a small LED or a number of LED's (usually changing color from orange to red), or if you are watching an analog meter, it's the area of the line with the red shaded box.

Many people get confused and feel that their signal can never touch the red. This is not accurate.

Occasional clipping (the red lights flickering or the analog meter needle swinging far into and out of the red area of the dial) is okay. However, caution should be used to not exceed an occasional clip, as you will create distortion and possibly cause damage to equipment

Clipping is bad when the red led is constantly on – or is more solid than blinking (or in the case of the analog meter, the swing arm is pegged and remains stuck to the right side of the meter). Again, this is bad. This means you are pushing your system well past unity gain. You are sending a lot of signal down the line, driving everything to the point of distortion. Your mix is going to sound terrible and component damage is relatively soon to follow. Your equipment is just not made for that level of input distortion.

TIP

With clipping and gain structure alike, it ultimately comes down to common sense. Don't overdrive your equipment to the point of breaking it or causing damage, but use these tools to maximize your mix efficiency.

So, use the clip lights as an indicator of your system efficiency. Don't be afraid of them, but don't ignore them.

Rules in general are there for your overall good. The same is true with mathematical concepts for pro-audio systems. That being said, sometimes you break the rules. Even engineers will see and hear things that the system "shouldn't do," yet it sounds great. It's important for the sound engineer to have a working knowledge of the concepts that make the system work, but at the end of the day the job of the sound engineer is about achieving the best mix possible.

In the world of the House of Worship, the sound engineer's job is to make sure the message of the Gospel goes forth without hindrance and that there are no walls created during worship so the Spirit can work among the people without the hindrance of technology.

When a sound engineer is truly doing his or her job, the system disappears and the atmosphere that is created acoustically is one of confidence. What do

I mean by this? I mean the congregants have confidence in what they are hearing (lead vocals and lead instrument). **When you achieve a mix that creates this confidence, the walls that people create are torn down and they feel unafraid to worship. Every word can be heard, the melody can be followed, and there is an energy in the room that is created directly by the sound engineer.** This is the true job of the House of Worship engineer.

GAIN IS MORE THAN VOLUME

Gain affects more than simply volume. Normally in the concert world, the volume will start at its lowest and gradually build through the night until it reaches it's loudest point. In some cases, we can learn from this example in the area of worship. You can overcome some amount of listener fatigue as well as build the energy in the room.

However, it's important to realize that as your volume increases or decreases, your equalization tends to change as well. As the volume changes, so does the way your ears perceive tonality. Hence the reason you always see good concert engineers tweaking their equalization through the night.

BALANCING THE EQUALIZER

I am a firm believer in having both graphic and parametric equalizers at the front of house mix location. I believe these should be inserted through the various outputs of the console and sometimes, in extreme cases, inserted into individual channel strips.

These should be separate of the house equalization. The house equalization should be set and never altered (unless something dramatic changes in the room).

By having equalization inserted before the main house mix, you can start flat and alter the EQ as needed for that particular show and volume level. When you are done, the equalizer can once again be flattened and no adverse effects are done to the house settings. EQ should be inserted in the main Left, Right, and Center (if applicable) buses via the insert jack and insert cable. This will allow you to alter tonality in the room without changing the house settings permanently. A simply bypass of the EQ will revert the system back to the house standard.

It seems that people always like to tweak the house EQ, and in many places the room EQ is changed based on a person's preference. This EQ should be set by a qualified person, as discussed previously, and not altered. Inserting an EQ at this point on your mixer allows these engineers to adjust the room as they see fit but not change crucial settings to the actual room equalizer.

I also like to insert EQ into subgroups and occasionally into individual channels when extra tonal control or feedback elimination is needed. Likewise, EQ inserted in the AUX sends are a great idea for equalizing stage monitors, in-ears, and other sends from the console. If your console does not have an insert jack for the AUX send, you can send the AUX directly to the EQ then to the amplifier – essentially doing the same thing.

KNOW THY LAW

Most counties and cities have ordinances in place that dictate overall volume levels as well as start and end times for such public activities. For instance, one place I mix frequently has a 10 PM cutoff date for all concerts. Any concert exceeding 10 PM without special permits is in violation of the law and can be penalized.

DYNAMICS IN AUDIO

"One volume level for all things does not an interesting mix make."

Brad Herring

SOUND

58

You have probably heard the word "dynamics" as it pertains to audio, but what does it really mean? Dynamics is the natural shift of volume and intensity in the overall audio volume. You've seen dynamics in action – the pastor whispers and then he shouts. Most sound engineers become aggravated as they jump on the faders and clamp down the compressors. Sure, it creates a certain level of technical stress for the engineer – but you might be missing the point. That dynamic is with purposeful intent, and the intent is not to annoy you; the intent is to connect with the listener. The range of volume and delivery makes the speaker engaging. It keeps the delivery from being monotonous and it startles the listener back to paying attention. It also drives home points (both the whisper – by making the listener lean forward and listen intently to hear, and the shout – by being out of the normal and leaving a startling impression).

Music is the same way as is singing with the human voice. The dynamic makeup of the music creates interest and emotion.

> **TIP**
> Communicators use dynamics
> with purposeful intent – and the intent
> is not to annoy you as the sound engineer –
> the intent is to connect with
> the listener.

Many House of Worship sound engineers spend all their time trying to balance the audio and make it the same level. When this happens, the sound engineer is directly competing with the intent of the music! The engineer thinks he or she is doing a good thing but in reality, the engineer is actually detracting from his or her main goal.

Don't fret dynamics – embrace them. Sure, you still have to limit the extremes to keep your system performance within tolerances, but go with it – enhance it.

Likewise, a good sound engineer can create dynamics. For instance, imagine a scenario where the band is playing a song. In this example, you are alert and paying attention. You notice the lead guitarist steps forward. Thinking quickly, you realize he's about to let it rip! You decide that it's going to really add to the moment, so you discretely bring the guitar up in the mix just slightly over everything else. Suddenly, that instrument is engaged in one-on-one worship! The sound of that guitar rings through the room tastefully over the sound of the other instruments for a few measures. The neck of the guitar drops a little bit (an indicator that the moment is over), the guitarist slowly steps back into place, and you ease the guitar back into its place in the mix.

You have just created dynamics in the mix. You have just created an environment of worship.

I tell people all the time, the A/V team is critical to modern worship. They are a part of the worship team – it's not you and them. When you step behind that console you are playing an instrument as well, it's just a different type of instrument. Only, you have the most exciting musical instrument of all – you get to blend everyone together. You become the concertmaster! The responsibility of the full presentation of worship sits on your shoulders. The worship pastor has struggled all week (and in many cases much longer than that) to prepare context based on the movement of the Holy Spirit, and now, it is your job to communicate that context in an easy to absorb presentation that again eliminates people's walls and defenses and allows them to be easily reached by the Holy Spirit.

SOUND

59

That's not a small task. That makes you far more than a button pusher. You are an integral part of worship and teaching.

When you learn how to create dynamics in your mix, you learn how to make your instrument really sing. For instance, using a delay effect on the last word of a hanging vocal will make that word resonate and ring through the auditorium. Vocalists can't do that on their own – that's the task of the sound engineer. And that is the type of thing that a sound engineer gets to do that makes the hair on people's neck stand. The people don't know their neck hair is standing because of what you just did – it's imperceptible to them. You've created an environment. And with this environment, walls come down and worship manifests itself in supernatural ways because the flesh is no longer in the way.

Conversely, when you don't pay attention, you don't create dynamics, you allow feedback, you don't bring up microphones on time, etc., you create walls. Seriously – you create an environment where people are annoyed, they are sitting on the edge of their seat trying to hear, and they don't engage. They are timid. The worship leader struggles to engage the people, the pastor works feverishly to connect with the listener. The entire environment creates a situation of struggle and work to do the very that everyone has assembled together to do.

Sound really makes that big of a difference. If nothing else in this book resonates with you, I hope that this fact will. The two paragraphs above are a clear example of the impact you as a sound engineer have on worship.

The difference between the two scenarios is training, paying attention, having the heart of a servant and engaging with the worship team in practice.

Controlling Dynamics for Quality Audio

While dynamics are good for communicating and connecting with the audience, there is no denying the technical challenges it presents to the House of Worship engineer.

Unexpected or extreme volume changes can play havoc on a sound system. This is where the use of expanders, compressors, and limiters come into play. There is no way that a human operator can respond quickly enough to extreme changes – especially when the mix exceeds three or four channels. Sometimes, by the time you identify the specific channel the instance has happened and ceased. The audio engineer needs processing equipment that is always looking for these changes to help him or her out.

We will discuss compressors, limiters, and other signal processing tools later in the electronic processing section of this book. But for now, realize that there are tools that when utilized correctly can help you overcome the extreme dynamics for your mix integrity. The point that I want you to get from this section is that you should not fight dynamics nor should you try to compensate for them in your mix. Keep them under control, but realize the importance of dynamics in a mix and go with it.

PANNING AND EQUALIZATION

When it comes to dynamics, panning and equalization play a part of this as well.

TIP

Panning is the ability to move the signal from one channel to another. In its simplest form it is placing signal in the left, right, and center channels at various proportions. In a more technical and concise definition, it's the sending of a signal to multiple channels in variable amounts.

If you are mixing in a true stereo environment (or if you are mixing stereo for recording), you will find that panning sources around will create a broader-sounding mix. There are many theories on this, but the principle is that by panning sources you can help bring certain instruments more predominately into the mix as well as help the listener sound surrounded by the mix. In a live setting, panning can also help the listener with localization – that is, the ability for the listener to determine where the sound is coming from.

If a pastor enters stage left and starts to speak, the first reaction of the people is "Where is he?" Listeners then disengage while trying to orientate themselves to the speaker. As humans, we feel a need to connect visually to people speaking to us – especially when they are in the same room. Once listeners find the person speaking, they can then tune into what's being said. If you are able to pan the sound more dominantly in that direction, the ear automatically takes the listener to that side of the stage. (Coincidentally, as you add lighting to the mix and subtly bring up light in that area, the viewer will tend to locate the person more quickly as well – see how it all sums up for the overall connection to the audience?).

Now, obviously if you are not mixing in a stereo environment, panning is not used in the same way. In a mono environment, panning is often used to separate subgroup sends on many consoles. For instance, you might have an eight-subgroup console. Normally, these are linked in stereo (so subgroup 1 is left, subgroup 2 is right, subgroup 3 is left, 4 is right, and so on). By panning some instruments left and assigning them to subgroups 1 and 2, you have just assigned that channel to subgroup 1. Then take another group of channels and pan them right while assigning them to subgroups 1 and 2, and you have now placed them in the right subgroup. This will give you the maximum flexibility in your MONO mix.

One problem with many stereo PA systems is that only people in the center hear the true mix, while people sitting on either side hear dominantly from the speaker cabinet closest to them. These people actually hear a different mix than what is intended. There are ways around this with speaker placement and design, but due to the sheer cost of such a system most stereo systems suffer from these problems. Hence, most PA systems are mono systems and pan is used to control signal as it routes through the console (as described in the previous paragraph). Pan for actual mixing is used far more extensively in the recording areas of pro-audio.

Some higher-end consoles allow you to assign a channel into a single subgroup regardless of pan, but most consoles tend to link them in stereo pairs. If your console limits you in this way and you are using a MONO mix, it's another way that pan can help control dynamics. Remember that everything is summed when it comes to audio mixing – so, if you have a signal in subgroup 1 and that same signal in subgroup 2, when you bring up both subgroups, you will be doubly increasing the signal, whereas if you had the signal panned only to subgroup 1, you would mitigate this possibility.

Everything builds on everything else. It's important as a sound engineer to keep your head in the game at all times. Know where everything is set and have a plan for where you are going in the mix. This is the best way to keep out of trouble with the mix and create a dynamic mix that incorporates worship!

Equalization

We've talked a lot about equalization, but now it's time to really delve into what equalization is and how it affects your mix. There are several purposes of equalization and several different equalization types. Let's look at all of this to give you a better idea of what you are facing.

ROOM EQUALIZATION

Room equalization is accomplished with the main system equalizer. No doubt, at some point in your life, you have been told, "Don't touch that Equalization – it's been set." This can be really frustrating if it's the only equalizer in your system and you are experiencing a lot of tonal and feedback problems.

The equalization they are referring to is the room equalization. It's a primary part of the sound system. If the room equalization is done correctly, it will create a balance for the entire system that will allow you the maximum flexibility and the best sound quality. Once this is set properly, you should never mess with it again unless something dramatic changes in the sound system or the room (i.e., new speakers, amplifiers, or console or major room renovations or acoustic changes).

So, what is room equalization and why is it so special? When your sound system was installed, it should have been tweaked to the room. Probably your Audio Consultant used an RTA (short for real-time analyzer) to measure the loudspeaker/room frequency response. We see RTA's as a tool in pro-audio systems. The concept is similar, but a room RTA is often more precise and takes into account several locations.

When the contractor or consultant RTA's your room, he or she follows a series of steps. Generally speaking, they will take a highly tuned computer-based RTA and set it to a narrow bandwidth (this means they will see many more individual frequencies than the 31 you see reflected on your basic graphic equalizer). After calibrating their equipment, they will place a highly sensitive test microphone in the room at listener position (so, if the average person were sitting in a chair and his or her ear were 45 inches from the floor, the microphone would be placed at this level; likewise if the person were standing and his or her ear were at an average of 70 inches from the floor, the microphone would be placed at that level).

The engineer would then excite the room with pink noise. Pink noise is all frequencies at the same overall level per octave. The microphone hears this pink noise and then visually represents on the computer RTA the level of each octave or third-octave band. When the engineer looks at the screen, he or she will normally see peaks and dips in the room at various frequencies.

The engineer will then move the microphone to various locations in the room and note the average response he or she sees as the microphone sits in different positions (such as house left, house right, under the balcony, in the balcony, center front, the very back row, etc.).

Once the common frequencies are identified, the engineer will then boost or cut these ranges with the system equalizer. He or she will continue to do that until the room starts to flatten out visually. This means that all frequencies are responding similarly relative to each other.

This is the starting point of room equalization. Next, most engineers will do signal sweeps. Playing a range of frequencies into the house, they will find rattles and hums that are often generated by specific frequencies and emanate from items such as loose air vents, metal work, and so on.

Finally, you should play back music of various styles. Find music that you are familiar with and play it over the PA system. You should listen to the nuances and details of the music as well as the overall mix of the songs. By listening to music you are familiar with, you know what you should be hearing. You can then make minor adjustments based on what you hear. This is relative. For instance, the type of tonal qualities one person likes in a sound system will not necessarily be what someone else likes. So, you want to take an unbiased approach as much as possible. Think about your audience.

For instance, if your audience is 65 years old and over, you will most likely not want a huge amount of bass and super-loud volumes – even if this might be your personal preference. Likewise, if you are trying to reach 20- to 30-year-olds in a contemporary setting, you are very likely going to push the bass response in the room. You will find that bass response often correlates with excitement and energy in a mix. Also, in a contemporary setting, you will have a desire to push louder volumes and run worship more like a concert setting. Again, this might be against your personal taste, but you want to think about your audience and your mission goal of whom you are trying to attract – and mix toward that.

If you are in a blended setting, like so many of our churches are, you will need to find a happy medium in the mix – something that drives the mix for the younger audiences and something that smoothes the mix for the older members.

Listening to music over the PA system will tell you a lot more about how the room will sound – not just how the room will respond (as the RTA shows you). Now that you have listened to music that you know, I believe it's important to listen to music similar to your style of worship. I would encourage you to not listen to your own recordings, but to listen to professionally produced music within the genre of your style of worship. This will help ensure that you are listening to a correctly balanced mix and therefore not compensating for recording inadequacies.

SOUND
64

TIP
It's important to listen to music with a variety of musical range to give you a good feel of the response in the room.

There are two things that are important about setting your room EQ.

When it comes to setting your room EQ, this should be left to a professional who has the equipment and training to do the job correctly. Once the EQ is set for the room it SHOULD NOT BE ADJUSTED unless there is a major acoustic change in the room or a huge renovation of the sound system. Tonal quality and event feedback notching should be done via inserted equalizers and channel equalization – not the room equalizer. This is one reason many installers place the main house EQ away from the mixing console – so the mix engineer is not tempted to modify it!

TIP
When you listen to music, your changes should
be very subtle. The idea of room equalization is to get
the room responding to the best of its ability. When all
frequencies in a room react in a similar and predictable manner,
you have the most control over your mix. You know the room is
RTA'd properly when you are able to make minor adjustments on
the individual channel EQ and hear the effects in the room. Assuming
the EQ is enabled and you are adjusting frequencies within the
range you are hearing, if you are cranking the EQ like
crazy and hearing very little affect to the signal, you
most likely have a room EQ issue.

SYSTEM EQUALIZATION

With your room equalizer (the one that we just covered that has been set for the room acoustics), you should then layer equalization on top of it for feedback notching and tonal control.

TIP
As a rule, you should judiciously choose your equalizer
settings. Extreme equalizer alterations will usually do more harm
than good. If you find yourself making large equalization corrections
over a broad section of the equalizer, you should inspect your
room equalizer for accuracy.

There are two primary types of outboard equalizers – graphic and parametric.

Each band of a graphic equalizer is easily recognized because it has a set number of faders that represent various frequencies and generally a fader that controls the overall gain of the unit. Graphic equalizers come in various sizes, but they are most commonly 15-band and 31-band flavors. The number of bands is equal to the number of faders on the face of the unit.

A graphic equalizer has a set range (also referred to as "Q" or "bandwidth") that each fader manipulates. For instance, if you alter the gain on 1.2 KHz by adjusting the 1.2 KHz fader, you are not simply adjusting 1.2 KHz; you are also

SOUND

66

affecting many of the frequencies on either side. A standard configuration for a graphic equalizer is a one-third octave equalizer. In this setting, if you were to move the 1.2 KHz fader as mentioned above, you would also be affecting the one-third octave of frequencies centered at 1.2 kHz. On some equalizers, you affect a broad section of frequencies at small boosts and cuts and a smaller area of frequencies on a larger boost or cut.

Other common configurations are one-octave and one-half octave widths.

> **TIP**
> What's important to realize is that when you alter the fader of your selected frequency, you are actually affecting other frequencies as well.

A parametric equalizer (sometimes referred to as a "variable-Q equalizer") generally offers the user fewer individual bands, but far more control of the sound by allowing each band to select the frequency AND the bandwidth (or Q) that your selection will affect.

For instance, you can select the same frequency as above (1.2 KHz) and then select the bandwidth you wish to affect. You can select a very narrow bandwidth (often called a "notch" if you apply a cut) or a very wide bandwidth to affect a large number of frequencies.

A parametric equalizer can be a real lifesaver in many applications for the House of Worship. It is an excellent tool for minimizing feedback (by notching out the offending frequencies one by one) and it can be used for tonal control (using a wide-Q selection). While it's not as easy to look at and grab a frequency as a graphic equalizer, it certainly offers the engineer a great addition to his or her bag of tricks.

Using a parametric equalizer is as simple as selecting the frequency via the Frequency control, selecting your bandwidth via the Bandwidth or Q control, and then selecting the amount of boost or cut with the Gain control. Once you have your settings, you can roll the Frequency control back and forth and sweep those setting on various frequencies as you move the knob. This can be helpful in finding a specific offending frequency.

CHANNEL EQUALIZATION

When you look at the individual input channels on your mixing console, you will see that each channel has a section for equalization. On larger consoles, you find semi-parametric (typically a sweepable frequency and boost/cut). Rarely, and only on large, expensive consoles, will you find true fully parametric EQ. Most of your smaller analog consoles have three to four fixed bands of EQ. The better ones have two swept mids. Normally, you are limited to two or three frequencies. On less-expensive consoles these frequencies are locked and you cannot select your own frequencies. Some consoles have parametric EQ – they allow you to have complete control over both the frequency and the bandwidth – especially on newer digital consoles. The gamut can be anywhere in between, depending on your console.

TIP

In general, it is better to cut frequencies when altering system EQ rather than boosting them.

So, while you might have a limited number of bands of equalization per channel, you still have a fairly powerful amount of equalization per channel.

Sometimes, however you need more equalization for specific purposes (such as equalizing a difficult voice or notching individual channel feedback, or any number of other reasons). Most consoles have an Insert Connection on the back. By using an insert cable (this is a ¼-inch Tip-Ring-Sleeve connection that branches out to two ¼-inch Tip-Sleeve connections; one Tip-Sleeve connection is the send, the other is the return), you can connect any piece of outboard processing to the individual input or output that has the insert connection.

So, you would take the insert cable and insert the Tip-Ring-Sleeve (TRS) end of the cable into the insert connection. Then, depending on your console, either the Tip or Sleeve connection will be the send, while the other is the return. Insert the Tip-Sleeve connector for the SEND connection into the INPUT of the processing equipment and insert the Tip-Sleeve connector for the RETURN connection into the output of the unit. You can also chain equipment together by connecting the output of the first piece of equipment in the input of the next, then taking the output of that component to the RETURN connection of the insert cable. Now you have two components inserted into this channel. You can continue to do this as need be.

However, whatever you insert will only be available on that one channel. Sometimes, people will insert equipment on a subgroup (such as a compressor or effects processor). This will allow you to affect any channel going into the subgroups with the processing equipment inserted and allow you more bang for your buck (although limiting a lot of flexibility).

FIGURE 5.3
Channel EQ on face of console.

CHAPTER 6
Electronic Processing

Most churches in America (and elsewhere for that matter) are primarily using a microphone, a mixer, a systems equalizer, and loudspeakers. Many churches are fighting to maintain some level of control with just a few components and would be quick to ask, "Why would I want to add more components into the equation?"

My first response would be, if your church can't get a most basic mix without feedback, dropped microphone cues, and the other mere basics, then you probably shouldn't add anything else to the mix.

However, electronic processing can offer huge advantages to your mix. Therefore, if you fall into the category of churches that can't keep their head above water (technically speaking), you should do everything within your power to get there so you can really start to craft your mix and improve your ability to communicate with your audience.

The mark of a successful mix should not be that you did not get feedback. It shouldn't even be about getting compliments on a good blend or being able to hear a vocalist. These might be short-term accolades and definitely accomplishments on your way, but the real goal should be to create an amazing mix that breaks down the walls of insecurity in public worship! Creating a mix that sweeps people into the environment and provides them confidence and excitement should be the ultimate goal, because as we've mentioned earlier in this book, this is the place where people really begin to experience corporate worship, let their defenses down, and allow the Holy Spirit to work within them!

Electronic processing goes a long way in helping you achieve this kind of dynamic mix.

So, with this in mind, let's take a look at some of the most typical electronic processing components and discuss how you might use them.

AN EASY WAY TO LEARN ELECTRONIC PROCESSING

One great way to learn how various effects work in your sanctuary is to record someone from your church singing. Ideally, record just that person and a piano or guitar. Record the instrument on the left and the vocal on the right. Now, you can set that track to loop and bring the left side in on one channel of the board, and the right track on another channel. You now have a test bed to play with effects all day long while no one is growing impatient with you (or looking over your shoulder). You can now add effects to the voice, the instrument, or both! This will go a long way toward helping you understand how and when to use electronic processing.

SOUND

70

EQUALIZATION

We just took a good look at equalizers, so we won't go into much detail here. However, it's important to realize that equalization is a form of electronic processing. It takes the original signal and alters it (hopefully improving it) and colors it to achieve a specific sound as desired by the engineer.

REVERB

Reverb is another class of effects processors. Have you ever sung in the shower? You've probably heard the old saying, "Everyone sounds good when they sing in the shower," right? The reason for this is a long reverberation time that is created by the large number of hard surfaces and right angles. This allows the sound wave you create with your voice to bounce around all over the place. The echoes (or reflections) that are created when you sing in the shower result in what is known as "reverberation."

Too much reverberation will kill intelligibility in the room (or in laymen terms, it will make it very difficult to understand what is being said). However, a little reverberation will allow you to create an environment that blends vocals and helps performers. It can make them sound like they are performing in a large open room as opposed to a small tightly packed room. It can add space and dynamics to your mix and really help create a feeling of excitement.

Reverb is great for the vocalist as he or she is singing – but it is not great for the spoken word. So, you might want to add some reverb while the person is singing, but you will need to remove it when he or she speaks to the audience directly. Again, this is due to diction and being able to understand what is being said.

Reverb will have many settings – usually referred to as "plates," or "rooms". For instance, a large plate or a large room will have a long reverb time that rings through the room, while a small plate or a small room will have a fairly quick reverb time.

There are a ton of settings on most reverbs. When starting out, I'd recommend that you stick to the factory presets and then slowly venture out on your own as you get more comfortable with the settings.

CHORUS

When used tastefully, chorus is in many ways similar to reverb, but the sound is a little different. Chorus adds a signal to its detuned replica, creating a wavy or shimmering effect. The chorus effect can make a vocal or instrument sound like there are several of them versus creating a reverberation of the original signal. One of my favorite places to use a chorus effect is with an acoustic guitar (especially when the instrument is being plucked versus strummed).

Chorus will really add to the richness of the sound and help bring the instrument to life. It will add dimension to the mix and make it sound more like a polished performance that you would expect to hear on a professional recording.

Again, like with the reverb, your effects processor will come with several factory presets. Use them as you begin to experiment with the sounds you can get before venturing on your own.

SOUND

71

FLANGE

Flanging is an old favorite for guitarists in particular. It gives a very hollow, swishing sound to the source. Usually, the instrumentalist will choose this effect to match the style he or she is playing. However, most effects processors will offer flange effects. Flanging is created by adding a signal to its delayed replica, where the delay is swept continuously from about 0 to 15 milliseconds (ms).

It is yet another tool to enrich the sound of your mix and help make certain instruments stand out during certain segments.

DELAY

Delay is used both as an effect and an environmental control. Don't be confused by the two.

First, system delay is used as an environmental control. Sound is relatively slow. If you have a row of speakers at your stage and another row midway back in your auditorium, odds are you are going to have a time issue. Without a delay, the speakers will fire at the same time. By the time the content of the first speaker reaches the second row of speakers, the second row of speakers is already that distance ahead of it. So, the audience perceives this as an echo. It makes for terrible intelligibility.

So, the key is to place a delay processor on the second row of speakers. This way, they wait until the first row of speakers catch up to them and then they fire. This keeps all the signals time aligned. So you get rid of unwanted echoes and phasing issues.

A delay effect is totally different. A delay effect (basically a controlled echo) will take the original signal and play it again at a time specified by the user. It will continue to play this delayed sound until its duration is reached. How the delayed signal is reproduced is up to the engineer. It can delay for a set duration of time and fade in volume as desired.

Delay can make for a memorable effect when used correctly. It is commonly used in concert vocalists to echo a last word or phrase and can add a lot of effect and dimension to a performance.

COMPRESSOR/LIMITER

Perhaps the most misunderstood (and possibly most feared) piece of electronic processing is the compressor/limiter. It's really unfortunate, because these two components can go a long way toward helping you achieve a better mix.

In its most basic explanation, a compressor allows you to set a certain threshold (or volume) that you are willing to accept. Once that threshold is reached, the compressor allows you to set how quickly it grabs the volume, how hard it pulls the volume down, how long it keeps it attenuated before releasing it, and how quickly it releases it once it does.

SOUND

72

A limiter is like a compressor on steroids. A limiter allows you to set a volume threshold you are willing to allow and then, no matter what, never allow that signal to peak above that setting – regardless of how aggressive it has to be in its methods to keep the signal below that point.

It's not uncommon for a beginner to seek help and get responses such as, "Just play with it until it does what you want." Not exactly a helpful answer, is it?

Don't be discouraged.

First, understand that the natural tendency (once you understand what these devices do) is to set them way too conservatively and expect them to mix for you. Remember when your momma taught you that nothing is free and nothing is easy? Apply that here.

With compressors and limiters come tradeoffs, and the tradeoffs here are artifacts. Some artifacts are "pumping" and "breathing." You will be able to actually hear the compressor/limiter as it begins to do its job.

For instance, if you have it set to compress anything above –15 dB on the console meter, then you send it a –3 dB signal; it's going to sound squashed as this piece of equipment tries to compress a –3 dB signal down to –15 dB. However, this is a great example of why you would want a limiter in the system to begin with. Let's say that you get a feedback spike at 125 dB, but you've set your limiter threshold for an equivalence of 90 dB. Perhaps you've done this to protect your loudspeakers or perhaps you've done it for overall volume control. That limiter is going to grab that noise and keep it below your setting. This is going to protect your equipment. It's not going to sound pretty, but it's going to save the day and prevent expensive repair and/or replacement.

Now, the real purpose for a compressor is taking sudden spikes and reducing them. For example, an extra-aggressive hit on the cymbals, or an out of the ordinary loud shout from the pulpit, or a screeching soloist who has gone real wrong on a bad note – all of these are examples of judicial use of compressors. The compressor will react quicker than you can on the loud and unexpected peaks, attenuate the spike, and return it to normal operating level once the spike is gone. This is essentially what you would do at the volume fader if you were quick enough (it's really difficult to be that quick sometimes – especially on a complicated mix).

There are several schools of thought as to how to best set a compressor or a limiter. The practical side suggests that during sound check you listen for the loud spikes and conservatively set your threshold so that the compressor will just barely grab them. Most engineers for Houses of Worship would probably lean toward using a soft knee on vocals (this will tend to grab the signal with more of a natural sound, albeit a little slower) and a hard knee on instruments like drums and piano where the compression transition can be very quick.

TIP
A compressor helps control your mix, and a limiter helps protect equipment and hearing.

SOUND

73

How long you hold the sound in its attenuated state (sustain) is a personal preference, as is how quickly it releases (decay).

If you set the compressor too hard, you'll know it because your mix will suffer. You'll lose all the dynamics in the voice or the instrument along with all the strength of the signal. Using the example at the top of this section, play your recording and crank in the compressor and limiter. Listen to them at their extremes to understand what they do and how they do it, then back off to a conservative setting and listen to how they help you maintain order in the mix.

TIP
A well-set compressor will keep you from constantly grabbing faders and yanking them down just to slowly reset them, and a well-placed limiter will keep you from dropping a speaker cluster to replace a smoked-out voice coil.

As a starting point, you might want to set your threshold at 0, your ratio at 1:3, the attack at 30 ms and the release at 100 ms. Then, as you are playing your content at full level, turn the threshold setting down until you begin to see 2–4 dB of compression on the signal. This will get you in the ballpark and provide some level of dynamic control. If you want to control larger peaks, raise the threshold, raise the ratio to 1:5 or 1:8, and turn the attack and release down a bit.

GATES

Gates are often misunderstood and commonly left out of the mix. A gate can be a great tool – and it can also have devastating results.

A gate is a component that mutes the channel it is on until that channel reaches a certain threshold (volume). Once this signal reaches the threshold that has been set, it opens the channel.

Sound systems with too many microphones open and high stage volume can sound terrible (and most often do). So, what happens is you have a loud source on stage; in this example, we'll use the kick drum. The kick drum is miked with a kick drum microphone usually sitting inside the drum itself.

When the large foot mallet slams into the backside of the kick drum, the drum emanates a loud low-frequency response. But does only the kick drum microphone hear this sound? Of course not – the snare mic, tom mics, cymbal mics, hi-hat mics, and overhead mics all hear it too – and they hear it all out of time with each other. The result? Mud.

SOUND

74

So, what do you do when you have microphones in close proximity and they are going to pick up ambient sounds, but you have to have them all up at once (such as in a drum cage)? You place a gate on them. This way, the cymbal mic is muted unless it hears a signal that is loud enough to only be from the instrument it is nearest to (the cymbal), and the same goes for the tom mics and the snare. Your overhead microphones are a little trickier because you are using them to round off the entire sound of the kit; but normally speaking, the overheads are run fairly softly, so they don't give you as much problem in the mix.

Choir microphones are another killer. Even with a gate, once they open up, they pick up everything that they hear – and this is usually 25 percent choir and 75 percent everything else in the room. If you SOLO or PFL a choir microphone, just listen. You will most likely hear the entire mix in that one microphone – commonly you'll find the organ, the B3, the trumpet, the drums, and anything else that's screaming around the stage. This is why controlling the stage volume is so important (and we'll look at that in the next section when we discuss stage monitoring).

A gate is easy enough to set – the exact setting is up to the engineer. Too conservatively and it will be mostly ineffective, too liberally and it will cut off the first semblance of the sound. In other words, it'll open too late and you'll miss something.

Perhaps the best thing about using gates is that they give you more overall gain before feedback as well as a tighter sounding mix. Essentially, they reduce your noise floor by reducing the number of open microphones that are just picking up the room, and they improve the tightness of your mix by doing the same thing.

HOOKING IT ALL UP

So, now that you are aware of these components, how do you go about hooking them all up? That's a great question, and there are several ways to do so.

The best place to start is the manufacture's instruction manual. I know, no one wants to read the book, but it is usually where the vital piece of information is found at 3 AM when you could have found it at midnight and gone home. Can I get an amen from the choir?

Most manufactures will suggest the ideal ways to connect their equipment to your sound system, but listed below are the most common methods.

Auxiliary Sends and Returns

This is one of the most common ways to hook up external processing devices. Simply take the auxiliary output from the back of the console and route it to the INPUT of the piece of equipment you wish to use. Then, take the OUTPUT of the processing component and route it back to the mixing console. This can be done in one of two ways: On some consoles you can route the auxiliary back to an auxiliary return, or you can return the signal to any of your normal input channels.

Personally, I prefer to route the return into a channel because I have full control of the equalization, the signal routing, and the metering. These advantages make it worthwhile for me to eat up an input channel whenever possible.

Once the unit is plugged in, you simply select the channel you wish to add to the effect and dial up the corresponding auxiliary knob. You will also need to make sure the MASTER AUXILIARY knob is up as well. If you are not getting a lot of effect, turn the master up first, then work on the individual channel sends. Some processors require a lot more input than you would expect, but as with all things, begin with a little and work your way up to where you need to be. It is important when using the AUX system to control delay-based effects that the effects unit be set to 100 percent wet at the device itself.

Insert Cables

Perhaps the second most popular way to connect outboard equipment is via an insert cable and the insert connection on the back of the console.

An insert cable works by utilizing a ¼-inch Tip-Ring-Sleeve (TRS) connection at one end and two ¼-inch Tip-Sleeve (TS) connections at the other. We discussed the insert cable earlier in this book, but to recap, the TRS connection contains the send and receive, while one TS connection on the other side is a send and the other is a return.

The use of an insert cable allows you to take the raw signal, send it to the processing unit, and return it to that same channel affected by the processor.

FIGURE 6.1
Auxiliary control knob on face of console.

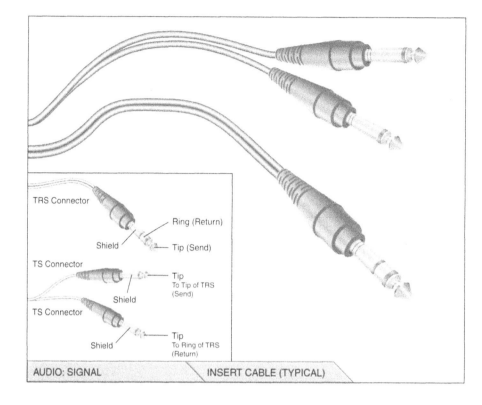

FIGURE 6.2
Insert cable.

This method is commonly used for compressors, limiters, parametric equalizers, gates, and other such devices, but not for delay-based effects.

The benefit is that it doesn't use up auxiliary outputs and other critical output paths; the negative side to this is that you can only use the processor on that one individual channel. So, it's really up to the end user if this is a viable option or not.

As a general rule of thumb, delay-based effects (such as echo, chorus, flanging, reverb, etc.) should be connected via the auxiliary bus, and dynamic-based effects (such as compressors, limiters, and gates) should be connected via the insert jack.

Personally, I use inserts on either individual channels or subgroups for my outboard compressors, limiters, and parametric equalizers.

Direct Outs and Channel Returns

Another option for routing signal to your external processors is using the direct output of the channel (if your console has direct outs). Some lower cost consoles have a "workaround" that allows you to half-patch a Tip-Sleeve cable into the insert connection. This will use the channel's send without connecting to a return. It's a cheap way to achieve the result, but with manufacturers looking to provide low-cost alternatives, it's a creative way of solving the problem.

The direct out will allow you to take the raw signal on that channel and send it wherever you need while still having the unaffected signal at the channel to control as desired. Direct outs are sometimes useful for recording scenarios where you want to split the signal to in-ear monitors and other similar purposes.

Again, if the signal is to be processed and returned to the console, you can send it back via an available input channel, as described above. Normally, a direct out connection is used to get the signal to another source and not necessarily to bring it back into the mix.

FINAL THOUGHTS ON PROCESSING

I cannot stress enough that when it comes to any form of electronic processing, less is more. When you start cranking effects everywhere, your mix gets muddy and the goal of presenting a clear mix is missed. The other thing that will happen is the effect will take precedence over the actual signal. So, it will be obtrusive and suddenly will sound like you got a new toy and can't wait to try it out – and put it everywhere. The goal is to use effects judiciously to help make the mix really pop. They should be subtle and barely noticeable. Ideally, the effect should be perceived as a room acoustic and not a trick. For instance, when you run delay through a vocal and the voice rings on the last couple of words, it should feel normal – not forced.

FIGURE 6.3
Direct out of console.

SOUND

77

Also, keep in mind that with each additional processor, you are summing or subtracting your overall system gain. So, in other words, with the use of external processing you are altering your gain structure along the way. You must keep in mind your gain structure and your noise floor as you implement more complexity into your mix.

Finally, processing should be a part of your mix – it should not be the mix. Processing should be a subtle addition to the raw mix that helps the mix dynamically and emotionally. It should flavor the mix and help make it interesting. If your mix is nothing but the processing, your mix is going to sound terrible. Make sure you keep everything in perspective as you mix.

CHAPTER 7

Stage Monitors and
In-Ear Monitors

I continue to be surprised by the number of churches that don't understand or use stage mixes. So, let's take a moment and talk about what a stage mix is and why it's important.

When you mix your service, the audience needs to hear a polished, well-rounded mix of the instruments and vocals. This mix is what creates an environment that encourages worship.

Alternatively, the musicians on your stage need to hear something very different. They need to hear components of the mix. For instance, the worship leader is going to need to hear your primary instrument (most likely a piano or guitar) and certain vocals. He or she might want to hear the drums or specifically the kick drum to help keep time. The worship leader may not care to hear the bass guitar or other parts of the mix. It's just not necessary to do the job.

It's your job as the engineer to find out what each musician and vocalist needs in the mix and provide it. When the stage monitor mix goes haywire, it's a very scary thing for the performer. It's like taking a security blanket away from a baby – only with real consequences.

I am not a musician. However, I was once "strongly encouraged" by a pastor to lead worship for a youth camp. I recall getting caught up in the moment and venturing off stage and into the crowd. I was using wedge monitors, and suddenly I found myself in the house unable to hear my monitor mix. It didn't take long for that song to go in the tank. I couldn't hear my primary vocalist and I couldn't hear the keyboards. I was so far off that the song was unrecoverable. This was a strong lesson to me in the value of consistent stage monitors.

So, stage mixes are critical, but even more critical to the overall mix is how you control the stage volume. I like to teach that mixing sound is all about controlling the acoustic energy in the room. If your stage volume is out of control, you are sunk.

Many churches find themselves mixing sound with the main speaker output all the way down or barely up at all! If this is where you find yourself, you need to reevaluate your on-stage instrument and monitor levels, and make significant changes to the way you mix worship. When you are not using your house mix, the audience is only hearing the monitors. This (as we just discussed) is not a balanced mix. On top of it all, it's not a direct mix – this is sound that is heard after it bounces off a back wall and then comes out to the audience. It's going to sound like mud, regardless of what you do.

If you are using wedge monitors, the rule of thumb is that your front-of-house sound plus the stage-monitor sound has to be a minimum of 12 dB louder than the stage monitors by themselves. What do I mean by this? Simple. Take a basic SPL (Sound Pressure Level) meter and position it near the mix position. Bring your master volume down and get a reading in the house with everyone on stage playing and singing away. Let's assume this reads at 80 dB. In order to get intelligible sound, when you bring up your main master, your new reading should be at least 92 dB. Actually, the larger the separation you have between those two readings, the better off you are. There is some argument as to the exact number, and like everything with sound, it's relative to your venue; however, 12 dB is generally the lowest number tossed around.

It's also not uncommon to need more than one monitor mix. For instance, your worship leader will need a mix, but your praise team might need to hear something totally different. Likewise, your choir or drummer will need to hear something else. So, it's not unheard of to have two to six stage monitor mixes at any given time.

WEDGE MONITORS

Perhaps the most common form of stage monitor is the wedge monitor. The wedge monitor is usually contained in a box that allows it to sit on the stage at one, two, or three different positions. This allows the wedge to be aimed more directly at the person(s) using the monitor. They are most commonly floor mounted and positioned around the stage with regard to the location of both the performer and the microphone.

When using wedge monitors, it's important to be aware of the polar pattern of the microphone. For instance, if you are using a hyper-cardioid microphone, you will most likely want the speakers pointed at 70 degrees to the back of the microphone, as the hyper-cardioid pattern also picks up sound from directly behind the microphone. If the monitor were directly behind the microphone, this would increase your stage clutter in the mix as well as make you more prone to feedback.

It is not uncommon for a lead vocalist (or sometimes a pastor) to want two monitors offset 45 degrees from his or her position. This will give

FIGURE 7.1
EAW MicroWedge.
Photo courtesy of EAW.
All rights reserved.

equal coverage in each ear and it will also extend the person's ability to hear if he or she moves from side to side. With other groups, it might be easier to have multiple people share the same monitor (such as an electric guitar and a bass player). The end setup will be determined based on the needs of your people, the limit of your equipment, and the capability of your sound engineer.

All Wedge Monitors Are Not Created Equal

Knowing what to look for in a wedge monitor is key. For instance, sometimes you need a small footprint or you need it to be stand mounted. Here you would select a near field monitor, also known as a "hot spot." However, for your worship leader you are going to want a full-range sound, so here you want to place the best monitor you can afford.

Things you should look for in a monitor include:

- The physical weight
- Frequency response
- Overall size
- Power handling
- Type of driver

The physical weight is a factor – remember, you are going to be lugging these things around. Make sure that you can handle the load. Also, think about scene shifts: You might have a smaller person expected to move some of the stage equipment – will he or she be able to? But also realize that a heavier speaker is often a better speaker. It's going to have larger magnets and better construction, and it tends to be more robust. This is not a hard-and-fast rule, but it's a general standard.

Frequency response is important because the cabinet needs to be able to reproduce the quality of sound needed for the job. For instance, can it handle the higher-end spectrum of your orchestra? Will it handle the low frequencies to a reasonable enough level for your taste? Most monitors are full-range speakers; nonetheless, it's a good specification to check.

Overall size is often more important in the House of Worship than in the concert world. Oftentimes we have to deal with aesthetics as well as smaller stage sizes. The physical size of the monitor might be a concern. Likewise, if you are a mobile ministry, you have to consider roadboxes and trailer space.

Power handling is a feature often overlooked by many churches. Many churches purchase small 100 W or 150 W speakers for monitor speakers. While this is fine in some cases, if you are doing any type of contemporary worship, you will probably be happier with a monitor that can handle more power. Power and clarity often travel together. Just because you purchase a 500 W cabinet doesn't mean it's going knock the wind out of your lungs when it turns on, but it does mean the signal reproduced will most likely be of higher volume quality (than a speaker with lower power handling) if matched to an appropriate amplifier.

Likewise, the components inside will often be of higher quality. This will yield you a better product in the long term as well.

Finally, the type of driver is an important quality to look at. Some monitors have horns, others have coaxial designs, while still others use ribbon speakers. Each of these components has its good and bad side. For instance, a horn is very directional and can be easily controlled, but it can tend to be harsh sounding. This is not always bad; sometimes a harsh sound helps cut through the stage clutter, but some people will not prefer the sound. A coaxial design is going to give a more blended sound, but it's going to have a very wide coverage (usually at least 100 degrees), and this could make it difficult to control in proximity to other speakers and microphones. A ribbon speaker will produce a very nice sound, but they tend to be very susceptible to moisture. They are also usually more expensive.

Hands down, most people use a horn-based, two-way wedge monitor. You can get them in 8-, 10-, 12-, or 15-inch varieties fairly easily. The size refers to the woofer diameter. Most ministries would be well suited with a nice two-way 12-inch solution, but the 15-inch will provide you a lower frequency response and usually a louder overall volume should it be needed. Of course, a 15-inch cabinet is going to be significantly larger as well.

Advantages to Wedge Monitors

Wedge monitors have several advantages. Primarily they are inexpensive when compared to in-ear monitors. They are portable and their purpose can change from week to week. Another advantage is that multiple people can share a wedge monitor.

Generally speaking, using wedge monitors will result in fewer individual mixes as more people are listening to the same source. Of course, this is not always the case, but it tends to be true, especially in smaller and medium-size Houses of Worship.

Wedge monitors can also be mixed more easily from the front-of-house location than other dedicated solutions. This is a must for many churches that struggle just to get someone to mix sound, much less those trying to find someone who can mix monitors as well.

The biggest drawback to using wedge monitors is the stage volume and how it has a direct negative impact on the quality of the main house mix.

Mixing Wedge Monitors

Generally speaking, when mixing wedge monitors from the front-of-house position, you should use an auxiliary channel for each mix. It is imperative that the auxiliary mix be PRE-FADER. Otherwise, every change made in the house will be tracked in the monitor mix, and your musicians and vocalists will be pulling their hair out. You will get flooded with complaints, and the front-of-house engineer will quickly tire and become burned out.

When mixing the wedge monitors in the PRE-FADE position, the monitor mix will not change regardless of what you do to the other mixes on the console. This way nothing fluctuates, and the stage level and proportional mix remain consistent.

It is also worth mentioning that altering the gain after you have the monitor mix set is not a good idea. Even pre-fade mixes are affected by the gain. So, if you haven't set up your channel properly to begin with, making large changes to the channel via the gain control can still mess up your monitor mix.

While it is difficult to get the musicians on board, you will find more success if you mix the house FIRST. Give the monitors a rough mix just so the musicians and vocalists can hear key instruments and vocals, but mix the house BEFORE you mix the monitors.

Remember, the concept about mixing sound is to control the energy in the room. When you begin to push level to out of the front-of-house speakers, the room will fill with energy. The musicians and vocalists will hear more of themselves in the main house mix than they expect to. Now, when you start mixing the monitors, they will need fewer overall monitors because they can hear better.

If you start with the monitors, they can't hear anything – so they ask for more and more volume, and the result is that you don't ever get the main house volume up, thus creating the problem we mention in the beginning of this section.

Realize also that people don't always know how to communicate with you. For instance, when they ask you to turn the bass up, what they might really need is for you to turn the piano *down*. If everyone starts demanding more volume, you are soon going to find yourself spiraling out of control and the mix going out the window. Instead, remember that you are there to control energy and the environment. Work closely with your team to establish trust and relationships. Understand their needs and make sure they understand yours as well.

IN-EAR MONITORS

Until recently, in-ear monitors were the holy grail of church sound systems. Everybody wanted them, but very few could afford them. Each person had to have his or her own mix, the cost of good wireless receivers were out of sight, and finding people who knew how to use them was even more of a challenge. Add to that the cost of even more batteries, and the whole idea was quickly shot down.

So, why would people want to use in-ear monitors? Simply put, so they can control their room energy by controlling the stage volume. When you remove those big monitor wedges from the stage, your stage volume reduces exponentially. This immediately makes the front-of-house mix better.

Before we look at some of the newer options on the market that make in-ear monitors very viable for even the smallest church budgets, let's talk about how to use in-ear monitors safely and properly.

Proper Use of In-Ear Monitors

First, your musicians and vocalists should use both earplugs. This is for safety. Using only one ear bud leaves the other ear open to all the ambient noise. Plus, without the second ear plugged in, the other ear is usually cranked up louder. Both conditions can cause hearing problems or hearing damage. Second, using only one ear creates an odd imbalance that is very irritating and uncomfortable to the musician.

If you want in-ears to be successful, plug up both ears of your performer. Now when you do this, you create a problem – a huge disconnect for the musician or vocalists from the audience. This can be a deal breaker. The symptoms are the same: A look of panic is seen on the face, and worship usually starts to suffer. The performer will then reach up and flip out one of the ear buds in order to once again connect with the audience. Now all of a sudden this individual experiences that imbalance we just mentioned, and in an annoying attempt to regain some control, he or she pops out the remaining ear bud. No longer having the stage monitors to rely on, the performer is using all of his or her musical fortitude to get through the service. At the end of the service, the musician tosses you the in-ears, telling you they're horrible, and asks for the wedge monitors back.

You can't simply plug up both ears without solving this problem of disconnect.

Relax: It's an easy problem to solve. Just take two microphones and place them on the front of the stage aligned with your musicians and vocalists. Point these microphones out toward the audience. I prefer to use a condenser microphone for this as it will give a broader, deeper sound to the musician, but anything is better than nothing (as long as they are reliable and work). Make sure you don't accidentally mix your audience microphones into your house mix. The result will be far less than ideal. Now, take these two microphones and add them to the in-ear mix. This will rebuild the room sound that the performer has lost and will reconnect the performer with the audience.

It is important that these microphones be in line with the band and musician or you will get a timing issue. The band will hear an echo in the in-ears because the microphones are too far away from them. Because of this, your hanging audience microphones for crowd recording will usually not suffice.

Some people will not need the audience microphones. But key people (such as your worship leader) must have them in the mix to do their job.

Aside from that, traditional in-ear monitors are mixed very similarly to wedge monitors. They are usually fed out of a PRE-FADE auxiliary, but instead of going to an amplifier and speaker, they go to a wireless transmitter and receiver. Ideally, you will want some form of limiter in the system to protect your performer in the event of feedback or another super-loud signal being accidentally introduced into the in-ears. Remember, this sound is sitting right at the performer's eardrum. You don't want to cause hearing damage by doing something stupid (or making an innocent mistake).

With that in mind, let's look at some of the systems available to the House of Worship.

Types of In-Ear Monitors

TRADITIONAL IN-EAR MONITORS

These are the more expensive "flavors" of in-ear monitors. They work much like a wireless microphone. You have a wireless transmitter that sends signal to a wireless receiver that is worn on the belt. This receiver typically has a channel selector on it, a headphone jack, and a volume control.

The mix is sent to the wireless transmitter the same way a mix would be sent to a wedge monitor.

With some systems, multiple people can select the same receiver channel and share the same mix. Generally speaking, all persons would have their own individual monitor mix in their ears, but this is not always the case.

NEWER CAT5E-BASED SYSTEMS

Within the past few years, new personal monitor mixing solutions have come on the market. Several manufacturers make various solutions, but perhaps the most notable is the Aviom system.

What a tremendous breakthrough for Houses of Worship!

These systems take a set number of inputs (anywhere from 5 to 32 is standard depending on the manufacturer). The sound engineer provides either a direct send to the input or a small mix. For instance, the lead vocal might go into its own channel. The kick drum might have its own input as might the snare drum, but the rest of the kit might all be mixed down and put into a single channel. These inputs would then go down to the individual musician via a Cat5e cable. Now, each musician has a small station to balance his or her own mix!

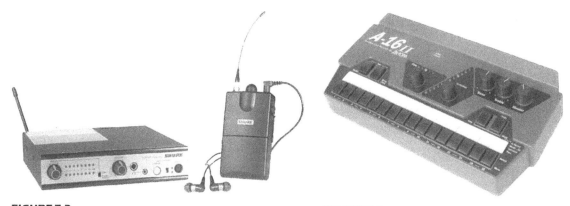

FIGURE 7.2
Shure in-ear monitor system.
Photo courtesy of Shure. All rights reserved.

FIGURE 7.3
Aviom A-16.
Photo courtesy of Aviom. All rights reserved.

This is tremendous. This is as close as we have come to "set it and forget it" stage monitoring. With these systems, the main engineer can get the feeds set, then allow the musicians and vocalists to do their own thing. These units can be tied to a headset or to a wireless solution.

They can even be tied to a loudspeaker, but I highly discourage this. Remember that getting a good mix is about controlling the room energy and the stage energy. If you have a loudspeaker controlled by a third party, you are just asking for troubles.

These systems are simple to set up. For optimal results you should use a console that allows you a pre-fader, post-EQ send. This way the musicians will receive a little of the color of the mix for accuracy (via the EQ) but will not be affected by your mix in the house. If you cannot provide pre-fader sends, in-ears will give you nothing but headaches. But then again, that's true of all monitor mixes.

Ideally, in-ear monitors (as well as complicated wedge monitor mixes) require a dedicated monitor engineer on a dedicated monitor console. This can be quite an expensive and complex solution for most Houses of Worship. Fortunately, these user-based Cat5e systems do away with this need. They are truly a remarkable solution for Houses of Worship.

Advantages to In-Ear Monitors

The many advantages to utilizing an in-ear solution are probably obvious to you by now. First and foremost, it lowers your stage volume. This fact alone is a good enough reason to make the switch. Also, in-ear monitors effectively lower your overall house mix. Now that you are not fighting your stage volume, your house mix can come down should you choose – and that's the important thing: if you *choose*. The choice is yours. You are no longer being driven by the acoustics of the room; you are now taking control of the acoustics of the room and dictating your mix.

In-ears also allow more specialized mixes for the musicians. The use of in-ears will also allow you more gain before feedback for the overall mix. This will allow you more control of your mix.

Another great point to using in-ears is that the stage clutter reduces greatly. With most of your wedges off the stage, you suddenly find yourself with more room and fewer cables. This is a win–win in a House of Worship environment.

I'd strongly encourage any House of Worship to consider this as a viable alternative to your sound solution strategy.

WHAT DOES A MONITOR ENGINEER DO?

If you've ever seen a large event or a big concert, odds are you've noticed the guy immediately off one side of the stage behind a mixing console. Behold the monitor engineer. With complicated monitor mixes, a monitor engineer is crucial to things working smoothly.

To make this work, the original signal is split before the front-of-house console ever alters the signal. This is usually done with an isolated transformed split at the stage, but with newer digital snake technology it is often done with a simple Cat5e hub. Depending on the system, one console generally provides phantom power while the other has phantom power turned off – but this is not always the case. It is important to know how your specific system works.

> **TIP**
> Digital snakes make splitting signals easy. Now, with relatively inexpensive equipment, you can route your original signal to the front of house, monitor console, recording console, and any other location you see fit – all with simple Cat5e routers and Ethernet cable.

The monitor engineer is almost always located adjacent to the stage in some way. This is done so the engineer can be close to the band and allows for easier communication between the two. It also gets the engineer closer to the action so he or she can actually hear a better representation of what is happening on stage. The monitor engineer will typically have a headset and at least one wedge monitor at his or her console. The monitor engineer is then able to listen in to any of the monitor mixes on either the headset or the wedge, thus mimicking how the performers are listening to the same material.

The console a monitor engineer uses is similar in function but different in format to a front-of-house console. Instead of having a handful of aux sends and a main output section, a monitor console will typically have at least 12 auxiliary outputs and several other types of outputs as well. This console is designed to send several individual mixes to different locations.

Perhaps the strongest point to the monitor engineer is that he or she is able to focus on just the monitors. The monitor engineer and front-of-house engineer work hand in hand to create a balanced mix, but monitor engineers focus their efforts on the monitor mixes on stage. This way, they are able to keep everything balanced for the performers and respond more quickly to needed changes on the stage.

For most Houses of Worship, a monitor engineer is a luxury you will not see. However, it's good to have a working knowledge of the concept in case there is ever a situation that would benefit from such a setup.

Importance of Clearly Communicating

Realize that most people don't understand how to communicate correctly with the sound engineer. Perhaps you will recall the story I mentioned in the very beginning of this book, where I was called to the church whose choir couldn't hear. The real problem was that the choir couldn't hear each other. However, the problem was presented as if they couldn't hear the stage monitors. In reality, the stage monitors were so loud they couldn't hear each other to sing properly – a perfect example of poor communication.

The choir was voicing a problem: They couldn't hear. The sound guy responded by bringing up the monitors so they could hear better. The problem worsened when it should have improved. It snowballed. The situation hit a climax because no one had thought to ask the basic question, "What can you not hear?" because they all assumed the answer.

We turned down the monitor mix, the choir was overwhelmed with excitement – and my work here was done.

This story illustrates a perfect point. Everyone comes from his or her own angle when communicating a concern. The key is to not assume and to put yourself in the other person's position. Find out what the real problem is and communicate with each other as to how you are going to resolve the problem.

This applies not only to monitor mixes, but to life in general. Scripture tells us to be slow to speak and quick to listen. The key to a strong A/V ministry is communicating well with people and being a servant to them. As we discussed earlier in this book, being a person who holds up those called to publicly proclaim the Gospel's message is our goal. Communication and patience is the key to success with this goal.

SOUND

88

CONTROLLING STAGE VOLUME

Remember, the key to getting a good house mix is to control the overall room energy; this includes the stage. While using in-ear monitors is a great way to start reducing stage volume, there are other things you should do as well.

Many churches all too quickly abandon acoustic drums in favor of electronic drums. Unfortunately, most electronic drums just lack the sound of a good acoustical set. Likewise, many drummers despise playing on them. Instead, the answer is to simply enclose the acoustic drum set in a complete drum cage with Plexiglas panels so the drummer can see out and the audience can see the drummer. This will reduce the ambient sound of the drums to such an extent that the drum will have to be miked and brought up in the mix to be heard.

Also, guitar amps can be placed in remote "amp rooms" and miked, or they can face the player from the front or side so the guitarist can hear them better and will not need them to be so loud.

Horns can be played with mutes and pointed down into acoustic material (versus up into the air) to control their acoustic volume as well.

There is almost always more than one simple fix for a problem when it comes to sound reinforcement. The more creative you are and the more time you put into the mix, the more it will pay huge dividends with the final product!

CHAPTER 8

Making the Move to Digital

Recently there has been quite a buzz for digital consoles, digital signal processors, and, perhaps most recently, digital snakes. Many churches ask, "Should we make the switch?"

Previously, manufacturers were making digital consoles that worked well in the recording realm but were a real nightmare for live mixing. Slowly but surely, the digital world has evolved for live sound – and now, as the role of the House of Worship grows at an unbelievable rate, more and more manufacturers have entire divisions dedicated to the House of Worship.

The world of digital offers a lot of positives for the House of Worship. First, the signal-to-noise ratio is drastically improved over analog. There's also the issue of being able to split signals much more easily than with older analog solutions. With digital consoles, you can create users and lockout features – this is great for funerals, weddings, and other special occasions. You can also preset a setting for each person; so if you mix on Wednesday and come back Sunday just to find that the youth band was in the room Saturday, insert your USB key and all the settings fly back to where you left off on Wednesday. These are huge advantages to the House of Worship.

Making the move to digital is inevitable. It is important that you understand this: It's only a matter of time. Manufacturers are offering more and more consoles with formats that are very appealing to live mixing. These consoles are also integrating with the digital snakes, in-ear systems, and digital signal processing in unparallel ways.

DIGITAL CONSOLES

Digital consoles are quickly becoming commonplace. Digital consoles come with Digital Signal Processing (DSP). Earlier in this book we talked about outboard processing equipment. In the old days, signal processing took rack upon rack of space and was very costly. However, with the advent of digital consoles, now you have an amazing amount of processing available to you at the touch of a screen.

Most digital consoles allow you equalization, compression, and usually noise gates on each channel! When you consider the cost of a single middle-of-the road stereo compressor, you can quickly see the benefit in this one feature alone. Now every channel has the option of its own individual signal processing. Remember the previous discussion on making decisions about where you insert or patch compressors, limiters, effects processors, and so on? Those days are virtually gone with digital consoles. Limited only by the DSP-processing power of the console you choose, you can have access to processing only dreamed about before by the average House of Worship.

Things to Look for in a Digital Console

Digital consoles can be tricky – especially if you are converting from analog to digital. The newer digital consoles are second nature to newcomers, particularly younger generations who have grown up around computers.

The first thing you must realize is that the process of mixing on a digital console is different than it is for analog. Now one must think a little like an audiophile and a little like a computer geek. This means you have to think about page locations, soft buttons, and layers. They way you mix will change, but the value of making the jump will pay huge dividends in your ministry.

Because a digital console is a computer inside, most of them tend to operate on pages. By pages, I mean that the information is stored in different locations that can be pulled up on the central screen (such as EQ settings, aux settings, soft patches, etc.) A soft button is a physical button on the console, but its function changes depending on what page you looking at. The soft button will usually have its function identified via the screen. And finally, when I talk about layers, I am referring to the actual faders. Say, for instance, you purchase a 48-channel console, but it only has 24 faders. Faders 1 through 24 are on layer 1, and faders 25 through 48 would be on layer 2. By pressing the layer button, the faders will snap to place where you left them. So, when you press the layer button to select layer 1, the faders snap to position for the settings on

channels 1 through 24. Likewise, when you press the layer button again, the faders will snap into position for channels 25 through 40. The motion of the faders moving automatically is often referred to as "flying faders."

First, I urge churches to look for digital consoles with as few layers as possible. Many consoles boast about 48 to 96 channels in a 3-foot-long desk. Well, by the time you account for a master output section, LCD screen, and other common features, you quickly realize that you are going to be working on three or more layers to access those channels. When a House of Worship engineer has to flip through multiple pages to get to a specific channel (and remember which page it was on), this is a recipe for potential disaster. Likewise, imagine your operator on a auxiliary return layer when a microphone begins to feedback. Now the engineer has to identify the microphone, identify the layer, and fix the problem. This is much more complicated than grabbing some faders on a console and fixing the problem.

I urge churches not to get more than two layers deep whenever possible. Then, I urge them to take all of the primary microphones and place them on layer 1 and link the secondary microphones to layer 2. For instance, let's say you have four choir microphones. In reality, you rarely mess with them on an individual basis; you generally bring them all up to the same mix, only on occasion altering an individual setting once you have it set. So, my advice is to put one choir microphone on layer 1 and then link the other three on layer 2. This way, the engineer can spend more of his or her time on the first layer. If a tweak is necessary, the engineer can jump over to the second layer and make the adjustment, but he or she isn't constantly bouncing back and forth in the main mix. The same concept can carry on other groups of microphones such as drums, strings, brass, and other similar sections. This will help simplify the mix.

Having a console with digital-naming ability per channel is helpful as well. This way, when you do jump layers, the channel name is displayed. It's hard enough for a House of Worship engineer to navigate pages, but it makes it a lot easier when channels are properly named (such as KICK, SNARE, TOM1, TOM2, CHOIR1, CHOIR2, etc.) versus having a cryptic code that doesn't relate to the purpose at all.

Another option to look at is how the console is controlled via a computer. Most manufacturers offer proprietary software that offers the ability to control the console remotely. The way it does this varies across the industry. For instance, some consoles share with the computer real time, so if I am in the house and looking at the equalization for channel 12 and someone on the console pulls up channel 32, my screen on the computer jumps to channel 32, regardless of what I am in the middle of. Other controllers allow multiple people to work at once, so in this example, I would remain on channel 12 while the console operator works on channel 32.

Some consoles allow for wireless integration more easily than others. This might be something that is of value to you. Some allow you to tie in via your church Wi-Fi network, while others do not.

The integration of a USB key for each user is another great feature found in a lot of consoles. We mentioned USB keys earlier in this chapter. The USB key gives you the ability to record individual settings, patches, and equalization for your console. You can then issue this USB key to as many people as you wish, and with each preset these people will have only as much access as you give them. Plus, it serves as a master reset to your specific settings every time you insert an individual key. This is an amazing feature for the House of Worship. Imagine a situation where you have a deacon running sound for a funeral. You can assign the deacon a key that allows him to use channels 1 thru 4, monitor A, and the Master Left/Right bus. He has no access to any other part of the console or configurations. Then, regardless of what he might do to channels 1 thru 4 during the funeral, when you show up on Sunday and insert your USB key, the console is just the way you left it the last time you mixed. What a great feature that we only wish we had on analog consoles!

The digital console should be able to interface with digital snakes, in-ear monitor systems, extra DSP power, and more. Make sure you know where you are going long term with your A/V ministry and buy a console that will keep up. Some consoles will integrate more easily with recording applications, while others are meant to be strictly a front-of-house console.

Many resellers will oversell the reset feature. I call this the mythical magic button. The idea is that if settings get messed up, you can hit the reset button and reload all the settings back to the original. While it is true that you can do this and it is a great feature, it's not the end-all of digital mixing. Without adequate training for your people, these features are a wash. Sure, you can go back to the original settings for your church, but you are not solving the problem that got you there in the first place. The reset key is a great feature for "zeroing out" the console and starting over, but the real answer is to train your people how to run the sound system, troubleshoot the sound system, and mix. There are times when the reset button is the right choice, but it should not supercede your people being adequately trained on how to properly run the system.

Generally, when people start looking for a "one-button solution," it's because there are other problems that they haven't fixed. Invest the time and resources in your people to train them well and your service will see the investment pay off hugely.

DIGITAL SNAKES

Digital snakes are the way of the future. Gone are the days of running hundreds of analog microphone lines and stage returns. Now all of this information can be carried over one or two Ethernet cables. With each day that passes, newer technology allows for more bandwidth, better fidelity and more flexibility.

A digital snake will utilize standard Ethernet cable or fiber-optic cable to transmit your audio and control data. These cables will interface with a stage box that

holds your preamps and a console box that has preamp controls, channel signal data, and a fan-out for the console (if needed). Now, instead of lugging huge analog cables around, you can do the same job with a couple of Ethernet cables or fiber-optic cables while getting the clean digital signal path at the same time.

The signal-to-noise ratio on digital snakes is much better than our old analog sidekicks. You can get a better sound in the room, with much more volume and far less noise due to the naturally quiet digital circuits. Another great feature for many of these snakes is a better resistance to picking up interference from AC (Alternating Current) and RF (Radio Frequency) noise. Many high-quality snakes offer redundant connections, so if one connection fails, the other takes over – transparently.

With rooms that require setups or with mobile churches, a digital snake is a lifesaver! Not only are they lighter to carry, but they are so much easier to set up and use. When coupled with a digital console, the benefits get even better as the signal path remains digital and the signal-to-noise ratio is even stronger.

One concern with digital snakes – and digital devices as a whole for that matter – is the issue of latency – that is, how long it takes the signal to find its way from the source to the destination as it travels through audio to digital conversion, digital to audio conversion, as well as through various DSP calculations. In audio, as we've already discussed, sound travels fairly slowly as it is. When you add unwanted delays to the signal path, the end result is far less than ideal.

An example of latency would be using a standard off-the-shelf USB micro-phone, running it through a computer, and speaking into it but listening at the same time via headphones that are also plugged into the computer. In most cases, you will say a sentence, and then halfway through the sentence you will begin to hear it in the headset. This delay is latency, and latency will create a disaster for any type of live sound.

However, as technology evolves, more manufacturers are overcoming these hurdles. To date, there are high-quality digital snakes with less than 1 millisec-ond latency. This is acceptable for pro-audio solutions. So, be aware of latency

FIGURE 8.2
Roland digital snake.
Photo courtesy of
Roland. All rights
reserved.

issues with your DSP, digital console, and especially your digital snake, and purchase accordingly.

One of the most exciting features with digital snakes that utilize Ethernet cable as their model of signal transmission is the ability to split the signal via Ethernet hubs. If you are new to the world of networking, an Ethernet hub allows you to take one Cat5 signal and split it into several signal paths. Commonly, you will find hubs that allow you to take one input and split it to 4, 5, 8, 16, or more signal paths! Some manufacturers allow you to use standard network hubs that you can buy off the shelf, while others require you to use a proprietary hub. Either way, digital snakes make it far more economical to do splits to multiple locations. With the advent of digital snake technology, it is now well within the average House of Worship to create a separate recording mix as well as monitor mixes (should they have the need).

Often times, the preamps found in the head units of a digital snake exceed what you would find on an average- to low-cost console. This alone will increase the quality of your sound and become yet another factor in reducing your noise ratio.

DIGITAL SIGNAL PROCESSING

We've talked about digital signal processors (DSPs) but haven't really defined what they are. A DSP is basically a computer that utilizes its processing power to manipulate your audio signal. What used to be rack upon rack of equipment is now contained within a one- or two- rack space unit that controls your system equalization, matrix mixing, routing, delay, limiting, and a large number of other processes.

With the advent of digital consoles, this concept has been applied to the console itself, so now a console can have digital signal processing that can be applied to the mix the same way a DSP handles the front-of-house system.

One word of caution: If you are designing a sound system utilizing a DSP, make sure to order a second one as well for backup. When you are about to have a service and a lightning storm comes that destroys the DSP, you don't want to be waiting on repair or shipping. Have the second DSP programmed and ready to go, swap over cables, and you are back up and running. Systems become very dependant on the DSP, and redundancy is key. Likewise, as stated earlier, it's a great idea to employ UPS's and proper surge protection on all sound systems, but especially ones utilizing digital mixing and digital signal processing.

Digital signal processing is a wonderful thing for the House of Worship. By utilizing this approach, you can get a lot more sound system for the ministry dollar.

TRAINING

The key to good sound system performance is training for the people running it. Making the move to digital technology requires a little bit of a learning curve. As each day passes, it also requires greater knowledge about basic networking and server control. Mixing digital is different than mixing analog. You should plan on receiving adequate training by someone who understands the needs of the church and the dynamics of a House of Worship engineer.

Regardless, it's important to stay on top of your game when mixing on a digital console. It is imperative that you keep track of which layer you are on, where your microphones are, and how things are patched. However, if you are mixing on the right type of console, you will most likely find it easier than mixing on an analog console, once you get used to it.

If you are adding a digital console as part of your system installation, you should make sure your contractor includes solid training as a part of the sales package. Otherwise, there are excellent opportunities for hands-on training at many conferences and with companies that specialize in training and will come to you; on-demand and DVD training options are available as well. The training is available regardless of your budget or schedule, but it is important to get trained.

SOUND

95

TIP
Remember: You are more than a button pusher! When you move to digital, don't fall into the trap of only selecting preset buttons – it's a recipe for disaster! Learn your craft and take control of your mix.

CHAPTER 9
Conclusion of Sound Section

CONCLUSION TO THE SOUND FOR WORSHIP SECTION

Sound engineers should realize their full importance in worship. By how you execute your area of ministry, you either create walls or tear them down. You either facilitate worship or you greatly diminish it. You are a part of the solution or a part of the problem.

This is no small task. You are not merely a button pusher. Your role in the ministry is a vital one.

When the audio is right, people let their guard down. It just happens. The audio becomes transparent and the people are drawn into a spirit of worship. There are no distractions to encumber them. They simply worship. Their confidence is boosted by the quality of the mix, and the fear of the person next to them hearing or seeing them worship dissipates. This process makes it easier for the Holy Spirit to speak to their souls and stir up within them the reason He has brought them there.

Anything we do to reduce distractions will ultimately help facilitate corporate worship, but I believe none is stronger in facilitating worship than working hard to execute a flawless audio mix that helps usher people into the Throne room.

PART 2
LIGHTING

CHAPTER 10
Anatomy of a Lighting System

WHAT IS A LIGHTING SYSTEM?

A lighting system is a system of control, power, and usually dimming and lighting fixtures that allow you to control your architectural and stage illumination. Many churches underestimate the power and effectiveness of adequate lighting for worship.

First, let's look at how a lighting system breaks down.

You can see in Figure 10.1 that your main power comes to the dimmer rack. Large-gauge wire runs from the dimmer to the outlets (called circuits). Your lighting fixtures then plug into these circuits, and your control surface connects to the dimmer via a standard protocol to control their function. Your control surface can also send control signal to other devices (such as motors, fans, effects machines, moving lights, color changers, etc.) as well.

As far as the system routing goes, you have dimmers (the physical dimming devices within your dimming panel), the circuits (the actual drops that the lighting fixtures plug into), and channels (on the control console). In most cases, your circuit number will be the same as your dimmer number. However, it is possible (especially in smaller systems) to have more circuits than dimmers. This would be done for cost savings. For instance, you might have two areas of your lighting that never get used at the same time (this could be because of your room setup or any number of other factors). So, why would you spend the money on dimmers that never get used at the same time when you can patch those circuits over to the dimmers when you need them?

In this example, your circuit number and dimmer number would most likely not be the same.

Let's take an overview of each of the main components that make up a lighting system.

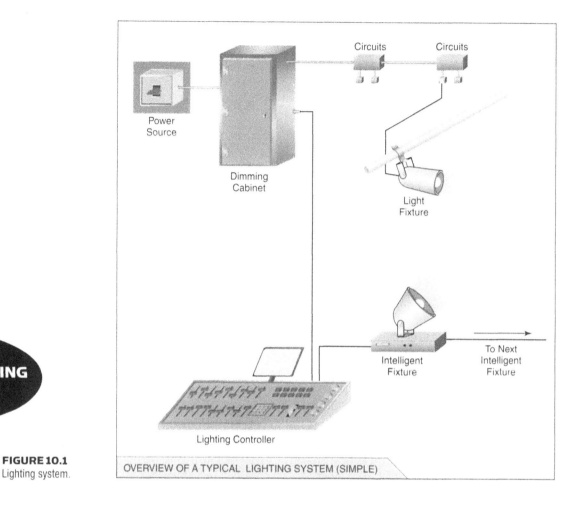

FIGURE 10.1
Lighting system.

Lighting Controllers

Most controllers today are computer-based devices. In the old days, lighting was controlled via manual control surfaces. The industry began with large rheostat devices that were controlled via large levers. This was shrunk down most commonly to a two-scene manual controller.

However, as computer technology became more accessible, we began to see the trend move toward computer consoles. The first models were very crude compared to the consoles of today. Many computer consoles today also offer functionality that was found on the original two-scene manual boards. Most computer consoles still have manual faders, some offer A/B scene selection on top of the automated cue feature, and several now have encoders for using special effects that go beyond dimmer control.

As technology continues to progress, we see consoles now controlling scenery, intelligent lighting, motors, automated trussing, and every other show-control

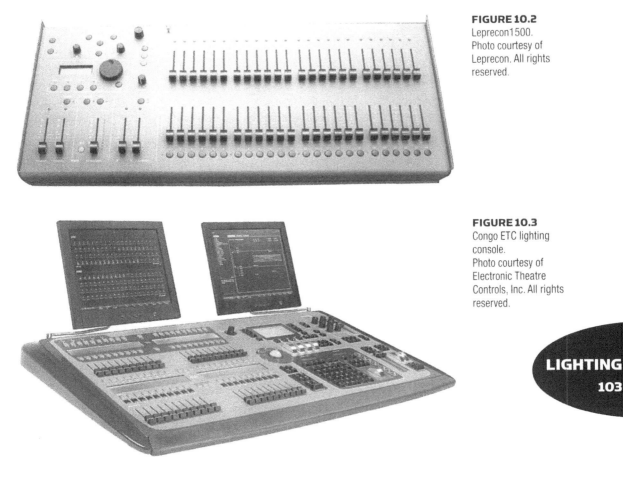

LIGHTING

103

contraption you can imagine. Consoles are no longer bound by physical expectations. Now, control can come from a laptop, personal computer, and – in some cases – a smart phone.

Dimming

Dimmers come in a variety of "flavors." A dimmer is basically a device that regulates power by controlling the current dispensed to an electrical light to control brightness.

When you think about dimmers as they pertain to the House of Worship, you are going to be dealing with one of three kinds – satellite, portable, and permanent.

SATELLITE DIMMERS

Satellite dimmers are often favored by smaller Houses of Worship because they are lightweight, inexpensive, and able to move with the lighting rig.

FIGURE 10.4
Satellite dimmer.
Photo courtesy of
Leviton

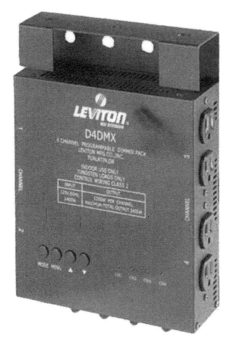

Generally speaking, a satellite dimmer is powered by 120 V via a regular 15 or 20 amp Edison (household) plug. So, the dimmer can plug into virtually any wall outlet and power a handful of lights. They usually range in power from 500 W to 2400 W per channel. Again, the dimmer is limited to the outlet amperage and the quality of the extension cable used in the application. Obviously, the larger the amperage capacity and the better the quality of cable, the better your results will be.

It's important to use no less than 12-gauge grounded extension cables. Anything less can build excessive heat and cause a risk of fire. Lower-grade extension cables will also tend to pop a circuit breaker more quickly due to the excessive amount of resistance they provide over a larger cable.

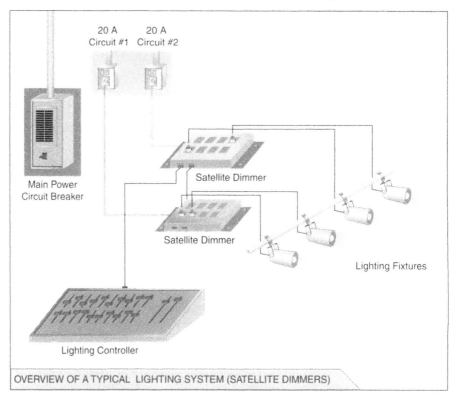

FIGURE 10.5
Lighting system
(satellite).

A satellite dimmer can easily be mounted to a light pipe, truss, or ceiling. They are usually lightweight and easy to work with. These dimmers can have channels assigned to them so the controller can communicate with them individually. For instance, a 4-channel satellite dimmer can be set on channels in groups of four. So, if the first one were channels 1 through 4, the next satellite might be 5 through 8, the next one might be 17 through 20, and the next one 9 through 12. No, that was not a typo – they do not have to be in order sequentially in the chain. The control system will control the dimmer, whatever channel you give it, regardless of its position in the system physically.

FIGURE 10.6
ETS sensor dimming system in roadbox. Image courtesy of Electronic Theatre Controls, Inc. All rights reserved.

PORTABLE DIMMERS

Portable dimmers are another variety of theatrical dimmers that utilize higher power sources but are contained in a unit that allows them to be temporarily installed and moved from event to event. These dimmers typically take single-phase or three-phase power and are "tied in" via cable tails that tie directly from the main feed of a circuit box.

Portable dimming systems contain large numbers of dimmers in one location. Usually, there will be between 12 and 48 dimmers in a portable system; however, there are no limits on either extreme.

There are several advantages to using a portable system over satellite systems.

- Power feeding the dimmers is often more stable.
- Dimmers tend to be at least 2.4k per channel.
- More industrial strength components – will tend to last longer.
- Easier to pack up and move around.
- Easier to troubleshoot.
- Dimmers are usually interchangeable and therefore easily replaceable.
- Not reliant on small fuses that easily blow.

Portable dimmers offer a lot of the benefits of a fully installed dimming system but still offer portability and usually cost less. The downside is that you need someone to tie the dimmer into raw power, you need access to single-phase or three-phase power (usually a minimum of 60 amps to upward of 400 amps depending on the number of dimmers), and you will need to make longer runs from the dimmer pack to the lighting fixtures – which requires a lot of cables and cable runs.

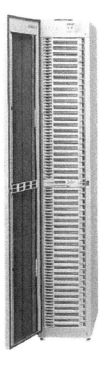

PERMANENT DIMMER SYSTEMS

Permanent dimming systems are by far the preferred method for any House of Worship that is going to utilize a lighting system for worship demands. A permanent system might cost more money initially, but the advantages pay off handsomely.

First, this is the only real way to get dimming control of your house lighting, which I would argue is absolutely imperative for modern worship. Being able to dim your house lights for stage focus, worship intimacy, or special productions is absolutely key. It is also critical to have all of your house lights controlled via one fader. This way they all come up together and go off together. So many churches are running their house lights via several rheostats on the wall and find it impossible to smoothly bring them up or down. This is just a distraction you don't need – not to mention a hassle. Getting your house lights under control should be one of the first steps you take in getting your lighting system in order. Using a permanent dimming solution is the only way to handle that many lights and amperage.

A permanent dimming system is always tied in to power – it's designed for the proper load and documented. Better yet, the cabling from the dimmers to the circuits is permanently wired inside conduit and clearly labeled. This reduces the amount of cable runs and safety worries – not to mention it makes everything look neater.

As with any permanent system, once installed and tested, there are many fewer failures; thus the system tends to be more reliable and predictable.

These systems will normally be fed from a three-phase 110 V per leg supply. The design will tend to evenly distribute your load if installed properly among all three legs.

CIRCUITS AND CHANNELS

We talked about the idea of circuits and channels in the overview. In the professional lighting world, a circuit is the connection that the light physically plugs into. This cable is, in most cases, run directly back to the dimmer that operates it. In this example, there is a one-to-one correlation between the two.

However, as previously mentioned, in some cases you could have a patch panel where your circuits would terminate. At this patch panel, the circuits would be hard-patched to a dimmer via a patch cable. In this example, you would have mismatched circuit/dimmer numbers. For instance, circuit 24 over stage might plug into dimmer 10. This is common when you have more connections in

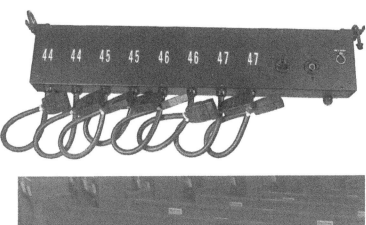

FIGURE 10.8
Cable drop and race-
way for a typical stage
circuit.
Photo by Brad Herring.

FIGURE 10.9
Computer light board
computer screen with
channels.

LIGHTING

107

your House of Worship than you have dimmers to support them. This is a cost-saving solution, or "value engineering." Proper documentation of the system will prevent a multitude of problems.

When you get to the console, it operates in channels. A channel consists of dimmers that are soft-patched via the control console.

Let's say you have 40 house light fixtures, each at 300 watts. If you are running 2.4k dimmers, you decide to allocate seven house lights per dimmer. You will need six dimmers total to manage your house lights.

When you get to the console, you wouldn't want to always manipulate those six dimmers individually – it would be a hassle. So, you would go into the software patch on the console and patch all six dimmers into one channel. Take the following example:

Your house lights are plugged into circuits 1 through 40. These circuits are hard-wired (since they are house lights), seven at a time, into dimmers 1 through 6. At the console, you patch dimmers 1 through 6 into channel 1. Now, when you tell the console to bring channel 1 to full, all of your house lights brighten to full power.

Conversely, you would have found yourself manipulating 6 dimmers – or, in a really worse case, *40* dimmers simply to bring up your house lights. Programming and consistency would be a real pain! Dimmers, circuits, and channels are all defined to allow the lighting designer a simplistic path for programming.

As you can imagine, paperwork is vital for successful lighting plots. We'll take a look at some of the paperwork you'd want to have later in the lighting section of this book.

Fixtures

Perhaps the most recognizable parts of a lighting system are the lighting fixtures themselves. Choosing the correct lighting fixture for the job is as important as an artist choosing the right brush for a stroke. Each lighting fixture performs its job differently and yields a different visual result for the designer. Let's take a look at each of the main categories of fixtures and identify what makes them different.

PAR CAN

Perhaps the simplest of all lighting fixtures is the PAR can. PAR stands for Parabolic Aluminized Reflector. In short, this light is often referred to as a coffee can with a floodlight inside it. And in fact, many a low-budget theater has made these lights by following that analogy.

Basically, this fixture is a can with a sealed beam light inside that looks much like

FIGURE 10.10
PAR 64.
Photo by Brad Herring.

an old-fashion headlight. These lamps come in Wide, Medium, and Narrow Spot configurations. Obviously a Wide lamp disperses light the most, while a Narrow Spot disperses light the least.

PAR can lamps are recognizable by the waffling on the front of the lamp.

PAR fixtures come in many different sizes. The most common are PAR 64, PAR 56, and PAR 38. Their sizes are derived from the diameter of their barrel, which is measured in eighths of an inch. So, if you were to take a PAR 56 and divide 56 by 8, you would get 7 inches – the diameter of a PAR 56.

Old school PAR cans have a known lighting characteristic: They typically disperse the light in a relatively uneven field, with a horizontal hot spot going through the

FIGURE 10.11
PAR lamps – wide/
medium/spot from the
front.
Photo by Brad Herring.

middle of the beam spread. From up in the air, you can see this hot spot easily. It is parallel with the ceramic back of the lamp. By grabbing the ceramic head of the lamp and twisting the lamp clockwise or counterclockwise, you can adjust the hot spot to where you desire. This is mandated by the object you are lighting. For instance, if you are lighting a tall piece of scenery, you will most likely want the hot spot running vertical to parallel the scenic item. This way, as much of the energy of the light spreads on the object as possible. If instead you were lighting a group of people, you would most likely want the hot spot to be horizontal and landing on the average height of the people's faces. This would tend to give you a more even-looking wash over the group.

PAR cans tend to be very inexpensive. They are the ultimate "point and shoot" fixtures.

LIGHTING

109

Pros: They can take a beating, there is very little inside of them that can break, and they are easy to maintain.
Cons: Overall poor quality of light, noticeable hot spots, and no ability to focus or shutter.

FRESNEL

The Fresnel is similar to a PAR can except it has a lens that sits in front of the lamp. This lens can be moved forward and backward, allowing the instrument to produce a tight spot or a wide flood. The lamp is a quartz halogen lamp and comes in many different wattages. Standard wattages for live theater are 500 and 100 W, but Fresnels are very popular in the film world and can easily be found in wattages up to 15,000 W.

Fresnels are referred to by their lens size. Most common sizes are 6- and 8-inch Fresnels. They are identifiable by the lens with ridges that form rings emanating out of its center and because the Fresnel lacks shutters for beam shaping.

FIGURE 10.12
8-inch Fresnel.
Photo by Brad Herring.

FIGURE 10.13
A Fresnel lens.
Photo by Brad Herring.

FIGURE 10.14
ETC PARNel.
Image courtesy of Electronic Theatre
Controls, Inc. All rights reserved.

The Fresnel is hardly more complicated than a PAR can, but it does have an actual base for the lamp that over time can corrode and will need maintenance. There is actually a small amount of internal wiring, whereas the PAR can is fully exposed.

These fixtures offer a more consistent spread of light, thus making them an ideal choice for fill light and for stages that will be utilized for television.

Pros: Relatively inexpensive, easy to focus, even beam spread, focusable beam size.

Cons: A little more maintenance required, lamp cost/lamp life, no shutters for beam shaping.

SOURCE FOUR PAR

Lighting sense made by ETC (Electronic Theater Controls), manufacturers the the Source Four PAR – a fairly new fixture on the lighting scene. This is a new-style PAR fixture that utilizes a 575 W or 750 W lamp. The field of light is much more efficient and more even. Heat dissipates out the rear of the fixture (versus the front of the fixture like a traditional PAR can would). This means that gel life is greatly lengthened and the fixture is a little easier to work with.

The Source Four PAR fixture uses one lamp, but unlike the traditional PAR, you get your various fields of light (narrow, medium, and wide) by changing

FIGURE 10.15
A PARNel lens kit.
Photo by Brad Herring.

lenses on the front of the fixture. This helps reduce lamp inventory and gives you more flexibility overall.

Pros: Only one lamp to buy, longer gel life, more compact size.

Cons: More expensive than traditional PAR can, more maintenance required.

ELLIPSOIDAL (ALSO KNOWN AS A LEIKO)

The Ellipsoidal is arguably the centerpiece of theatrical lighting design and a common fixture for the House of Worship. These fixtures offer a nice beam consistency and the ability to shutter and blur/sharpen the focus. Unless the Ellipsoidal is a zoom fixture (multiple focus length), the beam spread is set at a certain size (Figure 10.16).

Some manufacturers have interchangeable barrels for different focal lengths, while others make you purchase the entire light.

An Ellipsoidal is recognizable by the presence of shutters.

These fixtures have slots in them that will accept gobos and effects wheels. With these combinations, you can project patterns, words, and special effects. By being able to blur or sharpen, you can alter the way these effects look as well as how the lights blend with each other on stage.

One of the main selling points for an Ellipsoidal is the ability to use the shutters for beam shaping. This allows you to make "shutter cuts" off scenery and other areas that you don't want the light to spill onto.

Pros: Beam shaping, blur/sharpen focus, pattern and effects capability, even field of light.

Cons: Expensive, sometimes limited in beam spread, more maintenance required.

BORDER LIGHTS

Border lights are perhaps one of the oldest types of light we have from our history of theater and performance. In the early days, these lights were candles with reflectors around them that sat at the lip of the stage. Today, our technology has evolved far from candles, but the fixture still lives on the lip of the stage.

Border lights are another source of fill light. They are used to light the performer (and scenery) from below. The light then shines up on the performers' faces. This helps remove shadows under the chin and eyes. These lights go a long way toward helping the person on stage appear younger because they remove the exaggerated effect of "bags" under the eyes and chin.

Border lights come in a variety of styles – MR16 lamps, PAR lamps, floodlamps, and LED. The decision of which to use ultimately comes down to stage size, desired footprint, foot-candles needed, and budget.

These lights can bolt directly to the floor, be mounted to a floor base, or be held down via weight (sandbags or bricks). It is also possible to mount these lights from above via a C-clamp and use them as top fill, but their primary purpose is as border lights.

Prior to the days of quality cyc lights (discussed next), it was not uncommon to see a backdrop lit with these lights. The designer would mount them above and below the drop, usually focusing the lights so they slightly overlapped in the middle.

Typically these lights will come in a one-, two-, or three-circuit configuration. Perhaps most common is the three-circuit configuration where every third light belongs to a circuit. In a multi-circuit configuration, each circuit would be a different color. Many designers choose to use red, green, and blue so they can mix to virtually any color. However, the color is ultimately determined by your design need. Generally speaking, when used as a true boundary light, at least one channel would be no color because it's being used as a fill light for shadows.

Pros: Easy to use, cheap to maintain, small footprint, easy to hide, multi-color options.
Cons: When used for backdrops they give a scalloping appearance, often dim compared to other lights.

FIGURE 10.17
Border light (sometimes called a strip light).
Photo by Brad Herring.

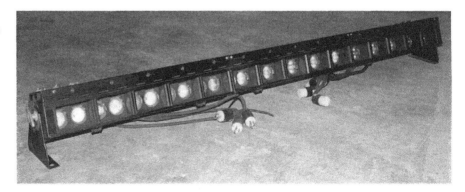

CYC LIGHTS

The Cyc light is one of the best and easiest to use fixtures for doing a full wall wash. These fixtures are great for back walls and backdrops.

The cyc light is typically a three-circuit fixture with each circuit having its own "cell." These lights are referred to as single-cell, dual-cell, three-cell, or four-cell fixtures. The fixture itself is very simple. Generally lamped at 1000 W, each cell has its own reflector and lamp. The cell produces a very even and wide wash of light. When properly placed with other fixtures, a very even wash is produced over a vertical surface.

There is a top and bottom to this fixture; the reflector inside will throw light further one distance than the other. This makes sense as the fixture is typically mounted via C-clamps on a pipe or truss and suspended approximately 6 feet in front of the object being lit. The light will throw a small field up but focus the majority of the field out and down to adequately cover the scenic element.

By locating the cells so closely to each other, color mixing is very effective. Again, utilizing red, green, and blue, a designer can mix to almost any color in the spectrum. Many people choose red, green, and amber as a primary pallet; these designers are looking for warmer tones and are not interested in achieving every color. Still others will use specific colors for their particular production needs. We will discuss this idea more in the color theory section of this book.

A cyc light is fairly lightweight and well worth the investment if you are lighting vertical components. They do tend to be a little clunky, making them more difficult to conceal than other types of lighting.

LIGHTING

113

Pros: Very even field of light, low maintenance, long lamp life, inexpensive lamp cost.

Cons: A bit clunky, generates heat, burns through gel fairly quickly, several required for an even wash.

FIGURE 10.18
Altman Sky Cyc.
Photo by Brad Herring.

FOLLOWSPOT

Perhaps one of the most iconic images in professional lighting, the Followspot is used in virtually every concert and many stage productions.

Followspots come in every size and wattage imaginable. These lights are operated by a person who visually tracks the target on stage. They can be wired so that the lamp is dimmed via the lighting control console or via the operator. They typically have iris and focus controls as well as a handful of color choices and a blackout panel.

FIGURE 10.19
Super Trouper.
Photo courtesy of
Strong Lighting.

Higher-end followspots incorporate laser sighting or telescopic sighting, while lower-end spots use an iron sight or lack sighting at all. Inexpensive solutions can be utilized, such as taping a straw down the top center line of the tube and taping a smaller straw vertically to the top center of the front opening, thus making an iron-type sight as found on an old rifle.

The operator must have some way to sight the followspots on the target or they will never be in the right spot at the right time. There is nothing more distracting or annoying than bad followspot work.

Followspots are used for highlights and front fill. In concerts they are very popular. The band can be lit via downlight and backlight in very sultry colors, moving lights can be used for wonderful effect lighting, and the follow spot can light up the few primary components (usually the lead singer) for front light.

A well-used followspot can have a very strong effect; a poorly utilized followspot will leave you very frustrated.

Pros: Bright light, can be pointed anywhere, not fixed to one location, can follow a moving target.
Cons: Usually expensive, difficult to train good operators, consistency can be a challenge, location for the unit can be a challenge.

WORKLIGHTS

All too often worklights are overlooked in lighting systems. It's important to realize that stage lighting is expensive to run, when you calculate the amount of power needed and the relatively short (but expensive) lamp life. There is no need to run stage lighting when you are not in a rehearsal, production, or service.

For instance, if a typical lamp costs $30 on average (some are much more expensive, others are considerably cheaper) and has an average life of 1000 lamp hours, this lamp will last you approximately 71 weeks when used on average 14 hours a week (6 hours on Sunday, 5 hours for a mid-week service, and 3 hours for rehearsals during the week). If you ran that same lamp every time there was someone in the sanctuary (including during setup and cleaning), your average time could easily be reduced to as little as 20 weeks. If someone were to accidentally leave the lights on all day and night (which happens more frequently than you would imagine, with cleaning crews alone), this time can be brought down to a handful of weeks.

That's based on a 1000-lamp-hour life. Many lighting fixtures use lamps that have a 250- or a 500-hour life. As you can see, the cost would increase significantly. Likewise, remember that you are possibly burning anywhere from 15 to 200 fixtures at a time (depending on your size and type of house light).

One modern-day trend is to use a theatrical fixture (like an ETC PARNel) for house lights. While they are very versatile and provide an excellent field of light, they are far more expensive to operate than standard floodlights. If you were to utilize a fixture like this for your house lights, you would most definitely want a good fluorescent fixture or other type of inexpensive light to use for day-to-day operations such as setups and building maintenance.

FIGURE 10.20
Worklight.
Photo by Brad Herring.

All too frequently Houses of Worship forget to install some sort of low-cost worklight solution for their altar and audience areas. This means they are constantly running high-voltage short-life fixtures. The cost of this adds up over time in both utility bills and lamp replacement. Likewise, the fixtures themselves get more wear and tear as a result of the constant heat and have to be replaced or repaired on a more regular basis. Also, any gel or patterns in the lights will tend to expire much more rapidly, once again resulting in high operation costs.

LIGHTING
115

Any House of Worship utilizing a stage lighting system should have an inexpensive incandescent or fluorescent worklight solution that can be illuminated by a standard light switch. This will protect your investment, lower your operating costs, and your fixtures will have a longer lifespan – all of which saves your ministry dollar for more important uses. Having these lights controlled via a standard light switch will keep unnecessary people off your lighting console. You will want to have some sort of cover or lockout switch on these lights so they don't get flipped on when you are in the middle of a service or production.

Pros: Cost savings.
Cons: Sometimes not as bright.

LEDS

Perhaps one of the newest innovations to the lighting world is the advent of LED lighting. With each day that passes, manufacturers are learning how to make LED's brighter and cooler. The long lamp life and ability to color change are huge motivations for progressive work in this field.

An LED fixture consumes less power, usually emits less heat, and allows full-spectrum color changes. The limits have always been about making them bright enough to compete with stage lighting. We are now seeing more LED solutions.

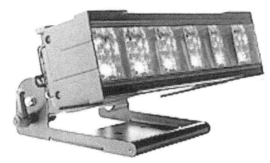

Any of the fixtures mentioned in this section have LED counterparts, and most likely one day they will all be LED based.

Presently, LED fixtures tend to be costly and, as already mentioned, considerably dimmer than a quartz-halogen product. However, LED fixtures are commonly used to light scenery and walls as well as for backlight and boundary lighting. As more and more fixtures become brighter, they will soon be used for front light as well as side light.

LED technology is definitely something to keep your eye on as the industry moves forward with this technology.

Pros: Low heat, long lamp life, little maintenance required, color changing.
Cons: Tends to be more expensive, tends to be dimmer, and offers less quality of light with current availabilities.

Fixture Accessories

What makes theatrical lighting "theatrical" is how the designer can affect the quality of light to set mood and build environments. Theatrical lighting offers a number of accessories that help a designer to set that mood and to build that environment.

GOBO HOLDERS

A Gobo is a metal or glass disc that contains an image. This metal or glass disc can be inserted into any ellipsoidal by the use of a gobo holder. The holder is typically a metal sleeve with a round opening that allows the gobo to sit inside it. When inserted into the light, this image is projected through the light onto whatever surface you point at.

Metal patterns are dye-cut, while glass patterns are more of a screen-press product. Glass patterns can reproduce photo-realistic color images, logos, and other impressive-looking projections. Metal discs offer half-tones and gradients that can allow for nice graphics, but are most commonly created in a stencil-type fashion and limited to the color of the gel placed on the light.

Either pattern is available via catalogs in hundreds of predesigned patterns or can be custom ordered with your specific artwork. Over time, a glass pattern will hold up better and last longer but is more expensive initially.

SNOOTS

A snoot (also sometimes called a "top hat") is attached at the end of the barrel of a fixture. A snoot will block unwanted light from hitting undesired objects by helping to focus the light on the desired object only.

A snoot is useful in helping to aim the light and reduce unwanted spills.

FIGURE 10.23
Altman snoot.
Photo by Brad Herring.

BLACK WRAP (CINEFOIL)

Black wrap (also known as "cinefoil") is the aluminum foil of professional lighting. Theatrical lights have many openings and opportunities for light to escape from the instrument other than from the end of the barrel. Oftentimes, this light bounces off the ceiling and other areas, and is a distraction to the audience.

FIGURE 10.24
Rosco black wrap.
Photo courtesy of RoscoLux. All rights reserved.

Black wrap looks and acts like a strong aluminum foil, but it is black in color and dissipates heat better than its aluminum counterpart. The black wrap does not reflect light and can be wrapped around the light much like aluminum foil wraps around a potato.

Black wrap can also be used as a make-shift barn door, snoot, or any other method to help you shape and control where the light spills and where it doesn't.

FIGURE 10.25
Altman barn door.
Photo by Brad Herring.

BARN DOORS

Barn Doors are most commonly used on Fresnels and PAR cans. They slip into the gel frame slot on the end of the barrel and offer four hinged flaps – one on each side of the barrel ring.

The barn door tries to make up for the fact that these instruments do not have shutters. They give you a crude but effective means of shaping the light and eliminating light spill. Barn doors are commonly used to keep light spill off the audience area, side walls, and other scenic components that you might

FIGURE 10.26
Altman doughnut.
Photo by Brad Herring.

FIGURE 10.27
Wybron color scroller.
Photo courtesy of
Wybron. All rights
reserved.

not want indirectly lit by the large spill of light from a non-shutterable illumination source.

DOUGHNUTS

A doughnut is a thin piece of metal that slips in the gel frame slot of a fixture. It has a small diameter hole in the dead center that is smaller than the barrel opening itself.

The doughnut eliminates reflections created within the barrel and produces a sharper edge on the beam of light when sharp-focused by the instrument. The doughnut is most commonly used on an Ellipsoidal with a gobo projection. The doughnut will eliminate the soft blur on the edges of a hard-shaped gobo projection.

COLOR SCROLLERS

Color scrollers are a way of allowing one fixture to produce a lot of different colors. The unit sits inside the gel frame holder of the fixture and works like an old scroll. Different colors of gel are taped together to the size of the barrel opening. The color scroller is then controlled via the lighting control board and moves as the control value is increased or decreased for its channel.

The color scroller is often used in concerts and theater where you have a group of lights focused on a certain area but want different colors in that area throughout the night. It eliminates the need for hanging a different light aimed at the same point on stage simply to achieve a different color.

Color scrollers can be difficult to work with at times. They have a tendency to drop accuracy and have to be reset from time to time to stay in sync with each other. Because it is dependant on the gel, the gel still burns through as usual and has to be replaced.

With color scrollers, you tend to get what you pay for.

As LED and CMYK* color mixing technology improves, color scrollers will slowly be replaced by these new technologies.

* CMYK mixing uses cyan, magenta, yellow, and black palettes for color mixing versus the standard red, blue, and green palette. CMYK utilizes a subtractive color system. Starting with white, the three colors (cyan, magenta, and yellow) are added to the light to block certain color waveforms. In the printing world, K is actually the color black, but in lighting, black is achieved by turning the fixture off. We will look at both the additive (RGB) and subtractive (CMYK) color theories in Chapter 11 in the Color Mixing and Color Theory section.

SAFETY CABLE

Remember, as a lighting designer you are responsible for the safety of those below! It is a reality that you are hanging a fixture weighing anywhere from 3 to 150 pounds in the air above people's heads. Accidents do happen and failure occurs from time to time.

Manufacturers make safety cables for their lights. They are generic, but effective. These safety cables easily clip and unclip from the instrument. Typically they are connected through the yoke and around the light bar or truss. In case of a C-clamp failure of some sort, the safety cable would arrest the instrument and keep it from falling.

Safety cables should always be used. Likewise, any type of backup restraint device (such as a gel frame clip) should always be employed when working with lighting. Even if the object doesn't weigh much, the metal corners and sheer velocity of the drop could cause severe injury to anyone below.

Remember – safety first!

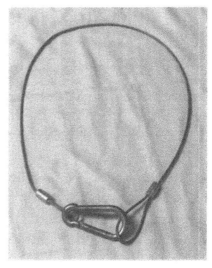

FIGURE 10.28
A safety cable.
Photo by Brad Herring.

Gel

A gel is a thin sheet of colored material that is slipped into a gel frame and inserted into the gel frame holder at the end of the barrel of the instrument. This substrate will alter the color or the color temperature of the light. The result is an artistic alteration of color and a technical alteration of color temperature.

Gel is produced by several different manufacturers. Each color has a name, but they are identified by a number

FIGURE 10.29
Gel cut and placed inside gel frames. Photo courtesy of RoscoLux. All rights reserved.

that is designated for each specific gel. To add to the confusion, each manufacturer has their own numbering system. The major players in the gel market are Rosco, GAM (Great American Market), and Apollo. Each manufacturer offers their own take on how they make the gel; some gels tend to have more color depth, while others hold up better to the heat of the lamp.

Generally speaking, the more saturated the color, the more quickly it will deteriorate. All gel will eventually burn out – some faster than others. This will depend on color saturation, maintenance of your lighting fixture, and type of lighting fixture.

Manufacturers offer free swatch books that contain everything they make. These swatch books are indispensable to the designer in choosing the right color for the right scene.

For more permanent displays or for colors that never change, glass gels can be purchased for most lights. While very expensive initially, the glass gels will last virtually forever, thus never needing to be replaced.

Gel works by being inserted in the direct path of your light beam. The gel actually filters the light to produce the colors within the spectrum of the material. You will notice on your swatch book several factoids. One of these is "transmission." The lower the transmission number, the dimmer the light will be. For instance, using a Rosco 80 (Primary Blue) will greatly diminish the normal output of the light. The color is also very saturated, so it will tend to burn through more quickly than, say, a shade of light amber. When all is said and done, it will take a stronger fixture to push through the dark filter and make it to the stage than it would for a lighter-colored gel.

Another form of "gel" is diffusion. Diffusion filters work to diffuse the light. Diffusion is commonly used for television and live stage to help blend light sources together and to help the lighting fixture reach further than it optically can in one direction or another.

The color corrector gel works by blocking certain frequencies of light as it passes through the filter. Color correction is necessary for matching the color temperature of the film negative or the white balance of a digital imager. Different lamps create different color temperatures. These changes are not noticeable to the human eye but are very noticeable to a camera. They will tend to shift from amber to blue and will be very dramatic. If all of your lamps are not the same color temperature, a correction gel can be used in most cases to solve the problem for the camera.

LIGHTING

120

CHAPTER 11
Color Mixing Theory

COLOR MIXING AND COLOR THEORY

While lighting may sometimes be thought of as being similar to paint, they are indeed very different. The entire spectrum of color for lighting is different. For instance, in paint, the color black is the presence of all colors, but in lighting, the color black is the absence of all colors. As video and lighting begin to emerge, this line gets a little blurry. You might notice that many of the newer fixtures on the market use CMYK color mixing – a palette that until recently was reserved for the printing world. We'll look at both RGB and CMYK as they pertain to lighting.

Different colors of lighting can be mixed to achieve different colors (just like when you mixed watercolors as a child), but the primary colors are different and the way they interact with each other is different as well.

The three primary colors in lighting are red, green, and blue. With these three colors, in theory you can mix to any other color you wish. Mix all three of them together at the same intensity, and in theory you will get white. This is often referred to as Additive Color Theory. Look at the color wheel in Figure 11.1 to see how these colors interact with each other to make up different colors.

FIGURE 11.1
Additive color theory.

You can see from Figure 11.1 that your primary colors (red, green, and blue) are the outer circles. As they move on top of each other, you can see the colors they create (assuming a 100 percent intensity value of each primary color). Red and blue make magenta, green and blue make cyan, and green and red form yellow. All three primary colors together make white.

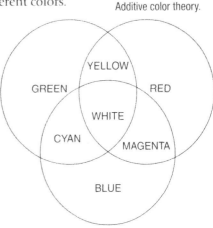

By varying the intensity of each primary color, you can alter the combined color within the spectrum, favoring the primary color that is the most intense.

So, you might ask, if you can do all this, why so many gel colors? The reason is that the color mixing theory is just that – theory. While it's true that light reacts this way, the color sources have to be emitting from the exact location to truly mix colors (as we see in technologies such as CMYK and RGB color-mixing fixtures). However, if the lights are beside each other, you will tend to see halos of color. You will also get some really interesting color shadows as the object moves through the light.

Color mixing like that described above works best with inanimate objects such as walls, cycloramas, and scenic elements. This theory works well for backlight and side light as well, when you want to create a dramatic effect of shadows and stage coloration.

The CMYK model uses what is known as Subtractive Color Mixing Theory. In subtractive color mixing, all colors combine to make black. This harks back to the print world, where mixing all the colors together yields black. In lighting, this is not really the case – you still get a grayish color, but because it is being projected, there is always some luminance to it. In lighting, to get black, we turn the fixture off (absence of light).

Subtractive color mixing works with white being the main color. To change colors, different filters are placed in front of the light to block the wavelengths of certain spectrums and produce a different color. You can see from looking at the subtractive color chart in Figure 11.2 that colors are achieved by different methods from those used in the additive color theory.

You will notice here that when the cyan and magenta are mixed together, you get blue. In the additive color theory, blue is a primary color, but in subtractive color you have to mix colors filters to get blue, thus making it a secondary color in subtractive theory.

CMYK color theory is necessary because many of the new intelligent fixtures utilize subtractive theory as their way of color mixing. When working with a CMYK fixture, you will be working with this color system as opposed to the additive system, when you work with traditional lights utilizing gel or RGB color mixing.

We will discuss color mixing and design choices later in this section, but for now it's important for you to realize the importance that color plays in lighting and how to use color to achieve the desired results.

ALTERNATIVES TO GEL

There are several methods available to the lighting designer to change the color of the light emanating from the lighting fixture. While gel is the most common method to do this, the designer has other options as well.

One of these, we have already mentioned – glass filters. Glass that is painted or dipped to a certain color can be

FIGURE 11.2
Subtractive color theory.

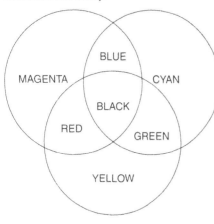

used in place of actual gel. While costly up front, glass filters will never wear out, so in the long run they are very cost-effective solutions. Obviously, being glass they are more fragile and can be broken, but the overall longevity of glass filters far exceeds a cut gel.

Some manufacturers also make a gel paint that is heat resistant. This gel can be applied directly to many lamp sources, glass, or lenses. This allows you to mix different colors to get your own color and also allows more flexibility in how you achieve your color with the light instead of simply using a filter. For instance, you could paint a window on the set with this gel paint and then shine the light through the window to pick up the color.

Likewise, if you are trying to do an illuminated cube or other similar effect, you could paint the translucent material of the cube with the gel paint and then illuminate using fluorescent or incandescent fixtures from within to give the cube a glow effect. Gel paint allows you not only to make your own glass filters but also to truly think outside the box with color and design.

CHAPTER 12

Common Power Connections of a Lighting System

There are several power connections that are common to lighting systems. Each of these connections has its own pros and cons. It is up to the individual user's taste, budget, and power consumption requirements in choosing the right connection.

You will also find adapters that will take you from one type of a connection to another – so if your lighting system uses only one type of connection, it is possible for you to use a device with a different connection on it without have to rewire one end or the other.

Let's take a look at the most common lighting connections for power.

2P&G (ALSO KNOWN AS STAGE PIN)

2P&G stands for "two-prongs and a ground." This is a very common lighting connection and is usually seen in a professionally designed lighting system. The connection is relatively flat, with three large brass pins, measuring about ¼ inch each, spread between the edges of the pin. The ground pin is just slightly off center so that you can only plug the connection in one way. The ground pin is also slightly longer than the other two pins to ensure it connects first.

FIGURE 12.1
2P&G connection.
Photo by Brad Herring.

Being relatively flat, these connections are easier to tape down and do not create a big bulky mess that can be easily tripped over. Their large brass pins also make a solid connection and are not easily bent or broken. The connector itself is cost effective (usually ranging from $3 to $8).

One downfall of this connection is that it does not actually lock together, so there is a small chance of it separating. Some manufacturers have molded holes through the connector so you can tie them together with trick-line (also known as "tie-line"); however, most people use a small piece of gaff tape to hold the two together.

TIP
When using tape, use gaff tape – it leaves
no residue and removes more easily. Also, take one
side of the tape and fold it over on itself by at least ¼ inch.
This will create a tab on the tape that will allow you to take it
off quickly when you are done and not have to try
to peel under it to get it started.

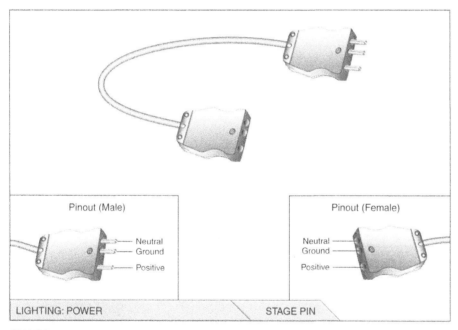

Pinout (Male)

— Neutral
— Ground
— Positive

Pinout (Female)

Neutral —
Ground —

Positive —

LIGHTING: POWER   STAGE PIN

LIGHTING

127

FIGURE 12.2
Illustration of 2P&G pinout.

TWIST LOCK

Twist lock connections (such as an L5-20) are also very common in lighting systems. These connections are built for commercial and industrial power needs. Utilizing a set of curved blades, the connections interlock and then twist to create a positive lock position. To remove them, you twist the connection in the opposite direction and pull.

FIGURE 12.3
Twist Lock NEMA L5-20 connector.
Photo by Brad Herring.

Twist locks make for very reliable and robust connections. They are a little more expensive than other forms of connections and are significantly bulkier as well. They are good to use in catwalks and other non-trafficked areas and when dealing with a supercritical power connection.

Twist lock has come to be a common term for these type of connections. They are available for multiple power ratings. The "L" in the connection name stands for locking – for example, the L5-20. This is a locking (L), 120V (5), 20-amp (20) connection. NEMA (National Electrical Manufacturers Association) is a U.S.-based standard for electrical code.

Of all the locking-style connections, perhaps the L5-20 is one of the most common power connections found in House of Worship lighting systems. Its wiring description is shown in Figure 12.4. If you are using other configurations, make sure to contact the manufacturer for specific wiring information.

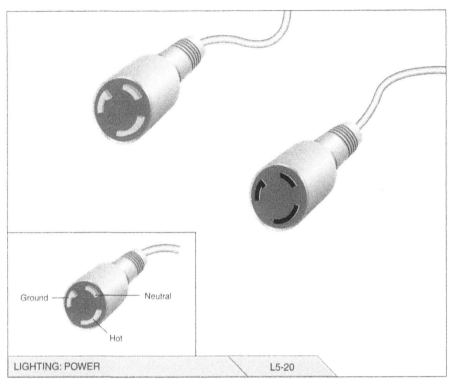

Ground — — Neutral

Hot

LIGHTING: POWER   L5-20

FIGURE 12.4
Illustration of NEMA L5-20 pinout.

LIGHTING

129

CAMLOCK

Camlock connections are very robust, well-insulated, high-power connections. In the world of entertainment lighting and the House of Worship, these connections are most commonly used for power tie-ins and high-voltage, three-phase power passing.

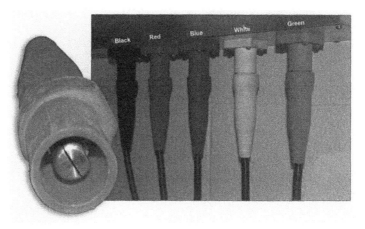

FIGURE 12.5
Camlock system.
Photo by Brad Herring.

You will notice that with most camlock systems, the green and white are opposite sex. The green is ground and the white is neutral. This is done as a safety measure to make sure a leg of hot power is not accidentally connected to the ground or neutral bus.

TIP
When wiring your own camlock connections, make sure to follow the safety standard of reversing the sex of the green and white connection to help ensure proper connection.

Camlocks require a special crimp tool. Generally speaking, most people purchase the camlocks with the necessary length and gauge cable already attached. It is fairly common to order a camlock connection with a specific length of cable terminating into a raw end. This allows the user to connect the cable to a power bus or any other termination while using a factory crimped camlock connector.

EDISON

Perhaps the most common type of power connector in the United States is the Edison connector. This is the standard three-prong power connection that you see in the wall outlets of your house and office.

20 Amp Connector   15 Amp Connector

FIGURE 12.6
Edison connector – 15 amp and 20 amp.
Photo by Brad Herring.

Edison connections are available in both 15 and 20 amp versions. You will notice from Figure 12.6, the 20-amp version takes the prong on the right of the outlet and flips it horizontal. The components that make up a 20-amp connection are a little bigger and stronger, to handle the extra current draw. If your equipment has a 20-amp connector, it is a BAD IDEA to remove it and replace it with a 15-amp connector so it will fit into an existing outlet. This is asking for trouble. Instead, upgrade the outlet to a 20-amp outlet and make sure the wire feeding that outlet is rated for at least 20-amp duty as well.

TIP
Nonsense such as putting a 15-amp connector on a 20-amp load is how best-case circuits are tripped and worst-case fires are started. Odds are, if you are pondering your insurance coverage, you should think of a new way to do the task.

Edison connectors are very easy to find, relatively inexpensive, and, while bulky, they are less bulky than most connections. Perhaps their biggest draw is that the outlets are already in the wall for plugging in accessories, and you can grab a connector at the local hardware store.

Edison connectors are good for some things, but for high-end lighting systems you should strongly consider other connection types. The plugs are made of smaller materials and tend to bend and break easily. There is also no easy way to keep the connector from pulling out of the connection.

Many lower-end dimmers and pro-sumer-type systems will use an Edison connection for lighting. This is also typical for small mobile rigs that might be in different locations with limited power accessibility. It is also tempting because extension cords are easy to find for an Edison connection.

If you are doing a permanent lighting system, spend wisely and utilize a 2P&G or twist lock connection for your system, and build an adapter for the special times you need an Edison connection.

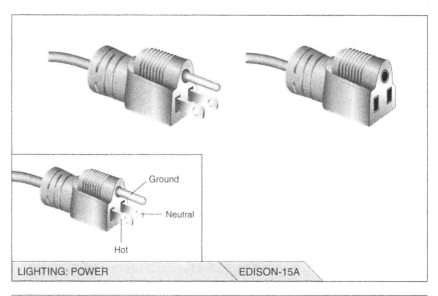

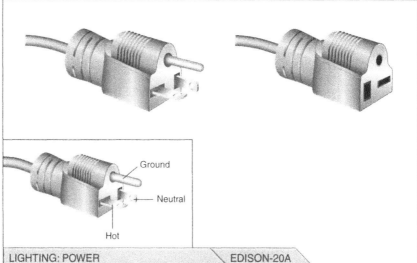

FIGURE 12.7
Pinout of Edison connector.

SOCAPEX CABLE (OR SOCO, AS THEY ARE COMMONLY KNOWN)

Soco cable is heavy, bulky cable, but it can save you a ton of work and hassle, not to mention it's a lot neater than stringing individual cables everywhere. The soco cable is the "audio snake" of lighting. This one thick cable contains six separate circuits. Soco cables have Veam-style connectors on each end (one male and one female). You can use a breakout that has the Veam connection on one side and six individual connectors on the other (most commonly Edison or 2P&G connectors, but it could be any type of power connector).

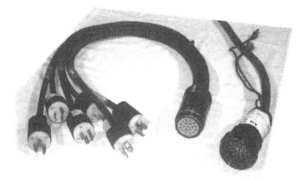

FIGURE 12.8
Socapex cable and breakouts.
Photo by Brad Herring.

Most professional-grade portable dimmers will offer a soco plug on the dimmer, so you can use the individual connectors or you can plug your soco cable right into the mass-pin connector, and away you go. This makes for quicker tie-ins and a neater connection point.

Remember, this is a multi-conductor cable that, unlike an audio snake, is containing many strands of 12-gauge wire. It's heavy, and you should think of smart ways to work with it to make your life easier, such as coiling it off the catwalks directly into a roadbox or hamper, using a rope to pull up the end, or other thoughtful ways of transporting it. Throwing 100 feet of this over your shoulder and hiking up the stairs (although done way too often) is not the way to enjoy your lighting career.

CHAPTER 13
Controllers and Protocols

LIGHTING CONTROLLERS AND PROTOCOLS

In this section, we are going to take a closer look at the various types of lighting controllers available on the market. Again, as technology is impacting our industry at a much faster pace than ever before, this information is continuously updating.

Two-Scene Manual Console

Once the modern-day staple of theatrical lighting, the two-scene manual console is slowly phasing out. However, this console is still found in many youth ministries, puppet ministries, and Houses of Worship across the land. They are cost effective, and if you aren't doing a ton of lighting cues, they can be very effective.

This type of console works by allowing you to set two looks – one that is active and one that is not. So, you would have a preset lighting cue that the audience would walk into; this would be on bank A. A second cue would be set on bank B based on written records for each channel. For instance, channel 1 would be at 45 percent, channel 3 would be at 30 percent, and channels 9 through 12 would be at 90 percent. But on bank A, the one the audience walks into, you might only have channel 3 through 8 at 90 percent.

FIGURE 13.1
Two-scene manual console.
Photo courtesy of Leprecon. All rights reserved.

You would then cross-fade from bank A to bank B at whatever pace you wish. The audience will now see the lights transform at the pace you cross-fade from the settings on bank A to bank B. Now that you are on bank B, the presets for bank A can be changed to the next cue. Now, when you cross-fade back up to bank A, the look will be different again. You would keep doing this through the entire show.

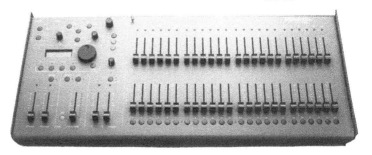

As consoles became more advanced, they began to offer more features such as a timer-based cross-fade for consistency, patching opportunities, and more scene banks (aside from simply A and B).

Manual lighting consoles are still available and are a viable option for small lighting systems, ones that don't require a lot of lighting changes, youth programs, puppet ministries, and other such applications.

TIP
The key to successful use of a two-scene manual console is good paperwork. Take the time to make a spreadsheet with a cell for each channel. Identify it by cue number. With all of your cue sheets laid out the same way, presetting the banks will be much simpler!

LIGHTING
136

Computer-Based Consoles

During the early 1990s, computer consoles were just getting their teeth in the marketplace. Initially, they were fairly bare bones, but today computerized lighting consoles are fairly complex. With these new control systems, we are able to control intelligent lighting, scene machines, foggers, hazers, color scrollers, color mixing, and a host of other non-life-safety items.

Now cues can be recorded and played back at the push of a button – identical every time in both content and timing.

Most computer-based controllers will allow you to see what you are programming via one or more computer monitors. If you are in the market for a computer console, you should make buying one with monitor support a must. Most computer-based consoles have this as a standard feature, but every once

FIGURE 13.2
EOS.
Photo courtesy of
Electronic Theatre
Controls, Inc. All rights
reserved.

in a while you will stumble upon a board that tries to make you hunt and peck without these vital tools. Having multiple monitors is ideal; this way you can see what's going on with the show while at the same time flipping around other parameters and seeing other things (such as patches, channel response, etc.).

Another great feature for most computer controllers that you should look for is the ability to control multiple universes. We will discuss this idea of universes later when we talk about the DMX protocol, but in a nutshell, the console should be able to send multiple outputs. You can also purchase splitters, but having the ability to control two or three outputs directly from the console is virtually a must for most lighting systems today.

If you are looking to buy a computer controller and are thinking about buying used, be aware of what you are purchasing. Many of the older computer controllers are very limited in what they can do (for instance, some only support a limited number of dimmers or channels, while others have limited fader options). For many ministries, these limits won't matter, as long as you make sure you know not only where you are, but where you are going when making a purchase decision. Don't buy something now that you'll regret later. Make smart use of your ministry dollar.

While most computer-controlled consoles have a myriad of functions, they are limited in their ability to control moving lights. If you are trying to program a dynamic, heavily cued moving light show, you will most likely want to use a moving light controller. As more consoles come to market, they are having the ability to program both static and moving lights, but when it gets down to individual control, nothing beats a true moving light console.

Moving Light Consoles

As moving lights have become more in demand, the need to control them has increased as well. There are several ways to achieve this. Some manufacturers, such as Martin, provide computer-based software for moving lights. This software is great for a youth group, special event, or smaller show. The software will control moving lights, hazers, static lights, or anything else that connects to a control protocol recognized by the software.

Software is only limited by its lack of hands-on controls, meaning that everything has to be grabbed via mouse or keyboard shortcut, and this greatly reduces the number of actions you can do at once. Some software is also limited in its ability to layer effects in real time.

Some manufactures have overcome these issues by using wing panels. These wing panels connect to your computer (usually by USB). They provide the touch control you desire, while using your desktop or laptop as the processing brain to run the software. One frontrunner in this technology is High End Systems, which produces the Whole Hog PC line of products.

FIGURE 13.3
Light jockey.
Photo courtesy of
Martin Professional A/S.

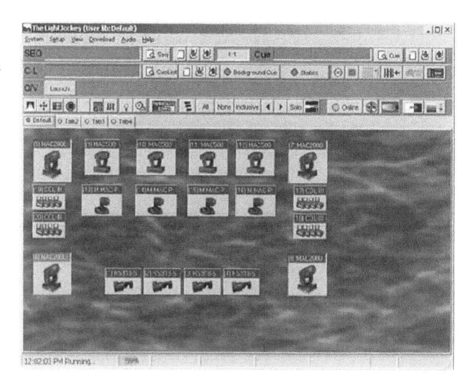

The Whole Hog is arguably the most notable moving light controller on the market. While not the only controller by any means, its name is synonymous with moving light control. The Whole Hog not only allows an operator to preset motions and cues, but to override these settings with manual inputs dynamically during a performance. This console truly gives you optimal control over the lighting. This is great if you are running a praise and worship segment and the pastor suddenly gets up to go to prayer; maybe you don't want the lights going nuts and you want to tone it down. With the gentle slide of a fader, they slowly transition to whatever you wish, even if what you wish is for them to fade down to black.

FIGURE 13.4
Whole Hog 3.
Photo courtesy of High
End Systems.

Many other companies offer budget-based solutions or solutions that control a fixed number of lights. For instance, some consoles will control up to 16 fixtures. For the average House of Worship, this is probably more than enough.

Many designers will run a conventional console for the static lights and a separate moving light console for the intelligent fixtures.

Your ultimate decision should be based on ministry need and budget. Remember, as with any other piece of equipment to gauge where you are, where you will be, and how long it will take you to get there when making a decision.

Automated Show Control

Automated show control really takes a step beyond lighting, but the controls are often lumped in with lighting packages.

Automated show control can literally control any aspect of the show that you want. For instance, many Las Vegas shows utilize show control. When it's time for the curtain to go, one button is pushed, which launches a series of commands that travel to all the various components. Music is played, click tracks are delivered, lighting is changed, and stage scenery moved – all on an automated timer in perfect synchronization. An operator is on standby to intervene should something get out of whack, but the entire performance is tightly choreographed.

That's one extreme of show control. Another could be that your lighting is triggered off CD markers, or your video content is switched based off time code. Show control can also be as simple as controlling hazers and foggers or automating CD playback with lighting cues.

LIGHTING

139

As we increasingly move to digital, it is becoming easier for us to slave components together so that change on one console will create a change with another.

Already we are seeing the move to smart sheet music. The sheet music software can control presets on some worship presentation software so that the song list is set with the music selection for the musicians. As our world continues to evolve with new technologies, this will become more standard in Houses of Worship.

Automated show control is definitely something to keep your eye on as we move into the future. While most Houses of Worship might not need to implement full-out show control (or even have the possibility given our dynamic nature), we will certainly reap benefits from this in certain areas of the work we do.

Control Protocols

Over the years, lighting has seen many protocols come and go. Originally, the standard was an analog system that has now faded out and given ways to new protocols.

You will still see some nonstandard proprietary protocols out there. NSI is one lighting manufacturer that has its own standard called Micro-Plex. Micro-Plex works off a three-conductor system and is proprietary to NSI equipment. It's worthy of mention that NSI also sells their equipment in the standard DMX format as well.

Oftentimes, protocols come either as a result of no set industry standard at the time, cost savings, or the attempt to force a user into a specific brand for future purchases.

Currently, the lighting standard is DMX. DMX is most commonly a five-wire XLR-style connector. In the early days of DMX, only the first three pins were used; therefore, the core standard of DMX is three-wire. However, as lighting systems have become more complex, the other two-wires (originally set aside for the future) are now being implemented.

DMX UNIVERSES

DMX systems work in what are called "universes." DMX512 (the full name of the standard) can work with 512 channels at a time. So, to maximize its efficiency we set 512 channels aside per universe. A typical console will have at least two universes built into it. Larger consoles will have more, and moving light consoles will usually have considerably more. Lighting systems will typically utilize universes in common sense ways. For instance, universe 1 might control all the conventional dimmers, universe 2 might control all the scanners, universe 3 might control all the moving heads, and universe 4 might control all the hazers, foggers, and other non-life-safety effects.

Of course, in simpler systems, universe 1 might run conventional dimmers while universe 2 runs everything else. In really simple systems, universe 1 will run all conventional dimmers until you reach the end of your house dimming (say 192) and then, starting at 193 (or 200 if you like to make the math easy) until you hit your 512 channel limit, will control everything else.

Universes are simply a way of overcoming a design limit in the DMX protocol. If your console does not have multiple universes, you can purchase a universe splitter box that will allow you multiple universes beyond what is built into your console.

DMX PIN CONFIGURATION

By using all five conductors of a DMX cable, it is now possible to control multiple universes via a single connection instead of having to utilize multiple DMX outputs for every universe. Obviously, this only works if your system is truly wired for five-pin DMX. Because the standard protocol only used three conductors, many contractors would only run three-conductor wire for DMX install. Therefore, you might see a five-pin connector, but in reality only three pins are wired up.

Many DMX fixtures (such as moving lights and hazers) utilize a three-conductor XLR-style DMX input. While this looks like regular microphone

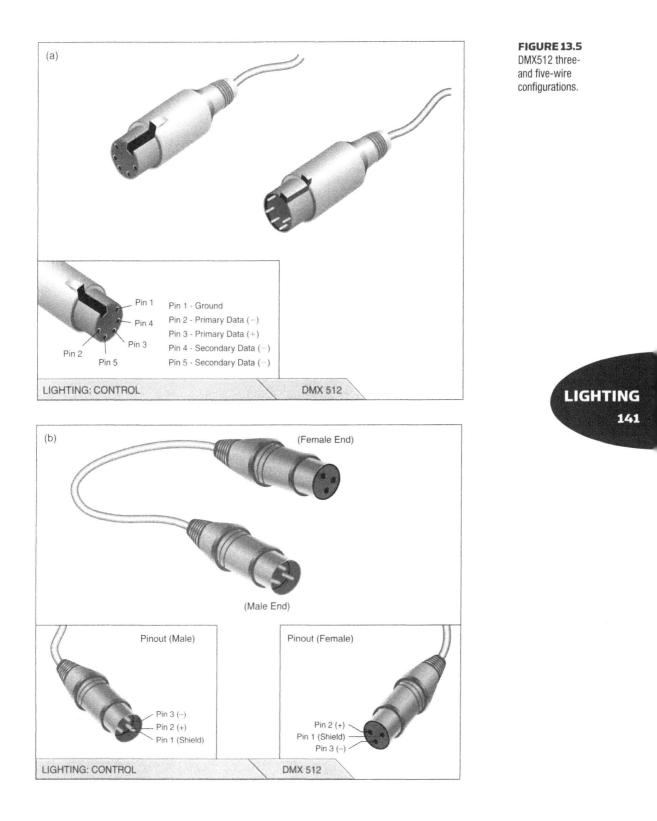

FIGURE 13.5
DMX512 three-
and five-wire
configurations.

(a)

Pin 1
Pin 4
Pin 3
Pin 2
Pin 5

Pin 1 - Ground
Pin 2 - Primary Data (−)
Pin 3 - Primary Data (+)
Pin 4 - Secondary Data (−)
Pin 5 - Secondary Data (−)

LIGHTING: CONTROL   DMX 512

LIGHTING
141

(b)

(Female End)

(Male End)

Pinout (Male)

Pin 3 (−)
Pin 2 (+)
Pin 1 (Shield)

Pinout (Female)

Pin 2 (+)
Pin 1 (Shield)
Pin 3 (−)

LIGHTING: CONTROL   DMX 512

cable, it is still DMX. Generally speaking, it is a bad idea to use standard microphone cable for these devices. Due to the differences in cable structure, a microphone XLR cable will not hold the DMX protocol tightly over long runs. This can result in position shift over all the values, thus rendering your cues slightly different each time.

If you are utilizing a three-pin fixture in a five-pin system, a simple five-to-three-pin adapter will hook it up and make everything run fine.

For those of you who really want to geek out on the standard, the United States Institute for Theatre Technology (USITT) publishes the full DMX512 standard on its web site (http://www.USITT.org). The standard is **USITT DMX512 1990**.

There has also been a lot of conversation over the years about using DMX over Cat5 cable. This might be confusing to some. By the phraseology, you would think this is sending DMX down an actual Ethernet line – not so. Instead, this is wiring for the future. USITT and Entertainment Services and Technology Association (ESTA) (both standards organizations) have tested and proved that DMX is capable of being sent down a Cat5 cable. Therefore, many facilities are installing Cat5 cable as their wiring infrastructure but still using the five-pin XLR connection to terminate.

There are currently no set standards for Ethernet connectivity. Barbizon, a major lighting reseller, in their Fall 2006 newsletter published a suggested good practice of termination by Barbizon Lighting Company:

Wire #	Wire Color	DMX512 Function
1	white/orange	data 1+
2	orange	data 1–
3	white/green	data 2+
6	green	data 2–
4	blue	Not Assigned
5	white/blue	Not Assigned
7	white/brown	Data Link Common for data 1
8	brown	Data Link Common for data 2
Drain		

The reason behind DMX over Cat5 is forward thinking. Lighting systems are evolving at a rapid rate. Already moving light manufacturers such as High End are creating full-blown moving data projectors with lighting capability. As these systems come online, there are more requirements that push past what DMX has to offer.

> **TIP**
> DMX512 is a one-way protocol. It cannot receive information from a device; it can only send information. Therefore, it is critical that DMX not be used to control any type of life-safety device such as chain motors, hoists, pyro, and other potentially life-safety devices.

Newer Protocols that are on the Way in

As newer systems and newer protocols are brought online in the future, having a facility wired via Cat5 will afford you the opportunity to convert to those standards.

Among the new formats being pursued by manufacturers are protocols known as ACN and RDM.

RDM (remote device management) is planned to offer two-way information, thus allowing you to control fixtures via your control center. For instance, you could conceivably get lamp-life information and set or reset fixture addresses without getting on a ladder and climbing up to the instrument, as well as obtaining other relevant information.

ACN (architecture for control networks) is planned to offer more features than the current DMX system allows. While not being confined to Ethernet protocols by current standards, it does lend itself well to Ethernet and is a recommended standard. One desired purpose for ACN is to control complex media systems as well as lighting and sound components. As of the time of this writing, the most recent official published information was ANSI E1.17 – 2006. For more detailed information about this standard, refer to that publication.

As for the scope of this book, realize that DMX is the standard protocol in the United States and many other countries for lighting system control. However, the market is changing quickly and newer technologies are forcing change. Control systems are something to keep an eye on and, if you are installing a new system running Cat5 or higher cabling, would be a wise investment for the future.

CHAPTER 14
Close-Up on Dimmers

We referred to dimmers in passing at the beginning of this section, but let's take a more in-depth look at their function and basic controls.

Dimmers have come a long way over the years. Much like everything else in our life, they have gone from large, heavy, cumbersome units to rather sleek, light-weight (relatively speaking) components that can be easily interchanged. There are several companies that manufacture lighting dimmers, but only one or two predominately used brands for entertainment systems.

A dimmer works by controlling the amount of current going through the circuit, thus allowing a lamp to dim. Without dimmers your lighting would simply be on or off. No fade, no variable intensities – just on or off.

Obviously, when using such high power, a dimmer needs to be fairly beefy to be able to handle the current draw and loads forced upon it – thus the bulky size. Newer dimmers are interchangeable; so you purchase the rack and then purchase individual dimmers that can slip in and out of the slots of the rack. This makes it really easy to have backups and to test potentially bad circuits. Also, with some systems, you can have a "dimmer module" that slips into the rack slot, but it actually functions as a relay or other control device. This adds a lot of flexibility to your system.

POWER NEEDS

Dimming requires a lot of power. I have yet to see an installation where the lighting designer didn't have to argue with an electrician about the reason for the power needs. Many people argue about the exact way to figure the load that you will require. Some say figure 80 percent

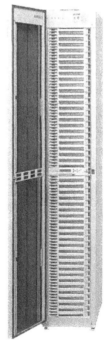

FIGURE 14.1
ETC sensor dimmer unit.
Image courtesy of Electronic Theatre Controls, Inc. All rights reserved.

systems full on – this assumes that all dimmers will never be loaded and few of them will be loaded to full capacity.

In a nutshell, you should think about your system and not limit yourself to how you currently use it, but imagine the worst-case "how it could be used" mentality. For instance, if you do a lot of productions, odds are your curtain call cue will be the brightest. You are likely to have the majority of your lights at a high intensity as well as all of your house lights potentially at full. This can be one serious load.

Every system is different, but the math is the same.

First, let's assume you are using a 2400W dimmer (commonly referred to as a 2.4k dimmer). This means the dimmer can handle 2400 watts. Now, keep in mind that you have resistance, so if you have 2000W worth of lights on a single dimmer, but they are located 300 feet away from the dimmer, your resistance load (depending on cable quality and connection integrity) could consume that overage on your dimmer.

Theatrical fixtures come in many wattages, but perhaps the most common for live production are 1000W, 575W, and 500W. Let's imagine that you have four 575W fixtures on a single 2.4k dimmer. That's 2300W, technically under the 2400W limit on the dimmer, but close enough that you might have problems if you have enough resistance on the line.

Now, when it comes to power in both audio and lighting systems, you are dealing with amperage (A). Amperage is equal to voltage divided by wattage, so the following formulas represents this.

For a single-phase system:

$$A = \text{Wattage}/\text{Volts}$$

For a three-phase system:

$$A = \text{Wattage}/(\mathbf{1.732} \times \mathbf{208}\,\text{Volts})$$

So, let's say you have 48 dimmers, each capable of 2400W (usually referred to as a 2.4k dimmer). If you loaded each dimmer to 80 percent (1920W each), you would have a total wattage draw of 92,160 watts. If your system is based on a 120V system, your total amperage draw will be 768 amps single phase, or approximately 384 amps per leg. If you were powering the dimmer system via a three-phase power-system, using the formula above your total amperage per leg would be approximately 256 amps, or roughly two-thirds the amperage required when using single-phase power. So, it's easy to see in a large lighting system how you could need a significant power supply.

Now with today's systems, it's unlikely that EVERY single dimmer would be loaded to capacity. Usually a dimmer will have one or two lights on it max, and the majority of newer lighting being produced is running 575W or lamps (while some older lights still run 1000W lamps). Also, if you had 48 dimmers,

a good portion of those dimmers would be servicing lights that you wouldn't use together. For instance, you would not have warm washes and cool washes, pattern washes, specials, multi-color units for scenery and backdrops, and so forth, all on at the same time. There would be no need to pull all of the circuits up at once, so the chances of finding yourself in this situation are slim. However, you do have to think about the reality of your specific install and be serious about the amount of power you need. It is better to assume the possibility that all of the lights may be brought to full at the same time and allow adequate amperage headroom just in case.

For permanent, installed systems, you are dealing with two basic load types: fixed and variable.

Fixed loads are typically house lights and, if run through the dimming system, worklights. In other words, a fixed load is any load wired directly to the dimmer rack. While variable loads are fixtures and devices used for production lighting – in other words, the devices you can plug, unplug, and move around – these are your variable loads per service.

If you are trying to determine the minimum required power feed for the entire system, calculate the fixed amperage load of the house and worklights based on the maximum rated wattage of the fixtures and the potential amperage draw of every production lighting fixture in the inventory, again based on the fixture maximum rated wattage. Add these two values. This is the minimum power feed for the system based solely on the attached and potential loads. As noted above, it is better to allow headroom in the system for adding fixtures that will increase the potential load on the system.

LIGHTING

147

The following power feeds are typical for installed dimming systems using 3 Phase 120/208 VAC Power: 24 dimmers at 2400 watts each – 125 amps-3 phase-120/208 VAC (these racks are typically rated for a maximum feed of 200 amps); 48 dimmers at 2400 watts each – 225 amps-3 phase-120/208 VAC (these racks are typically rated for a maximum feed of 400 amps); 96 dimmers at 2400 watts each – 400 amps-3 Phase-120/208 VAC (these racks are typically rated for a maximum feed of 800 amps). Maximum ratings may vary between manufacturers and are subject to other factors such as cross-bussing in multiple-rack systems.

Either a licensed electrical contractor or electrical engineer should confirm all power feed requirements. Preferably, the contractor or engineer should have some experience with production dimming systems.

CONFIGURING DIMMERS

It's also important to realize that dimmers can be configured to perform differently depending on your needs. Sometimes, there are physical switches on the dimmer itself that will make it a non-dim (meaning it's either on or off). With a non-dim, if the control system gives it a value of 0, it's off; with a value of anything other than 0, it's on full.

Likewise, dimmers can be set as to how they dim. While many dimmers make the claim to be "linear" in the way they dim, in reality most of them have a curve and it's usually on the lower end of the intensity sweep. You can adjust for this on most computer lighting consoles and on some dimmers themselves.

You can also set a dimmer to always be on, or to be "hot" all the time. This is useful when using them to power moving lights and other devices that you don't ever want to power off. This way, regardless of what the cue tells the dimmer to do, it will always stay on. This keeps you from accidentally shutting down critical show components at an inopportune or unplanned time.

ADDRESSING DIMMERS

Dimmers, like all controlled devices, work off addresses. We will discuss DMX since it is the industry standard. Generally speaking, your dimmer racks will start with address 001. They don't have to by any means, but this is common. If you have a 96-dimmer rack and you start the address at 001, the last dimmer will automatically be address 096. If you then wanted to put a portable dimmer rack in, say, another 12 channels, you would address it as 097 and – you guessed it – its first dimmer would be dimmer 97.

Now, we'll get into moving lights in the next section, but for argument's sake, let's say you have a moving light that has 16 channels to operate it. You could address it 098, or you could skip numbers. For instance, you could address it as 100. This would make sense if you had a string of other non-dimmer fixtures from this point on. Then your fixtures would start at address 100. The fixture in this example would automatically go until 116, and your next fixture could start at 117, or 120, or any higher number of your choosing.

If you were to address both dimmer packs (the 96- and the 12-channel units) as 001, then when you tell dimmer 1 to come up, the first dimmer in both packs would come up. Generally, this is not what you would want.

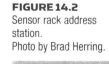

FIGURE 14.2
Sensor rack address station.
Photo by Brad Herring.

Likewise, if you were to address your first moving light at 100 and start the next moving light at 105, you would have constant conflicts of data and both lights would be uncontrollable, assuming the moving light has more than five channels.

The image here is a typical way of setting an address. In this case, you read from left to right, and the number in the window is the number that corresponds to that location -- in this case, it would be 001. Other manufacturers use dip switch settings and other methods to select the address. Some are more difficult than others, but if you consult the manufacturer's manual, you should be able to set the address rather quickly.

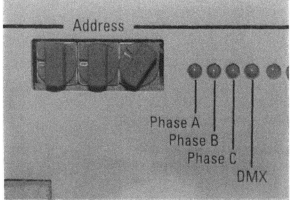

CHAPTER 15
An Overview of Moving Lights

More and more, we are beginning to see moving lights as a part of worship. They certainly have their place and have more than one function. When most people think of intelligent lighting, they think rock and roll and concerts. They imagine the lights moving all over the place with crazy color changes.

While moving lights can certainly work in this capacity, if that is all you can imagine them doing, you need to reconsider your way of thinking.

A moving light offers a House of Worship many advantages. First, it can be focused from the ground. This is a great liability savings in having volunteers or staff people working high up on a ladder every time an adjustment needs to be made. Also, this one light can have multiple focus points during a service, so the one light can do the function of several. And the moving light will give you a variety of color choices from the same instrument. Some fixtures will offer you a set number of colors within a wheel, while others will allow you to do full dichroic color mixing.

TIP
Dichroic color mixing uses glass filters to alter the perceived color value of the light. These filters allow light to change from one color to another all by controlling values via the lighting control board. Some of the advantages include never needing to climb a ladder to replace a gel, having any color available to each fixture at the touch of a button, and never having to replace the filters (unlike traditional gel).

FIGURE 15.1
MAC 550 moving light.
Image courtesy of Martin
Professional A/S.

LIGHTING

150

Moving lights do not have to appear to move at all. Imagine you have one focus for the praise and worship section. You might have the first song yellow, the second song orange, and the third song blue. Then, you fade to black to show a video and then come up on the pastor preaching.

On a small-size stage (let's assume 30 feet wide by 20 feet deep for the sake of this conversation), that entire scenario could be done with 10 lights – and that's assuming you want backlight! If you are not interested in front lighting every component on stage, you could probably do it with 7!

Imagine, each of the lights has a focus point for the band that gives a full stage wash – front and back lighting (we'll talk more about this later in this section). The first cue is yellow; then they slowly change to orange; then cue 3 slowly changes them to blue. Each song has transitioned visually into the next and your service is flowing nicely. Now, the third song is done, and you fade to black. During the blackout, the lights change focus. Three of the backlights swivel and pan to hit the pastor's primary area of teaching and change color to a light blue; and three of the front lights transition to point at the center of the stage (giving enough room for the pastor to easily walk on either side) and change color to white. All of this has happened invisibly to the audience. Now, the pastor steps up, the lights fade back up, and the cue looks as described earlier – no crazy motion or bizarre effects, but actual purpose and design.

Now, likewise, these same fixtures can move and change color and, in some cases, project patterns. Combined with an area hazer, you can see the beams of lights and create this majestic environment that sweeps through the audience. As the praise team (or choir) begins to sing a song about the resurrection, the lights slowly change to yellow and being to slowly tilt upward toward the sky. The lights themselves worship God, through design. Now this mood change has engaged the audience; they are subconsciously brought to this sense of awe as they are caught up in the moment of unencumbered worship (assuming the audio team isn't feeding back and the video screens are projecting the right words – see how it all ties together?).

How you choose to use the intelligent lighting will be up to your specific ministry and the way you communicate with people.

Now, be advised that intelligent lighting does have its drawbacks. These fixtures are expensive to purchase, they require a fair amount of maintenance (there have a lot of moving parts, gears, and belts), the lamps can be costly, and there is a learning curve to acquiring the knowledge to program them efficiently. However,

TIP
Don't use moving lights for the sake of using them. Motion in worship (be it lighting, cameras, or people) can be a huge distraction. You must use taste and guidance from the Holy Spirit in choosing the best time and method of using such design elements!

the payoffs for using intelligent fixtures can be extremely worth it in the long run.

COMMON TYPES OF INTELLIGENT FIXTURES

There are several types of intelligent fixtures on the market and they vary in cost, effectiveness, and longevity. Let's take a look at some of the fixture types that you will encounter and perhaps be tempted by.

Club Style (one-trick ponies and other cheapies)

If you see a moving light for under $300 (some would argue under $1500), it falls in this category. It's a cheaply made fixture that is designed to throw light and sometimes produce patterns. These fixtures are often purchased in bulk by clubs and restaurants to create a fun atmosphere. Oftentimes they are not controlled and are randomly running an internal program or at best are taking preprogrammed internal steps based off the beat of the music they hear on a cheap internal microphone.

If you are looking for something fun for a youth group or children's ministry or are specifically looking for a one-time special effect for a production, these fixtures might be what you are looking for. They are not what you need if you are trying to do serious intelligent lighting control for worship or if you need a delicate touch (Figure 15.2).

LIGHTING

151

Scanners (moving mirrors)

The scanners are what started it all (Figure 15.3). The idea was simple enough: All of the components are stored inside a nonmoving housing, and the lens projects an image onto a small mirror that then acts like a periscope for the lights. Move the mirror and you move the light. They are fast and quiet, but a little more limited in their movement. They cannot rotate 360 degrees; Normally, somewhere around 180 degrees is the extent of their travel, and their tilt is usually limited as well.

FIGURE 15.2
American DJ club light.
Photo by Brad Herring.

There are many uses for scanners in the House of Worship. They hang easily, blend in, and offer some nice design opportunities. Not all scanners have a good douser (ability to appear as though they are fading). Having a scanner with the ability to fade as well as open and close the shutter is a critical component for most Houses of Worship. By nature of what we do, there is often a need to transition slowly into or out of a scene. If your fixture can't do this, then you are stuck with a slam on or slam off effect – sometimes okay for youth services but usually not ideal for a worship service.

FIGURE 15.3
Moving mirror or
scanner.
Photo by Brad Herring.

FIGURE 15.4
Moving Head.
Photo courtesy of Vari-
Lite. All rights reserved.

Moving Heads (spots and washes)

Next on the scene was moving-light technology (Figure 15.4). These took the industry by storm and are what you most often see today in Houses of Worship. Over time, their movement has become very quiet and their flexibility offers a lot to the House of Worship. They can be hung from a truss or pipe, but they can also be floor mounted by simply sitting them on their bases. Likewise, they can sit on top of roadboxes or scenic elements and add a nice high-tech look all by themselves.

These lights can change color, pan and tilt in almost every direction, move slow, move fast (although not as fast as a scanner), and create spectacular effects.

A spot fixture can produce patterns as well as colors. This gives you the option of doing stage breakups for interesting looks or shaping the beam so that it has interest as it pierces through the air in a cloud of light haze. The spot fixtures most commonly offer the ability to spin and rotate the patterns as well, which adds a whole new dynamic to the environment.

A wash fixture typically produces color washes and does not project patterns. However, the beam it creates is usually wider (more like a Fresnel) and has a larger area of coverage. They usually excel in color mixing and can create stunning color shifts and vibrant displays. They are great to use on backdrops, scenery, or for stage washes.

Static Color-Changing Instruments

Color changer fixtures work like most conventional fixtures and come in Fresnel and Ellipsoidal varieties. You would aim these fixtures as usual, but instead of using gel, they have full CMYK color mixing built in. They are normally cheaper than full-out moving lights and require a little less maintenance as there are not so many moving parts within them (Figure 15.5).

Some companies are actually coming up with color changers that fit within existing static lights to modify them to change color.

These newcomers are a great option for the House of Worship – especially one that wants the advantage of color mixing but doesn't want to spend the budget on full-out moving lights.

LEDs

LED technology, as we have mentioned earlier, is making quite a move into the marketplace. The original problem with LEDs was brightness. They simply weren't bright enough to compete with your typical stage lighting. Then, they became acceptable for wall washes or background washes in certain applications (Figure 15.6).

However, LEDs are becoming commonplace in lighting plots around America and the rest of the world. They provide a long lamp life, give off low heat, and do not require dimmers. They can be plugged into the wall and controlled via DMX or other various protocols.

LEDs can also offer a smaller footprint, which can make them very viable for the House of Worship, where appearance is virtually always a concern.

PROGRAMMING INTELLIGENT LIGHTS

Intelligent lighting can be programmed via a static light board or a moving light board; however, it would be difficult to use them with anything less than a computer-based programmable console. If you are simply working with color changers, a good computer-controlled static light board will do everything you need. However, as you start to move into full-motion lighting and dynamic cueing, you are going to want to step up to a moving light console.

It would be well past the scope of this book to try to instruct how to program all of the various consoles on the market. Instead, it is profitable for you to know that there are different types of controllers for static and intelligent lighting alike.

Static Lighting Consoles

A static console strictly manipulates values for channels. In a typical setup, you might have 1024 channels. These channels normally relate to a dimmer, but they don't have to. For instance, on a one-to-one patch, channel 1 at full would bring dimmer 1 up to full.

FIGURE 15.5
Wybron Nexera.
Photo courtesy of
Wybron.

FIGURE 15.6
LED light.
Photo by Brad Herring.

LIGHTING

153

However, let's say that the static console is connected to a 16-channel moving head. For the sake of this example, the following channels are the functions of the light:

Channel	Light Function	Channel	Light Function
1	Pan Coarse	9	Pattern Wheel 2 Rotate
2	Pan Fine	10	Pattern Wheel 2 Index
3	Tilt Coarse	11	Effects
4	Tilt Fine	12	Lamp Strike
5	Color Wheel 1	13	Shutter
6	Color Wheel 2	14	Douser
7	Pattern Wheel 1	15	Iris
8	Pattern Wheel 2	16	Test Mode

Okay, so now that you know what each channel does for our fictitious fixture, you also need to know what each value of each channel relates to! For instance, channel 12 is the lamp strike, but only values 10 through 25 strike the lamp (actually turn on the lamp). Values 26 through 90 try to restrike, and values 91 through 100 turn the lamp off.

Likewise, channel 13 opens and closes the shutter... well, sort of. Values 1 through 15 close the shutter, 16 through 75 strobe the shutter at various speeds, 76 through 80 pulse the shutter (some very slowly), and 81 through 100 actually open the shutter.

Every channel is like this. So, you can't just, say, set channel 12 at full and strike the lamp. And, oh yeah, even if you could, chances are the strike needs to be no more than 5 seconds and then the value should reset to zero; otherwise it will continue to try to strike the lamp over and over, ultimately causing damage to the fixture or the lamp.

Now, once you do get the fixture on, pointed where it needs to go, and to the right settings, you write the cue. If you are doing a theatrical-style show with continuous cues, now you have to write a cue previous to this one in order to move the fixtures to this point, then time them to move, and THEN them turn on. So it can take up to three cues to get one look.

It's very possible to do. It will really help you get an answer to your prayer for patience. I've programmed many a show this way – it's possible, but it's not fun. It's also not dynamic.

Newer static consoles offer a moving light section. This allows you to load a fixture library and then control the attributes via encoder wheels. This keeps you from having to know in detail how each individual channel works. It's a huge leap above programming each channel by hand, but it's still very time consuming and requires a fair amount of programming skill and patience. Plus, you still have the dilemma of needing to program a move cue in between each visual cue, unless you want to see the lights randomly move from one spot to the other while changing all their attributes. Remember, the lights might have panned 360 degrees to point where they point. They will not just make a nice, smooth, straight-line track to the next position unless you spend a lot of time programming them to do so.

Moving Light Consoles

A moving light console is an example of having the right tool for the job if you ever intend to do a dynamic show with full moving light control.

Moving light consoles are designed for use with moving lights (imagine that). There are many types of moving light consoles on the market, and each of them works significantly differently from the others. As a designer or operator, you need to figure out which one best suits your ministry and learn it well. Then stick with it.

Now, you can load fixture libraries, and assign actions and triggers to fader response. At your fingertips are page upon page of actions. With most consoles, you can grab your fixture and assign it a motion path. You can move all of them together, some of them together, or one light all by itself. While they are in motion, you can change color, change patterns, or alter the path of motion. You can grab your intensity fader and bring them down to a slow blackout or you can slam them down to a blackout. Likewise, you can bring them up on command just as easily.

You don't have to worry about what each value on each channel is doing – that's all handled in the library. You want to turn the lamp on? Push the button corresponding to that instrument to strike the lamp. Need to reset one fixture or a group of fixtures? Select the fixture or group of fixtures and hit the reset option.

LIGHTING

155

Moving light consoles take some time to learn and a lot of time to master, but once you do, you are in complete control of your show. You can make changes on the fly or continue on with your well-rehearsed script. The ability to manipulate the lighting at a moment's notice far surpasses anything you would do on a static light board.

Likewise, a moving light controller is capable of controlling dimmers and running static lights. However, it's often like driving a Ferrari on an old gravel road. Most people who have a lot of static fixtures to operate will either group all of the static lighting into a few simple presets and run them off the intelligent console, or they will run two separate consoles – one for the static lighting and one for the intelligent lighting.

The choice is yours. It will depend on your needs and the demands of your service as to how you run the lighting for your House of Worship.

ARE INTELLIGENT FIXTURES WORTH THE MONEY?

This is a question that only you can answer for your ministry. I believe that if moving lights are an option for you, it is a good path to take – perhaps not your entire inventory, but at least a few on hand. At minimum, I'd recommend color changers. The dynamic environments that you can create and the flexibility they afford are beyond words. But at the end of the day, it comes down to budget, personnel, and determining how you communicate with the people God has given you to reach.

WHAT'S THE DIFFERENCE BETWEEN A $3000 FIXTURE AND A $12,000 FIXTURE?

What's the difference between a Porsche and a Pinto? Or an $800,000 house and an $85,000 house?

Really, by and large, you get what you pay for. For most Houses of Worship wanting intelligent lighting, a $3000 to $5000 instrument is going to far exceed your expectations. As fixture cost goes up, so do features, lamp brightness, tracking features, and so on. For instance, some of the real high-end fixtures can lock onto an IR (Infra Red) transmitter and actually track a target automatically, thus acting like a followspot. Others offer smoother color mixing, and some offer full video playback and edge blending for multiple light sources to create one large video wall.

Some would argue the quality of the fixture improves significantly as the cost goes up.

LIGHTING

156

When it comes to using ministry dollars, we have to evaluate the best bang for the buck. For every dollar spent on ministry, that's a dollar that doesn't feed the homeless or fund a mission trip. It's a dollar that doesn't help a troubled teen or an unwed mother. It's a dollar that doesn't fund a counseling ministry so families can get back on track and learn about the love that God has for them.

On the other hand, every dollar invested in media ministry is a dollar that goes toward telling a story of God's love in a unique way and capturing the attention of someone who might not otherwise listen. It's a dollar that helps build environments that break down barriers and make it easier for the Holy Spirit to work.

The best you can do is educate yourself, understand the needs of your ministry, pray, and let the Spirit lead you in your decisions.

CHAPTER 16

Beyond Illumination – Using Lighting for Design

BEYOND ILLUMINATION

What makes lighting so appropriate for Houses of Worship isn't simply illumination; it's the ability to sculpt the light to create a mood and to build an atmosphere that fosters worship and breaks down barriers. Lighting helps the audience to focus; it can draw them in and remove the separation of the stage and the audience area. With proper lighting design, the setting can be as intimate as you desire. It can be upbeat, it can be solemn, or it can be neutral.

It's how you choose to utilize the illumination that makes or breaks the lighting ministry in your church.

Using Color for Design

Color for design has two functions – aesthetics and illumination. Obviously, the process of lighting design goes far beyond the scope of this book, but there are some simple concepts to keep in mind in regard to color.

First, realize that certain colors (green in particular) look really bad on human skin. These colors can bring out all the imperfections and flaws in the skin and make a person look very undesirable. Also, realize that different skin pigments illuminate differently. So, if you have very pale and very dark people on stage together, your lighting might look uneven if not properly gelled. Likewise, very bright and very dark costumes can present problems that will make the lighting appear to be imbalanced. You will want to gel accordingly to average the lighting out while at the same time staying true to the costume design and overall look of the event.

When it comes to lighting for effect (aesthetics), the sky is the limit.

One of the biggest things that Houses of Worship (particularly contemporary Houses of Worship) miss is the backlighting element. With backlighting you can make bold color choices. You can change from one color to another and mix colors to achieve beautiful results. With backlighting it doesn't matter if the color is bright enough to adequately illuminate someone. This is the real beauty of backlighting – especially with worship, concerts, and other special moments. The backlight will wash the stage as well as the musicians and vocalists. It will also create beautiful effects on the instruments themselves. Backlighting can really make the stage come alive and help to create a strong environment or a very stirring mood.

Typically, color brings out emotions in all of us. It's the reason that adding colored theatrical lighting in various degrees of intensity stirs us when we see it. The entire stage becomes dynamically charged by the simple addition of multicolored illumination – and the color doesn't have to be extreme or constantly changing to have an impact on the audience.

Just like with sound, subtle color and intensity differences will bring the audience into an atmosphere of worship and help to break down walls and barriers that many people have when engaging in corporate worship.

Lighting Angles

Considering your lighting angles is important to any solid lighting design. There are arguably five distinct angles for lighting designers to consider:

- Down
- Back
- Front
- Side
- Up

In order to properly light a subject or scenic element, it takes many of these angles to make a solid "look." Lighting should be thought of as sculpturing. As you apply light from any direction, you will emphasize certain areas and deemphasize others. As you begin to combine multiple angles of light, you begin to create dimension on stage so some things pop out more than others, and you begin to create an emotion based on the angles and color.

You can also achieve basic but needed effects such as time of day, time lapse, and environmental changes. All of these are important aspects of production lighting; many are important for worship as well.

DOWN LIGHT

Down light is hung above the stage and pointed, for the most part, straight down. If the focus is tilted one way or the other, the tilt is extremely slight. The idea of down light is to hit the top of a target directly and spill around it on the floor.

You will notice in Figure 16.1 that down light by itself creates very strong shadows under the eyes, nose, lips, and chin. It also creates a strong presence of light on the top of the head and shoulders.

Down light can also be very effective in lighting scenery or instruments.

FIGURE 16.1
Down light.

FIGURE 16.2
Backlight.

LIGHTING

159

BACKLIGHT

Backlight is very crucial and often overlooked. When lighting a subject with backlight, the lighting tends to create a halo around the subject. Backlight can be from above, directly behind, or from below. Each offers the same type of light on the subject, but the effect is dramatically different. In traditional back-lighting, the backlight most often comes from the top.

Many churches miss a great lighting opportunity by not utilizing backlight. With backlight you can create sultry colors on stage and make beautiful color washes on instruments and scenery – as well as people, without worrying about whether you can see their faces. If you are in an environment that wants to see bright faces, back-light provides an excellent way for you to bring a good color palette to your design.

FRONT LIGHT

Front light is the staple of most House of Worship lighting. This light is hung in front and above the subject. Typically, front light will be projected at a 45-degree angle or as close to that as possible. This will help to reduce unwanted shadows on the face (by not exceeding 45 degrees) but will greatly reduce the shadow throw by keeping it as steep as 45 degrees. So, when your front light is off from the 45-degree axis, these are the trade-offs you face.

Front light is the lighting you would use to see the face of someone. This is primarily the only form of lighting many Houses of Worship utilize, and that's

FIGURE 16.3
Front light.

really unfortunate. Front lighting is, for most Houses of Worship, the essential lighting. However, the real artistry and emotion comes from combining it with other forms.

Many times I will avoid the use of front light completely or use it as sparingly as possible. In a contemporary worship set, I light the worship leader with front light, as well as the soloists and maybe (depending on the situation) the praise team. Everything else is lit with back-light, top light, and side light. I achieve a strong color palette that can be easily altered with the mood of the song or can remain sterile and not change at all (depending upon the conviction of the church that I'm designing for).

For a more traditional service, I light the main stage with a fair amount of front light, as that is what people are going to expect. However, the primary area of focus is always just a little brighter. As the area of focus shifts, so does the intensity (slowly and subtly). This helps the viewer subconsciously concentrate on the primary area of focus. Depending upon the individual ministry, I prefer to light the orchestra with less intensity than the main stage (they are not usually the focus) and to keep the choir lights down or at the very least dim unless the choir is singing. Any time the choir is singing, they would normally be lit. I spend a lot of time trying to focus on the architectural points of the room (thus lighting greenery, walls, and staging) to create visual interest in the room. This lighting could change a little (if allowable) during the worship set to help create an energetic mood, and it could also change with each sermon series to match video graphics.

Front light, of all the lighting angles, has the most likeliness of washing your subject out. It tends to flatten the subject, whereas the other forms of lighting help to create a three-dimensional sculpture of the subject. The more front light you use, the flatter things will tend to feel. Front light without any other angle of supporting light is dull at best.

SIDE LIGHT

Side light is, as you might now expect, illumination that comes from the side of the stage. Generally, side lighting will be almost parallel to the floor in its purest forms, but sometimes will come in at a long angle from a ceiling or floor point.

FIGURE 16.4
Side light.

FIGURE 16.5
Up lighting.

Side light is useful for creating interesting angles of light as well as for creating true three-dimensional feeling. The drawback with true side lighting is that it requires stage space as it has to be hung from a floor-mounted stand or lowered on a vertical pipe from above. Either way, the lights tend to be in the way and the logistics can be problematic.

UP LIGHT

Up light, as we discussed earlier, is sometimes referred to as "boundary lighting" or "foot lights".

Up lighting is nice because it can take away dramatic shadows created by front, side, and top light. The removal of these shadows removes any "sinister" look and also helps make the person look younger. Almost all high-quality television broadcasts of large ministries will use some form of up light on the pastor.

The problem with up lighting can be location. Obviously, the lighting has to be in the lip of the stage and this can be unsightly in some Houses of Worship. Now there are much smaller versions available via MR16 lamps as well as LED. Some pastors might also complain that they feel blinded by all the light. It's simply a trade-off of what is important – being well lit, looking good, figuring out a mounting system that works, and being comfortable. All of these arguments have their place, and it is ultimately up to each House of Worship how they choose to answer them.

Creating Shadows

Perhaps as much as what is lit, what isn't lit can tell even more of the story. Purposeful use of shadows and darker lit areas can create a lot of stage tension as well as interest. It's a well-known fact in Hollywood that, when making a

FIGURE 16.6
Controlling shadows.

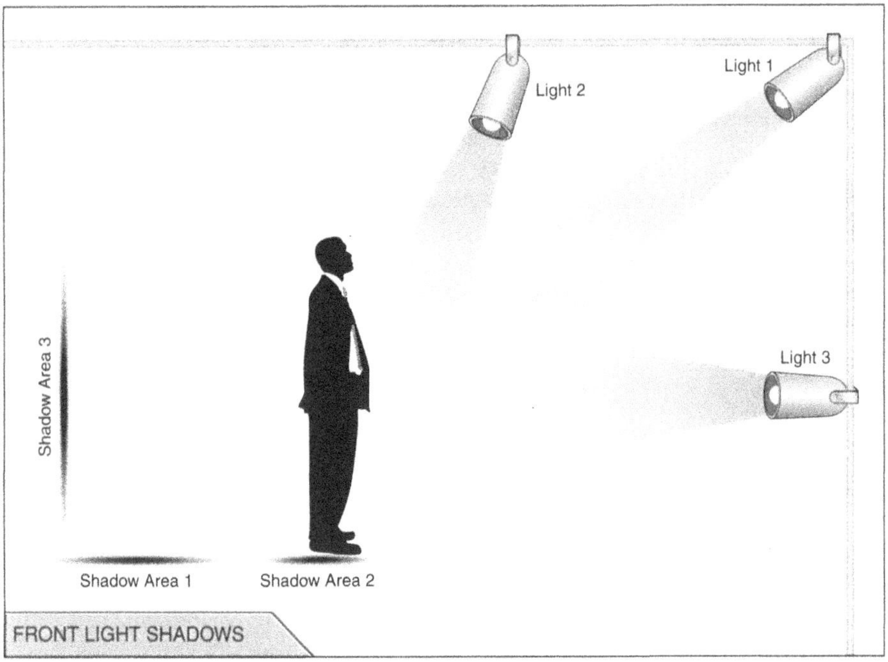

Light 1

Light 2

Shadow Area 3

Light 3

Shadow Area 1   Shadow Area 2

FRONT LIGHT SHADOWS

FIGURE 16.6
(Continued)

very dramatic movie, you can achieve a bigger effect by not showing the actual event but showing a shadow of the event, or hearing the sound of an event, and letting the viewers' imagination create the scene for themselves.

Likewise, as we briefly discussed in the Color Mixing Theory section, you can take a group of lights that are hung right next to each other and focus them at the same point on stage. Make each of these lights a different color and they will create multitone shadows over everything they touch on the stage. This can create a very dramatic (and aesthetically pleasing) look.

Many young designers become fixated on eliminating shadows, but real interest can come in the work when you manipulate your shadows and become very specific with them.

Controlling Shadows

There is difference in lighting with intentional shadows and relief versus not knowing what you are doing.

In general, if you are trying to control shadows, it is important to realize how a shadow is made. Clearly, objects casting shadows are not transparent and so, when struck with light, interfere with the illumination path. The result is a shadow. The lower the angle of light, the longer and more dramatic the shadow.

As a general rule, the closer your lighting angle is to 45 degrees, the better off you will be. This will tend to drop a shadow more directly behind the object while not creating harsh shadows that look unsightly.

It's also important to remember that the brighter the light, the more intense the shadow. For instance, if you create a shadow with ten 1000 W front light fixtures, ten 500 W fixtures from directly above are not going to wash it out.

Every light will create a shadow. This is simple physics. So, if your front light creates shadows going backward, backlight will create ones going forward, top light will create shadows that fall straight down, and so on. One of the jobs of the lighting designer is to understand the shadows and manipulate them as part of the environment creation process.

PHYSICS ARE FAIRLY SOLID

I originally entitled this section Physics Don't Change. But that's not really true. We know that the earth has stood still and rivers have parted, and I've seen with my own eyes the Spirit of the Lord work miracles in productions and services that literally betrayed every law of physics that I have ever learned. We serve the God of the Universe – and His powers are unlimited.

However, for the most part we have laws of physics. They operate within a set of predefined rules. For instance, the speed of sound is rather constant, the speed of light is a known quantity, and so on. In keeping with this, if you shine a light at a subject, there will be a shadow – and that won't change, even if you do have a backdrop behind the person.

I cannot tell you the number of times I have been asked if I can remove the shadow from the background because the director wanted a straight-on front light to wash out the actor. One common theme in this book has been the need for communication. The ministry of lighting is no different. We must be kindhearted in all cases, working as one who is a servant, but we must explain the facts to those who don't understand our world in a way that makes sense but is not condescending.

Backlight sometimes blinds people in the first row. You have to make a choice. Perhaps you don't seat the first row, or you fill it with ushers, or you readjust your backlight to an angle that doesn't work as well, or you move the worship leader upstage 4 or 5 feet *and* readjust your backlight. But, the rules stay the same: A bright light pointed at someone's face is going to be blinding.

Choir Complaints

This is probably the number one complaint for anyone trying to do lighting for worship – and undoubtedly the number one pain for someone lighting worship for television. It seems every time you turn a light on that's pointing anywhere near a choir member's face, the world stops spinning (but not the same way as accounted in the Bible) and the complaints come flooding in about everyone being blinded.

This is where your communication skills will really shine.

- Fact: You have to light the choir.
- Fact: Lights blind people when pointed in their direction.

How you handle this situation will determine your effectiveness as a lighting designer or lighting technician. The following three steps will help you be successful:

1. You should anticipate the problem and work with the worship leader and pastor to have a team-based solution.
2. You should have a layman's answer ready for the choir as to what you are achieving and why it's necessary.
3. You should be able to articulate what it is you are achieving (not only for yourself, but for the overall ministry that you are all engaged in together as a common body) and why it is necessary.

The list of potential roadblocks could go on and on, but the key is remembering the basics:

- You are a servant and should respond as one with a servant's heart.
- Your ability to communicate and not become emotional will be your make-or-break point.
- Your overall goal should be about the work of the ministry as a whole.
- You must be careful to be as much of a team player as you wish for everyone else to be.

You will see over time that, as you handle each issue with a servant's heart and a team perspective, God will begin to build a true spirit of teamwork and collaboration around your ministry. When this happens (if it hasn't already) is when things get really exciting! So, be mindful of yourself and you will see that God will use you as the catalyst for change.

Setting the Mood

Lighting is all about mood and environment. There are many things you can do to create an atmosphere with lighting. We've discussed some of them already (shadows, angle of light, fixture choices, intensity, etc.), but now we are going to talk more in detail about some standard design concepts that you can use.

USING COLOR

Now that you have an idea of how color mixes, let's talk about what you can do with that color. There are certain physiological traits to light. People associate color with different things. For instance, red usually signifies anger or murder (the color of blood). Red tends to be classified as a "hot" color, so it has a temperature associated with it. Yellows and purples are often associated with royalty. Blues are commonly reflective of elements such as water, sky, and nighttime. Likewise, blue is a calming color, so it tends to relax people and build trust.

You have warm colors – these are your ambers, oranges, reds, and pinks – and you have your cooler colors – blues, purples, and cyans. Daytime exterior scenes are typically lit with warmer colors, while nighttime exterior scenes are often lit with cooler ones. Cold climates tend to emphasize the cooler colors – or cool colors are added to a warm wash to give a subtle "chill" to the wash.

As humans, we associate color with temperature. When you think of a cold, snow-covered place, you tend to think of it more in shades of blue; however, if you imagine yourself on a sunny day running though a field in the middle of summer, you often have more of an amber tone to that scene. Likewise, for summer, yellows and orange and white pop out at you. The winter is blue and gray and – coincidentally – white. Some colors transcend to both warm and cool. A no-color light can give a warm feeling or a cold one depending on what it is paired with.

Especially in concert and dance lighting, it is common for a designer to combine a very hot color with a very cold color. Or to mix primaries in general – a primary red complimented with a primary blue will create a dynamic visual effect on stage. Likewise, so will a primary red and a primary yellow.

Color contrast is very important in creating an interesting stage look. If all of your lights are one color, it quickly becomes quite drab, even if that one color is bright yellow. However, if you have a rich blue background with magenta backlights, no-color face lights, and sweeping bright yellow shafts of light going over the heads of the worship team, you have just created a very dynamic look by mixing your color palette.

Color in lighting can build tension, define time of day, determine location, or simply build emotion. The right color with the right lighting will bring life to a song, add mystery to drama, and help the audience focus on the message.

GOBOS

The gobo is overlooked by too many House of Worship lighting designers. As we have discussed earlier, a gobo is a breakup pattern of some sort – be it branches, leaves, abstract, cityscapes, logos, or whatever, a gobo breaks up the light. This breakup of light can then be focused in a hard sharp focus or a very soft fuzzy focus. The resulting look will be very different with each focus.

In the real world, lighting is rarely without breakup. Take a walk outside and look for the effects of lighting. On the ground, you notice the shadows of leaves, power lines, and tree branches, and the general unevenness of lighting in general. The use of gobo patterns in lighting brings back that dimension of life to your design. People are accustomed to seeing this, and the lighting looks unnatural without it.

This is not to be confused with bad focus. A poorly focused wash where there are hot and cold spots of lighting is just poor lighting. This will distract from the message and look amateurish. This is not what we are talking about. Instead, we are looking for a well-focused wash with the pattern breakup resting nicely on top of it – or, in some cases, the pattern breakup being the wash.

Some uses of gobos for the House of Worship would include (but by no means be limited to) these:

- Casting the shape of a prison bar on the floor and over the face of an actor who is portraying Paul writing letters in prison.

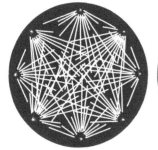
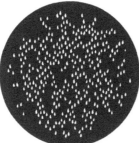

FIGURE 16.7
Breakup patterns.
Photo courtesy of GAM
Products. All rights
reserved.

879 Laser Lines

893 Teardrop Breakup

884 Bing Bong

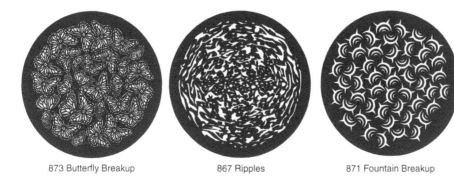

873 Butterfly Breakup

867 Ripples

871 Fountain Breakup

LIGHTING

167

- Shadows of leaves as a character playing the part of Jesus teaching under the trees in a garden.
- A logo for a retreat weekend taught by the pastor, projected on the walls at different sizes, angles, and colors.
- Several cityscape gobos on a blank canvas that's being lit by cyc lights of varying colors to portray the world that we live in.
- A series of windows casting over the stage as a man and wife play out a scene on the den sofa, watching television. The outside light is breaking through the windows that you can't see, which eliminates the need for building windows and complicating the scene change in some instances.
- Abstract breakups on the floor or back wall, sharp focused or soft focused for visual effect during a worship set.
- Your church name projected on the wall as people come in.

Obviously, the list could go on and on. The idea is to get you thinking about how to use gobos as a part of lighting for both worship and event production. When budgets get tight, lighting can compensate for a lot of scenic elements. This saves time and money in the long run.

SOMETIMES THE BEST LIGHTING IS NO LIGHTING AT ALL

Another common mistake is feeling that lighting must always be turned on. This is a misconception. For instance, if you want to have an interesting scene, let your actors come in with torches (assuming proper safety procedures are taken) and then allow the torches to light the scene. If there's not enough light, ghost some top light in at 10 or 15 percent intensity and maybe some front light at 10 percent or so, but by and large, let the torches do the work.

Likewise, if you are doing something more modern, consider giving your actors flashlights. As they work, they can shine the lights onto other actors' faces, and sometimes their own. They can also reveal things about the set as they shine their lights on these things. This can create a lot of interest and, by the mere fact of not using stage lighting at all, the flashlights can set the place and time. They can also add a sense of realism to the scene, depending on the content.

You can also choose to illuminate what are considered to be "practicals." A practical is anything on a set that would be used in real life that you choose to highlight. An example of this would be a lamp, headlights of a car (should the car be on the set), and so forth.

There are numerous ways to create environments with lighting – and it doesn't always have to be from the theatrical lighting in the air.

Blackouts are another form of lighting – actually, the absence of light. However, blackouts should be tastefully executed. Sometimes used to cover scene shifts, a blackout for such shifts should always be as brief as possible. Anything over 10 seconds begins to feel like an eternity. But a blackout doesn't have to simply cover something up; many times a blackout can occur at the climax of a scene for added effect.

Lighting design is only limited by your imagination. Even if you don't have tens of thousands of dollars worth of equipment at your disposal, you can create dynamic effects with a little ingenuity and hard work.

ATMOSPHERIC CONDITIONS – HAZE, FOG, AND DRY ICE

Hazers

Have you ever been to a concert and observed the beams of light as they sweep across the audience? Perhaps you've been to a contemporary worship service and witnessed the same thing. Have you wondered how they do this?

> **TIP**
> Chemical hazers and foggers will set off most commercial fire alarms!

Simple – they use a hazer. There are a couple of different types of hazers on the market. Some are oil based and others are water based.

A hazer simply puts a suspended particle in the air and the beam of light reflects off it, thus making the beam visible to the human eye. *The key to getting a hazer to work properly is using a fan in front of it.* Even if it comes loaded with an internal blower fan, results always seem to be better when an external box fan or the equivalent is used. The fan helps to make the particles even finer as they come out of the hazer.

A hazer will tend to make a mess around it. As the hazer (especially an oil-based hazer) starts to pump fluid, there is a natural spillage that will come out of the mouth of the hazer as it creates its particles. This is normal, but it can get messy and, in some cases, slippery. Normally a hazer is located somewhere on stage or mounted onto a lighting truss. You will want to observe how your hazer works and then decide. Not only should you consider the residue it might leave, but also what works best in your facility overall. Temperature, humidity, and air currents all play a factor in how the haze will function in the room. These factors will also affect hang time and height consistency of the atmosphere.

FIGURE 16.8
DF50 Hazer.
Photo by Reel Efx.

A word of warning: You are going to want to experiment with the haze. If you set it too high or leave it on too long, your sanctuary will tend to look more like a smoky bar than a House of Worship.It does not typically take a lot of haze to achieve the effect of seeing light beams in the air. Once the correct amount of haze is in the room, a small burst of haze periodically will usually keep enough volume in the air for your effect.

Also, when you use a hazer for the effect of seeing a lighting beam through the air, you will want to start working with sharp-focused patterns (such as the Rosco 77894 Beam Splitter Gobo or GAM 336 Balloons Gobo). Obviously, these patterns are just suggestions, but the idea is that they will break up the beam of light from a solid blob to a defined set of streaks. Different gobos will affect the light differently, giving a different visual effect in the air. Experiment and find your own favorite!

LIGHTING

169

Fog Machines

Fog machines are used primarily for effect. Fog machines produce a large amount of dense fog that looks a lot like smoke. It tends to rise in the air and fill a room. Fog machines work off a chemical that is heated and creates the illusion of fog.

Fog machines produce a much denser atmosphere than hazers. As a result, they are very prominent in the design and should be used with purposeful intent.

Some fog machines, especially ones that create large volume, are very loud when they are pumping. Fog machines can also be located offstage (or under stage), with the fog routed through large dryer hose or other venting systems.

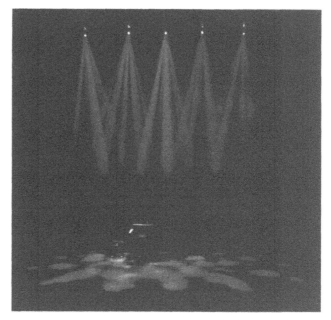

FIGURE 16.9
Haze effect.

FIGURE 16.10
Fog machine.

Fans are usually required to help push/pull the smoke through these systems, but again it depends on the effect you are going for.

Likewise, your fog machines can be routed through hoses and vents to force the fog to come out in a certain pattern or multiple locations.

Dry Ice Machines

Dry ice is a rather simple effect that often gets complicated. The premise is that when you drop a block of dry ice into a large heated body of water (usually boiling or close to boiling), the result will be a low-lying fog effect. There are some heater modules that work off 110V, but the 220V is far better if you have the power. The hotter the water, the better your result will be. Likewise, if you are doing multiple effects, the dry ice chills the water, so you need the ability to reheat fast.

There are several professional models available that you can purchase. Many people build their own, using 55-gallon drums, hot water heater elements, blower fans, and dryer hose. The image shown in Figure 16.11 is a much more recent model. One key part to success is having the lid of the barrel sealed securely so there is no fog escaping from the lid and all of it is coming out of the dryer hose.

FIGURE 16.11
Dry ice machine.

Dry ice can produce several dramatic effects for the stage. Heating and air systems are critical for consistent dry ice delivery. Any change in room temperature, humidity, or air currents will result in the dry ice reacting very differently in the room. Also, as the fog heats up, it tends to rise, so the warmer it gets, the less likely it is to hang low to the ground as desired. Clearly, stage lights tend to heat it up, so controlling your heating and air systems are critical. Many times people will tech a show with dry ice, but when the show goes into performance, the air systems get cranked down to compensate for crowds and the fog reacts differently.

It's also a wise idea to test the dry ice more than once to make sure that it responds predictably.

LIGHTING

171

Design Software and Reporting

Have you ever heard the saying "Plan your work and work your plan," or perhaps "Failing to plan is planning to fail"? These popular sayings apply directly to lighting design and proper planning for it.

When you get ready to design a show, there are several tools available to you. First, let's look at some of the components expected from a lighting designer, talk about how they integrate into the House of Worship, and then look at modern tools available to help make the process smoother.

LIGHTING PLOT

The image above is an example of a very simple lighting plot. The rectangle would represent the stage, and the pipes are drawn to location over the stage. Clearly, in a real stage plot you would most likely have more fixtures and positions, but this is just a sample. A lighting plot is a drawing that shows (to scale) the position and type of each fixture, its circuit number, dimmer number, channel number, pattern number (if any), and gel color. Some designers also put focus information at each fixture on this list. The idea is to have on paper, available at a glance, everything that is in the air.

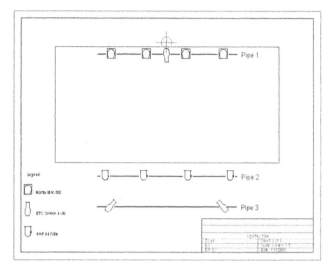

FIGURE 16.12
Lighting plot for a show.

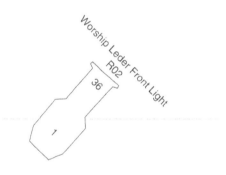

FIGURE 16.13
Lighting plot close-up.

This document is to scale so the technicians can pull scale measurements off the plot and hang the lighting accurately. Normally, a plot is printed on a 24- × 36-inch sheet of paper, much like a construction drawing. However, it can be on any size of paper.

The cleaner the drawing, the better you will be. Remember, technical ministry is all about communicating, and the lighting plot is one major way of communicating your design to other people (as well as referencing it yourself).

Typically, your lighting plot will be an overhead view of the theater. Each pipe and truss location will be drawn on the plot, and house circuit locations will be on the plot as well. This way the designer can make sure he or she is designing smartly. For instance, if you place a light near circuit 42, you wouldn't want to have it plug into circuit 10 on the other side of the house unless you could not help it. Likewise, the designer can tell when he or she is out of circuits during the design phase so as not to be surprised on location.

A second page of the lighting plot is the sectional. The sectional is a cross-section of the middle of the church. If your church varies widely in design across its lateral sections, then you might have multiple sectionals. The purpose of this document is two-fold. First, it allows you to see the design from your audience perspective and set all of your sight lines (sight lines are what your audience can see from the extreme positions). So, this allows you to set your lighting to the right height as well as determine the heights of any teasers or backdrops to hide the lights. You could also use the sectional to set up drum risers, guitar risers, choir risers, and so on.

A sectional will also let you determine your lighting angles. You can place a person of typical height (say, six feet) on the drawing and see where your lights will hit the person at various points on the stage. You can also get a better idea of your shadows.

DESIGN PAPERWORK

Along with the lighting plot, you should include a stack of paperwork. Paperwork is very important to a streamlined design. Paperwork will do many things. First, consider the hit-by-a-bus theory. If you get hit by a bus, the next guy could read the paperwork and maintain the show. This is important. While you will probably not get hit by a bus, you might come down with the flu.

Paperwork will also give you a quick cross-reference tool. Your paperwork, at a minimum, should include patch sheets, gel cut sheets, dimmer loading, channel lists, group lists, and a magic sheet.

Patch Sheets

A patch sheet is a spreadsheet that shows each fixture location (pipe/truss/catwalk ID, fixture number), the circuit it is plugged into, the dimmer that is patched into, and the channel the dimmer is patched into. This way, when a light suddenly doesn't work, you have all the information you need to troubleshoot right away.

Gel Cut Sheet

A gel cut sheet identifies each gel color and size used in the show. It then groups these by color and tells the technician how many cuts of gel to make for each color. This paperwork will often include calculations of the number of cuts you can get per sheet and the total number of sheets you need to buy to gel the show.

This is extremely useful for both the designer and the technician hanging the show. The technician can assign someone to cut gel based on the cut sheet, while the designer can keep track of the gel budget.

| Show Name: | Sample A | | Designer: | Joe Anyone |
| Date: | 1/1/09 | | Director: | Mr. Big Star |

Patch Sheet

Channel -> Dimmer Patch

Channel	Dimmer
1	5, 6, 7, 8
2	1, 4
9	9
10	10
11	11
12	12

end of report.

FIGURE 16.14
Patch sheet.

| Show Name: | Sample A | | Designer: | Joe Anyone |
| Date: | 1/1/09 | | Director: | Mr. Big Star |

Gel Cut Sheet

Gel Cut List

Qty	Color	Size	Name
3	R02	6 x 6	Bastard Amber

end of report.

FIGURE 16.15
Gel cut sheet.

Dimmer Loading

A dimmer loading sheet will help you realize how many fixtures are patched into a dimmer. This will allow you to make sure none of your dimmers are overloaded. If you are on a three-phase lighting system, it will also help you make sure your phases are fairly balanced as well, should that become a concern (assuming you know which dimmers are on which leg of power).

Show Name: Sample A   **Designer:** Joe Anyone
Date: 1/1/09   **Director:** Mr. Big Star

Dimmer Loading Report

Dimmer Loading Report

Dimmer	Circuit	Watts	Inst #	Location	Purpose
1	1	575	1	Pipe 3	Worship Leader Front Light
		575 Watts Total Load			
4	4	575	2	Pipe 3	Worship Leader Front Light
		575 Watts Total Load			
5	5	1000	1	Pipe 2	SR Front Fill
		1000 Watts Total Load			
6	6	1000	2	Pipe 2	RC Front Fill
		1000 Watts Total Load			
7	7	1000	3	Pipe 2	LC Front Fill
		1000 Watts Total Load			
8	8	1000	4	Pipe 2	SL Front Fill
		1000 Watts Total Load			

end of report.

FIGURE 16.16
Dimmer loading sheet.

Channel Lists

A channel list will identify fixtures by channels. This way you can quickly scan your channels and identify which fixtures will come up with that channel. This is helpful, for instance, when you see you have five fixtures in channel 1 but when you bring up channel 1, only four fixtures turn on. With this paperwork, you can quickly determine which locations you see, identify the one that is not working, and troubleshoot accordingly (Figure 16.7).

Group Lists

A group list is very similar to the channel list, except it displays the information by groups. Again, it's a quick reference for you when things aren't working or when you are trying to find something to light a specific area.

Wow, that's a Lot of Paperwork!

Yes, that is a lot of drafting and paperwork. But being organized is key to a quick light hang and cue session and to being on budget. When you are in the middle of rehearsal and the director wants more lighting in a certain area, or a fixture blew and you need to know which one, you don't want 50 plus people waiting around for half an hour while you figure out your job.

Show Name: Sample A			**Designer:**	Joe Anyone
Date: 1/1/09			**Director:**	Mr. Big Star

Channel Sheet

Channel List

Channel	Dimmer	Inst #	Location	Purpose
1	PAR 64		1 Pipe 2	SR Front Fill
	PAR 64		2 Pipe 2	RC Front Fill
	PAR 64		3 Pipe 2	LC Front Fill
	PAR 64		4 Pipe 2	SL Front Fill
2	ETC Source 4		1 Pipe 3	Worship Ldr Front Light
	ETC Source 4		2 Pipe 3	Worship Ldr Front Light
20	Mac500		1 Pipe 1	Back Light
40	Mac500		2 Pipe 1	Back Light
60	Mac500		3 Pipe 1	Back Light
80	Mac500		4 Pipe 1	Back Light

end of report.

FIGURE 16.17
Channel sheet.

This paperwork allows you to be organized and respond quickly. The planning and work ahead of time will save you countless hours of work, hassle, and stress on the backend.

In the old days, all of this paperwork was hand drafted and all of the reports were hand generated as well. That was a lot of work. Then, along came computers and spreadsheets. Now designers can enter the information and sort based on data in columns. This speeds things up a lot.

Then came CAD (computer-aided design) software. With the advent of programs like AutoCAD and Vectorworks, designers soon switched to using the automated drawing systems (making drafting revisions faster) along with the spreadsheets.

Finally, software developers merged the two. Add-ons for Vectorworks, AutoCAD, and designer-specific software such as Softplot and WYSIWYG became available that interpolate all of the data. You draw in a fixture and virtually connect it to a circuit, patch it to a dimmer, and patch it to a channel. Assign the fixture a color and pattern, and tell the software which fixture it is. Now the software knows everything there is to know – it knows lamp type, gel size, pattern size, dimmer, circuit, and channel. So, the software generates all the reports you could ever want and spits them out accordingly.

Now, when you make a change on the plot, the paperwork automatically updates. Suddenly, all that work isn't much work at all. What used to take designers days to do can now be done in hours. Updates and changes are a breeze. Sometimes it takes longer to print the reports and plots than it does to make the changes.

CHAPTER 17
Architectural Lighting and Integration with Stage Lighting

ARCHITECTURAL LIGHTING

So, up until now we have mostly been discussing stage lighting. Architectural lighting is considered anything that doesn't illuminate the stage – wall sconces, aisle lights, step lights, house lights, lobby lights, outdoor lighting, and so forth.

Architectural lighting is every bit as important as stage lighting. Audience safety and first impressions are as important as how the show itself looks. All of the lighting comes together to make an impression on the audience. All of it works in concert to create a mood and environment. You must be able to control all of this lighting.

Likewise, you want people to be able to control the architectural lighting without firing up the stage lighting system.

INTEGRATING ARCHITECTURAL AND STAGE SYSTEMS

Most new lighting systems allow for an integration of the two systems. You will typically have an architectural control panel. This panel usually utilizes the stage system to control all of the dimmers to set the looks desired. In a House of Worship, you might have one preset for cleaning, another for weddings, another for funerals and one for general meetings. Now, you can shut down the lighting system and someone can walk over to a wall panel, press a button, and get lighting – preset lighting.

Now, when you turn your board on (or on some systems, press a lockout button), the wall panels are bypassed. You have full control at the board and can run the show without worry of someone bumping into them and messing up the lighting cue.

This type of system works very well for allowing control over the architectural features but not turning over the keys to a complicated system. It's important

that you have architectural control as part of your lighting system, so figuring out how to integrate the two systems is well worth your time.

Another option for integrating your lighting is to use the world clock within the console. Most higher-end computer controllers allow for programming based on time and date. So, you could have your console control all interior and exterior lights. These lights could either be connected directly to your dimming system or controlled via relays from the rack. So, for example, a relay could be actuated by the control surface that would then turn on all of the exterior lights.

How you choose to integrate your architectural and stage systems is ultimately up to you and the flexibilities you wish to have. However, understand that you will need to address the issue one way or another.

CHAPTER 18

Conclusion of Lighting Section

CONCLUSION ON LIGHTING

You can see that lighting has a primary objective – to provide illumination so people can see and safely navigate the room. However, lighting goes well beyond this most basic requirement. With lighting, you can create an atmosphere and mood. You can shift the audience's focus on the stage to wherever you direct them. You can hide certain things and reveal them at your choosing. You can mystify the audience with a sense of awe as you create beautiful landscapes with light that glides through the air and across the stage.

With lighting, you can control the feel of a service. You also enhance the sound and video ministries by helping to enforce where the communicator is on stage (and resolving localization issues for the listener) and by shielding the video screens from excessive bounce light so the image really punches. Likewise, as you manipulate the house lights, you can draw the audience into a more intimate moment or you can put more emphasis on the video presentation that might be happening.

Lighting the exterior of your church can create a more welcoming feeling for guests and members alike after the sun has set. Likewise, the lighting of the lobby and other public areas is just as important for creating a welcoming atmosphere that helps people let their walls down so they can worship uninhibited.

Lighting is all too often overlooked by the House of Worship. Many churches just want to have enough light to read by or have the lights dim enough that the video can be seen. This is really missing the point. Lighting gives us a huge opportunity to communicate visually with the people who attend worship and to help guide them along the way of finding what it is they came for.

**PART 3
VIDEO**

CHAPTER 19

Anatomy of a Video System

WHAT IS A VIDEO PLAYBACK SYSTEM?

A video playback system is any number of devices that are brought together and displayed on a screen for the masses. This can be as simple as a computer-based system and a projector or as complicated as multiple cameras, multiple video decks, and multiple computers all running through a switching device out to an array of plasmas, LCDs, projectors, and recording devices. Ultimately, the one thing they all have in common is the final result – an image that is viewed by the masses.

Video playback systems are taking Houses of Worship by storm. If you don't have an integrated video screen in your worship service, you most likely want one. I have come across a few Houses of Worship that have no interest in video playback, but by and large, those Houses of Worship are few and far between.

Most fellowships recognize the advantages for video systems and they want them *now*! The problem is that people want a video playback system without understanding all that is entailed to get one working properly. Many Houses of Worship (especially smaller ones) ignore the fact that their sound system is poorly functioning and that they have no controllable lighting and 12 huge windows flooding light into the sanctuary – but they want video projection.

The result of this type of mentality is usually not stunning. Either the church spends way too much money buying a super-huge projector to overcome the ambient light in the room, or they buy a cheap projector that looks terrible and washes out. If the church opts for the brighter projector, the sound system is often still terrible, so the true effect of the video presentation is often lost. Even if the sound system starts to keep up, without controllable lighting it's hard to pull the congregation into what's happening on the screen because everything is a wash of light.

Likewise, if a House of Worship opts for a plasma or LCD screen, typically the screen is still washed out and, more commonly, too small to see! This makes the impact much less dynamic and minimizes the effect that video can have for your service.

FIGURE 19.1
Typical video system
block.

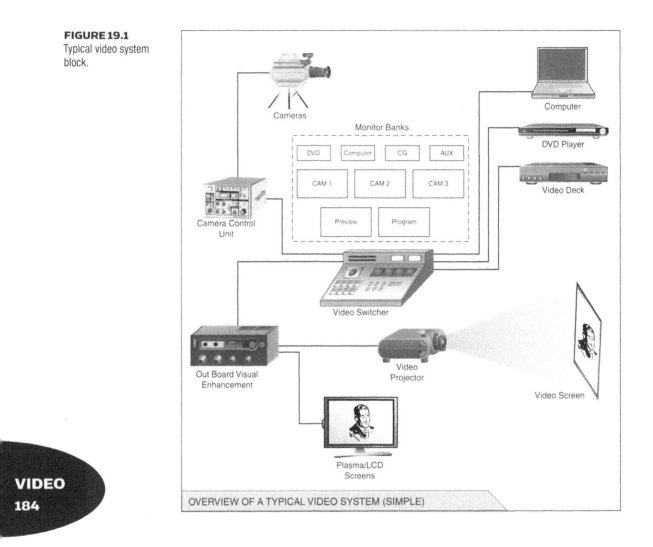

Assuming the House of Worship is skimping on the video playback system, odds are they are skimping all the way around – poor switching choices, poor worship presentation software choices, poor computer playback choices, and poor video playback choices. If they are thinking about Image Magnification (IMAG) via live cameras, odds are they are also looking for the cheapest cameras they can get their hands on.

There is a difference between being cheap and being frugal.

I hope by now you are starting to really understand that these three media systems are not stand-alone systems in a House of Worship. They truly build off each other. They are not three individual systems that you might or might not need; they are parts of one big system that works in concert to create a mood and environment that captures people's attention, communicates with them on different levels, and helps to remove barriers for worship.

There are many things to consider when installing a projection system. If you are looking to install a video system today, there is no option but to get widescreen 16:9 screens and native 16:9 projectors. Anything else is archaic and will soon be out of date.

The only question that even sort of remains is, Should you do high definition or standard definition? Chapter 21 addresses this issue.

TIP
The most important thing you can do for a video playback system is to control the amount of ambient light in the room! Likewise, you should make every effort to eliminate lighting spill on the screens (be it a flat panel or a projection screen). Ambient light and light spill on a screen will kill your image by washing it out. This is one reason having an adequate lighting system is so critical to a successful video playback system.

VIDEO
185

A video playback system consists of at least a few items. The absolute minimum would be a video projector (or flat panel display) and a computer. However, a minimal yet proper video playback system would consist of the main source that is being displayed, the switcher, the scaler, and the video projector (or plasma or LCD display). Let's take a look at each one of these in more detail.

Main Source

The main source is whatever is being played at the moment on the screen. This could be the computer, a DVD, a camera, or any other type of visual playback that you have connected to the system.

When thinking about your sources, the higher the quality of components you can afford, the better your signal is going to be. Also, like anything else, the quality of your cable and connections will make or break you.

You also want to use the highest resolution connection you can get. In ranking order from worst quality to best quality you have:

- Composite
- S-Video
- Component or VGA
- DVI
- HDMI

Let's take a brief look at each of these inputs.

COMPOSITE

Composite video is a single RCA phono-style connection. Composite video can also be delivered by a single BNC connection. All professional systems use BNC for composite video. All of the information within the video passes through this one connection.

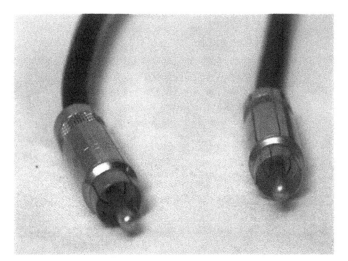

FIGURE 19.2
RCA composite cable.
Photo by Brad Herring.

This is by far the worst video connection you can make. It is not designed to travel long distances and maintain good quality; and it has lower bandwidth, making the signal degradation high. In the old days of 4:3 analog televisions, we could mostly get away with this, but try to project a large image on a high-end video projector – regardless of whether it's standard definition or high definition – and you are going to see a fairly ugly signal on the screen. Send this to a plasma or LCD display and the results are going to be equally bad.

This connection is found on the back of many consumer components and is usually yellow in color.

A composite connection carries intensity information as well as all three color channels (red, green, and blue).

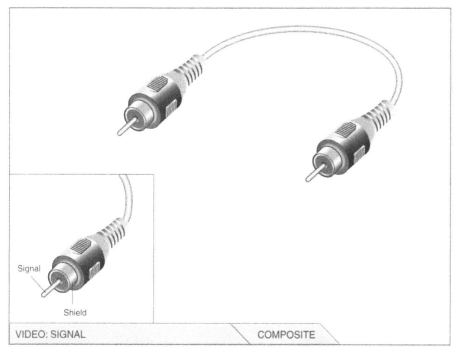

Signal

Shield

VIDEO: SIGNAL   COMPOSITE

VIDEO
187

FIGURE 19.3
Composite cable.

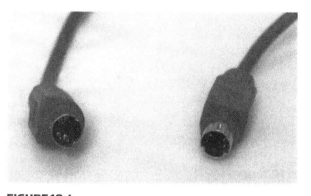

FIGURE 19.4
S-Video cable.
Photo by Brad Herring.

S-VIDEO

S-Video is a step up, that's for sure. It's still an analog signal, but at least it's beginning to separate the channels of information within the video, which will offer a higher-quality picture.

S-Video separates the video information into two channels – luma (luminance) and chroma (color).

S-Video connections are capable of carrying a 480i standard-definition signal. This is a much higher resolution than composite video, but, as you can see, it is quite low by many of today's emerging standards (720p, 1080p, 1080i, etc.).

For 4:3 standard-definition video, you can use S-Video without a lot of consequences. However, as you start to step up into widescreen, digital, and high-definition video, you are going to want a higher-quality connection.

VIDEO
188

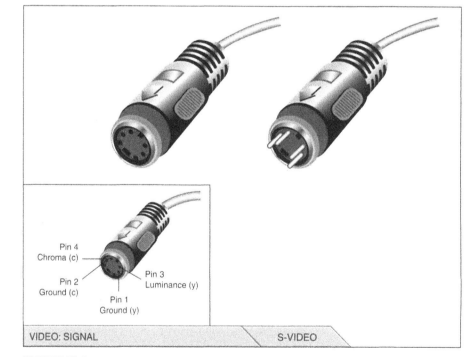

Pin 4
Chroma (c)

Pin 2
Ground (c)

Pin 3
Luminance (y)

Pin 1
Ground (y)

VIDEO: SIGNAL   S-VIDEO

FIGURE 19.5
Pinout of S-Video cable.

COMPONENT/VGA

Component video and VGA signals are still analog connections, but they present one of the best overall image qualities you can expect without going to the digital realm. Component connections are easily recognized by their three-color individual pathways. Component video comes in several standards, but the three that most commonly impact the House of Worship are RGB, RGBHV, and YP_bP_r (also known as YUV).

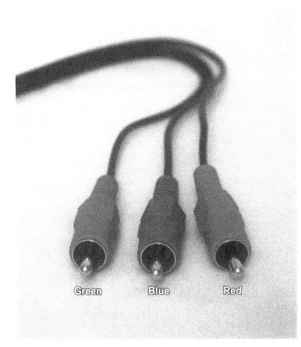

FIGURE 19.6
Component cable.
Photo by Brad Herring.

RGB cables carry the red, the green, and the blue color channels on individual conductors, thus maximizing the amount of bandwidth each conductor can contain with individual color channel information.

With RGB, the green channel contains the horizontal and vertical sync information.

RGBHV offers more flexibility by offering red, green, and blue information channels, and then two separate inputs in addition to the color inputs – one for horizontal sync and another for vertical sync. These connections are most commonly found in high-end pro-sumer and professional components.

YP_bP_r is another standard of the RGB family. In this standard, Y carries the luma (or brightness information), P_b carries the difference between the blue and the luma (hence the b subscript meaning b-y), and p_r carries the difference between the red and the luma (hence the r subscript meaning r-y). In an effort to save bandwidth, the green channel is interpolated using the blue, red, and luma channels.

On a normal YP_bP_r connection, the green cable will carry the y, the blue carries the P_b, and the red carries the P_r.

The YP_bP_r standard came about to conserve bandwidth within the RGB connection.

FIGURE 19.7
Component cable pinout.

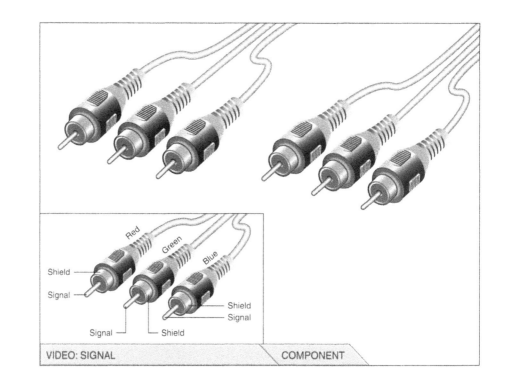

VGA signal is another form of RGB, only in a nine-pin D-Sub connector. Originating with computer display monitors, VGA was created as an easy method to carry RGB information to a computer monitor. Over time, the other pins were utilized for various purposes. Today, many projectors and other video devices will accept RGB via a VGA connection. For the purposes of video projection, I've included the following VGA pinout:

FIGURE 19.8
VGA cable.

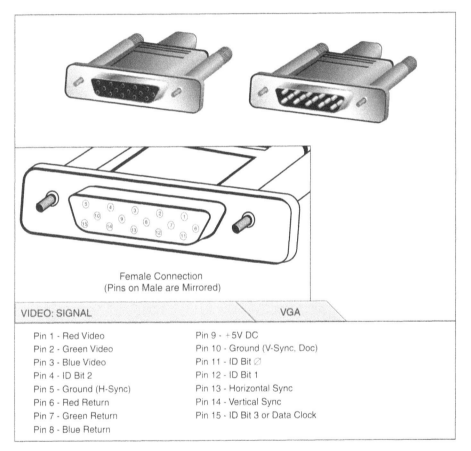

Female Connection
(Pins on Male are Mirrored)

VIDEO: SIGNAL	VGA
Pin 1 - Red Video	Pin 9 - +5V DC
Pin 2 - Green Video	Pin 10 - Ground (V-Sync, Doc)
Pin 3 - Blue Video	Pin 11 - ID Bit ∅
Pin 4 - ID Bit 2	Pin 12 - ID Bit 1
Pin 5 - Ground (H-Sync)	Pin 13 - Horizontal Sync
Pin 6 - Red Return	Pin 14 - Vertical Sync
Pin 7 - Green Return	Pin 15 - ID Bit 3 or Data Clock
Pin 8 - Blue Return	

FIGURE 19.9
Pinout of VGA connector.

VIDEO

191

DVI

Digital Visual Interface (DVI) is a true digital connection; however, its transmission distance (normally 15 feet or less) is very limited without some form of DVI amplifier. Cable quality will be a huge factor in how far your cable transmits. Typically, when you reach the threshold of your cable length, the signal will start to degrade with artifacting. Another 5 to 10 feet of cable after artifacting will generally yield no signal at all. There is generally very little tolerance for length of the cable – the signal will generally work or it won't. There are some standards (DVI-I) that will allow an analog signal for compatible components as well.

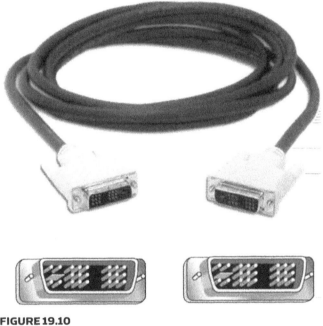

FIGURE 19.10
DVI cable.

DVI uses Transition Minimized Differential Signaling (TMDS) encoding to compress the video signal and send it from the source to the projector or plasma/LCD screen.

There are many arguments on the topic of quality. Some will argue that the DVI connection is better than component video because it is digital. A lot of people disagree with this. Component video is a very solid video signal path; DVI is solid as well. The individual choice is up to you.

The quality of DVI is very good. With longer lengths, you are going to need an amplifier.

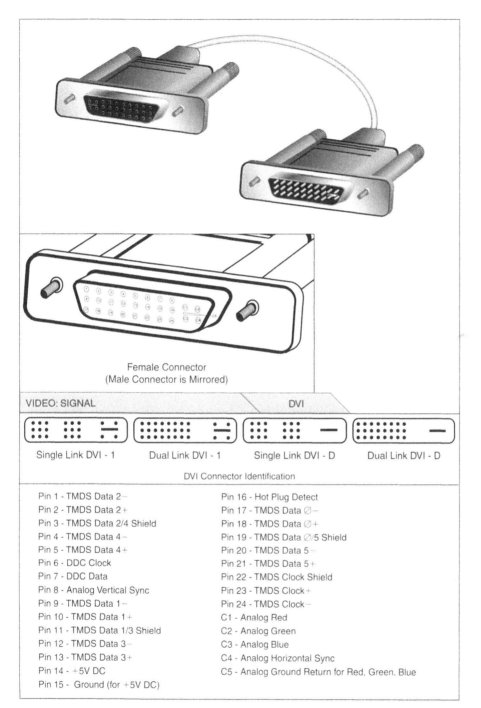

Female Connector
(Male Connector is Mirrored)

VIDEO: SIGNAL		DVI	
Single Link DVI - 1	Dual Link DVI - 1	Single Link DVI - D	Dual Link DVI - D

DVI Connector Identification

Pin 1 - TMDS Data 2−
Pin 2 - TMDS Data 2+
Pin 3 - TMDS Data 2/4 Shield
Pin 4 - TMDS Data 4−
Pin 5 - TMDS Data 4+
Pin 6 - DDC Clock
Pin 7 - DDC Data
Pin 8 - Analog Vertical Sync
Pin 9 - TMDS Data 1−
Pin 10 - TMDS Data 1+
Pin 11 - TMDS Data 1/3 Shield
Pin 12 - TMDS Data 3−
Pin 13 - TMDS Data 3+
Pin 14 - +5V DC
Pin 15 - Ground (for +5V DC)

Pin 16 - Hot Plug Detect
Pin 17 - TMDS Data ∅−
Pin 18 - TMDS Data ∅+
Pin 19 - TMDS Data ∅/5 Shield
Pin 20 - TMDS Data 5−
Pin 21 - TMDS Data 5+
Pin 22 - TMDS Clock Shield
Pin 23 - TMDS Clock+
Pin 24 - TMDS Clock−
C1 - Analog Red
C2 - Analog Green
C3 - Analog Blue
C4 - Analog Horizontal Sync
C5 - Analog Ground Return for Red, Green, Blue

VIDEO

193

FIGURE 19.11
Pinout of DVI connector.

HDMI

High Definition Multimedia Interface (HDMI) utilizes the same encoding as DVI: Transition Minimized Differential Signaling (TMDS). The primary difference is the actual connector *and* that HDMI also passes audio. HDMI is a digital connection capable of transmitting hi-def signals.

FIGURE 19.12
HDMI cable.
Photo by Brad Herring.

As a general rule, HDMI cable is very expensive. Long runs of this cable are often not cost effective, but for a shorter run to a projector or plasma screen, HDMI can be very simple and quick. The video quality is excellent and the audio signal (up to eight uncompressed digital channels) transmits with it. One cable, nice and neat, finished.

There are three different size connectors for HDMI – Types A, B, and C. Type A has 19 pins, Type B has 29, and Type C is a miniconnection with 19 pins as well.

For certain applications, HDMI is an excellent choice. For long runs, it's generally cost prohibitive. Most HDMI cables are limited to less than 50 feet without some sort of amplifier. Some studies have shown that when used with HDMI fiber-optic extenders, HDMI can travel over 300 feet.

Because HDMI and DVI are compatible, no special conversion boxes are required to adapt HDMI to DVI. However, DVI is not capable of transmitting the audio signals, so they are lost in the conversion.

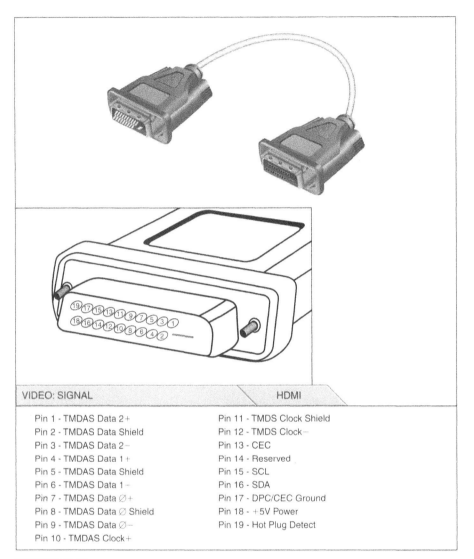

VIDEO: SIGNAL	HDMI
Pin 1 - TMDAS Data 2+	Pin 11 - TMDS Clock Shield
Pin 2 - TMDAS Data Shield	Pin 12 - TMDS Clock−
Pin 3 - TMDAS Data 2−	Pin 13 - CEC
Pin 4 - TMDAS Data 1+	Pin 14 - Reserved
Pin 5 - TMDAS Data Shield	Pin 15 - SCL
Pin 6 - TMDAS Data 1−	Pin 16 - SDA
Pin 7 - TMDAS Data ⌀+	Pin 17 - DPC/CEC Ground
Pin 8 - TMDAS Data ⌀ Shield	Pin 18 - +5V Power
Pin 9 - TMDAS Data ⌀−	Pin 19 - Hot Plug Detect
Pin 10 - TMDAS Clock+	

FIGURE 19.13
Pinout of HDMI connector.

SDI/HD-SDI/VIDEO OVER CAT5

The video industry is rapidly changing as technology evolves. There are a few other video standards that you will encounter in the future, but the aforementioned standards are the ones most prevalent in Houses of Worship. It is, however, worth mentioning these other standards so you are aware of them.

FIGURE 19.14
Video switcher.
Photo by Brad Herring.

Serial Digital Interface (SDI) is a broadcast standard for transmitting uncompressed standard-definition video, audio, and other data packets over a standard BNC connection. Newer on the scene is High Definition Serial Digital Interface (HD-SDI), which allows uncompressed high-definition video, audio, and various digital packets, generally over fiber-optic cables.

One of the new emerging standards that you will most likely interact with is video over Cat5. Cat5 cable is increasingly being integrated into A/V systems – video is no different. Many manufacturers make equipment that can convert regular video signal to Cat5 cable and back again. Depending on the equipment, you will sometimes need the converter, or it may be integrated directly into your devices. This saves a tremendous amount of money with regard to purchasing copper cable and still presents a good image. There is no doubt we will see more of video over Cat5 cable as this standard continues to evolve.

Switcher

A video switcher is the heart of a true video system. This is the "mixing board" of video signals, if you will.

The video switcher can take multiple video sources and allow a director the opportunity to transition (or "switch") from one source to another. The timing of the transition can happen via an automated timer or by a manual T-bar.

All of the various video inputs will have their own preview monitor so the director can see everything that is available at any given moment. Then, they can call up the desired input into the "preview" bank of the switcher. When they make the transition, whatever is selected in the "preview" monitor will transition to the "live" monitor. What you see on the "live" monitor (including transitions) is what will be broadcast or recorded; it is the final mix, if you will.

Most switchers allow for straight-cut edits (a simple, instantaneous splice from one source to another) or any number of transitions, from dissolves to fancy wipe patterns.

Some switchers will also allow for very rudimentary audio mixing, but this is not their primary function. And some switchers will allow you to color correct, mix to picture-in-picture (PIP), and create a host of effects for the image alteration.

Scaler

A scaler is an invaluable tool. A scaler will take various display resolutions and scale them to the image resolution you set as your final output resolution. A scaler does this by stretching and shrinking the material proportionally. Generally speaking, the more expensive the scaler, the better the results.

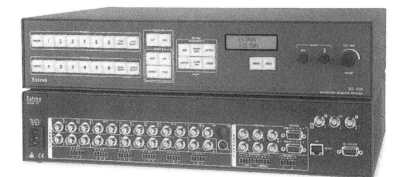

FIGURE 19.15
Scaler.
Photo courtesy of
Extron Electronics.

VIDEO
197

Scalers are often advertised as being a part of another component such as a video projector, switcher, plasma or LCD screen, or so forth, but these are generally not high-end scalers and do not always do a stand-up job at their task.

Your projector, or plasma or LCD monitor, is going to have a native resolution. For instance, many video projectors are 1024 × 768 native. This means that without any type of software interpolation, they project 1024 pixels wide by 768 pixels high. Your image quality will always be best when matched to the native resolution of your display device. So, you would use a scaler to "up-convert" or "down-convert" your source image to match the native image of your display. High-end scalers often give you better results because they are tasked with nothing but scaling. Therefore the components in the scaler are often higher quality and are tasked simply for that one purpose.

Using a high-end scaler is like taking a computer that is designed for GPS navigation and asking it to also run word processing and other tasks. The computer quickly gets overloaded and stops functioning as well as it can. However, if you take an out-of-the-box GPS unit and turn it on without asking it to do any other tasks, it works very well and efficiently for its intended purpose. The same is true with using an outboard scaler.

A good scaler will also offer you functions like pan, frame rate conversions, color alterations, detail enhancement, and other functions as well. So, once again, you get what you pay for when it comes to features and quality.

It is worth noting that the scaler can only operate to the quality of your display device. So, if you have a device that displays 1024 × 768 signal, as we used in our example above, a scaler cannot make that device show 1920 × 1080 pixels. The scaler can only operate within the confines of the display properties. Whenever possible, you want to make sure that your sources match the native resolution of your display monitor. However, this is not always possible – especially with the ever-changing standards in today's broadcast world. It is for these instances that a scaler exists.

Video Projector/Plasma/LCD

The final step is the actual display device. In most Houses of Worship this will be a video projector, but more and more Houses of Worship are turning to LCD and plasma displays as well. Sometimes a plasma or LCD screen is used instead of a projector, while other times a screen is used in conjunction with the projector.

FIGURE 19.16
Projector.
Photo by Brad Herring.

Whatever the source, it should be mounted at a viewing angle comfortable to the audience and should be as large enough for the image to be seen from the farthest seat. It is the second requirement that often eliminates a plasma or LCD monitor for most Houses of Worship. However, many facilities utilize plasma/LCD technology for the first few rows, the choir, or under the balcony. Many Houses of Worship will also choose to route their display to the lobby and nursery via plasma or LCD monitors as well.

Whatever your choice for your fellowship, you should make sure it is big enough and bright enough to do the job. We will look at specifics for projectors and flat-panel displays in the next section.

CHAPTER 20

Lumens, Brightness and Contrast – What Does it all Mean?

When it comes to projectors and flat panel displays, not all are created equal. Many will vary in color and brightness. Add to this that manufacturers measure their components differently! So, a projector by manufacturer A says it's 2500 lumens, and another projector by manufacture B says it's 2500 lumens. One projector will most likely look brighter and crisper than the other.

With this being said, one cannot choose by lumen alone. For that matter, one cannot choose by any one factor alone. When researching which display to purchase, you must take all of the specifications into account and then research your top choices. See what other users have to say about them, and finally contact the manufacture to try to arrange a demonstration of the product. You can even request a "shootout." This is where multiple manufactures bring their products to YOUR church and display YOUR content, thus allowing you to see for yourself, side by side, which one works best for you.

Oftentimes, Houses of Worship fail to understand the full buying potential they have. As we've stated earlier in this book, most manufacturers now have an entire team set up to serve the House of Worship market. We have exceeded theater and broadcast purchases in many ways; thus the companies are competing hard for your purchase. Use this to your advantage to make sure you make the right choice.

Also, it's important to realize that as a projector's lamp ages, its effective lumen output drops. Even though you might not be halfway through the advertised lamp hour for your projector, the image will be significantly dimmer in some cases.

A LOOK AT THE LUMEN

What is a lumen, anyway? A lumen is simply a way to measure the power of illumination. To put this in perspective, the amount of light that a single candle emits would be considered one candle. You have probably heard the expression "foot-candle". One foot-candle is the amount of light measured within a one-foot radius of a single candle.

Given this information, one lumen is equal to one foot-candle worth of light per square foot.

When it comes to projectors, American National Standards Institute (ANSI) standardized the procedure for determining lumens (hence the reason why you often see them referred to as "ANSI lumens"). There are other procedures for determining a lumen count for a projector, and manufacturers are not required to use ANSI lumens as their standard. If you see projectors with ANSI lumens listed, you can feel more comfortable that you are in the same ballpark with regards to how they were tested.

However, lumens are not the be-all and end-all of projectors by any means – this is only the general measurement of brightness. The amount of ambient light in the room, the type of screen, and the distance the projector is from the wall will dictate how bright the projector must be.

TIP

Just because your projector lamp is rated for a set duration of hours does not mean you should use it for that long. In order to keep a bright image, you should replace your lamp before the end of its life expectancy.

As we've already discussed, but which warrants stating again, as the projector ages, the lamp efficiency (i.e., lumen measurement) will decrease. This is vitally important if you are buying a used projector or if you have been using a projector for some time with the same lamp. The projector will become dimmer over time.

How Many Lumens Do I Need?

This is the million-dollar question. The best way to determine how many lumens you need is to try out the projector in your facility before you buy it. In general, the more lumens, the better off you will be. It is virtually impossible to purchase a "too bright" projector, but very common to purchase a "not bright enough" projector. Of course, the rub comes with budget constraints. We don't want to be wasteful in how we spend our difficult-to-come-by ministry dollars, but at the same time we want to do this once and get it right.

Here is a formula for finding your basic lumen needs:

1. Using a standard lighting meter (not a camera meter, but a true light meter), measure the ambient light that is hitting your screen. You should set your meter to read in foot-candles. (Note: 1 foot-candle = 1 lumen/sq feet.)
2. Determine the square footage for your screen (so, if your screen is 9 feet high × 16 feet wide, your total square footage would be 144 sq feet).
3. Utilizing SMPTE (the Society of Motion Picture and Television Engineers) recommendations, a good number for excellent video playback would be 20 lumens per square foot. (Their recommendations top out at 22 lumens per square foot, so you could alter this number if you want an even brighter screen; their low-end estimate is 12 lumens, so you can see 20 is fairly high.)

4. Using our base of 20 lumens per square foot, add to this your ambient light reading. For this example, let's assume your ambient light reads at an average of 5 lumens per square foot).

5. Take your answer to step 4 and multiply it by the total square footage of your screen found in step 2. In our example, this would be 3600.

So, the actual math formula is:

> [(Lumens Desired + Average Ambient Light Reading) × Screen Square Footage] = Total Lumens Needed with Ambient Lighting Consideration

Given the steps above, you would be looking at using a 3600-lumen projector as a minimum. This assumes you are using a screen with a gain of 1.0 (we will discuss screen choices and screen gains later in this section). If you are using a different screen gain, use the following formula for a calibrated lumen estimate:

> [(Lumens Needed for Ambient Light Conditions)/ Screen Gain] = Calibrated Lumen Need

However, even if you are using a screen with a gain higher than 1.0, I would still recommend the larger-size projector if possible. Make sure to read the section on Screen Gain for a better understanding of the pros and cons of using screen gain.

Remember also that as you adjust various settings and profiles, your projector will likely not output the full lumens advertised. Keep in mind that manufacturers will test lumens in the best possible scenario. These "ideal" conditions might not always be present in the real world. So, in general, it's always a good idea to estimate high on the lumens you need – as we discussed earlier, you can never have a projector that's too bright.

VIDEO
201

USING A LIGHT METER

We mentioned that you needed to find your ambient light level on the screen. You do this by utilizing a foot-candle light meter. There are also charts that allow you to use a photography meter and then translate the exposure reading to a foot-candle reading, but why not use the right tool for the job? A foot-candle light meter will run you around $120 to $160.

Foot-candle meters are also useful in establishing house light levels, classroom light levels, and office light levels. There are handbooks published by SMPTE and other standards organizations that tell you the amount of foot-candles required for certain conditions. Likewise, some building codes state the level of foot-candle certain areas must have for public safety (such as aisle lights, stairwells, etc.). A light meter is a very useful tool to have in your bag if you are doing lighting or video work.

FIGURE 20.1
Light meter.
Photo Courtesy of Extech.

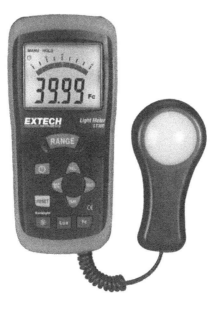

Likewise, a light meter can be used for stage readings. This can be especially helpful when lighting a stage for video.

A light meter has a light sensor and usually, these days, a digital display. This display will show you the number of foot-candles being read at the light sensor. Some of the more fancy models allow you to download your information into a computer and maintain fairly complex data logs, but for our purposes we simply need a meter that will show how bright the light is at the location of the light sensor. As you move the sensor around, you will find varying levels. This will also help you eliminate darks spots and hot spots.

One foot-candle is equal to one lumen, so the ability to read a foot-candle measurement works well for our calculations.

BRIGHTNESS

The brightness control of a projector (not to be confused with the brightness of the projector measured in lumens) will control the black level of the projector. The brightness should be set via a test chart. The chart will have a series of strips going from absolute black to white. The brightness is set correctly when the absolute black is still maintained but each individual level of black can be differentiated. Likewise, the white should remain white and not turn gray.

CONTRAST

The contrast control (not to be confused with contrast ratio) will control the white levels of the projector. The contrast should be set via a test chart. The chart (as used for the brightness level) will have a series of strips going from absolute white to black. The contrast is set correctly when the white is still maintained but each individual level of white can be differentiated. Likewise, the black should remain black and not turn gray or light black.

TIP

The Brightness and Contrast controls alter each other's settings. Setting them properly requires patience. A change in one will affect the other and require a tweak. Don't rush this. Once set correctly, your dynamic color range will be ideal for your display!

CONTRAST RATIO

Contrast is the measurement of the projectors blackest black in relation to its whitest white. In general, the higher the Contrast Ratio, the higher the detail in the image. Also, a higher contrast ratio will help you overcome the "wash out" effect in a room with ambient light bleeding onto your projection screen.

It is not uncommon to see contrast ratios exceeding 2000:1. The higher this number separation, the more defined your blacks will be. A higher contrast ratio is necessary in order to achieve good, crisp-looking video.

Perhaps you have noticed that when you turn a projector on without an image, in a dark room, you can see the gray box that it creates on the screen. This is a result of low contrast ratio. When you are seeing that box, you are seeing what your projector is defining as black. The higher the contrast ratio, the less noticeable this gray box will be when no image is being projected.

Contrast ratio works the same on both plasma and LCD displays. The bigger the number, the better the image quality, the darker the blacks, and the whiter the whites.

Specifically, when choosing a projector, contrast ratio is as important as the lumens!

CHAPTER 21

High Definition vs. Standard Definition

High Definition (HD) video is the new standard for video in the United States. As of the time of this writing, there are two primary formats for high-definition video – 720p and 1080i/1080p. The "p" indicates progressive scan, while the "i" indicates an interlaced image. We'll discuss this in more detail later in this section. High-definition video is also widescreen (16:9 screen ratio).

Standard Definition (SD) is what we've been watching pretty much since television was invented. The screen has far fewer lines of resolution and is traditionally a 4:3 ratio screen, although it can be presented in 16:9 format as well. Standard definition is on its way out (much like the days of black-and-white television).

Given this primer, clearly the biggest question on a lot of minds in Houses of Worship across America is, "To hi-def or not to hi-def?" In my mind, the answer is simple. If you are installing a new system, go hi-def. If you can't afford all of the hi-def components, then put in the hi-def infrastructure (projector, screens, cabling, etc.). At least get the hard part of a hi-def system in place and you can slowly upgrade your other components in the future. Many manufacturers offer SD/HD hybrid switchers that can get you by until you make the full swap.

If you are already established in standard definition, you should start planning your migration. Soon all content will be delivered in hi-def standards. As the video medium continues to grow for worship services, the need to deliver HD will become crucial. Remember, part of the reason a House of Worship uses the video medium in general is to speak to people in a relevant way. When everyone at home is watching content on 16:9 high-definition televisions, anything less will appear to be outmoded and dated.

If your church is only placing words on the screen and using text-based presentations, you don't have as much to worry about. You will by and large continue to be uninhibited because you are not showing produced video clips. Even if you are doing IMAG (image magnification), you are still limited to your own components.

Benefits to making the move to high definition include these:

- Crisper images and videos due to higher resolution
- Ability to play professionally produced clips
- Ability to integrate satellite and cable presentations or snippets thereof
- Continuing relevance to your audience and updated appearance
- Ability to create video recordings and archives that are forward compatible to the new standard

Continuing with standard-definition video systems over the long haul would be much like a church installing a black-and-white projector. You just don't do that.

THE DIFFERENCE BETWEEN STANDARD-DEFINITION AND HIGH-DEFINITION STANDARDS

All 4:3 aspect content is standard definition. Many people think when they see a 16:9 (widescreen) presentation they are watching high definition. This is not accurate. The aspect ratio of the screen size alone is not a determination of resolution and quality.

While it is true that high-definition programming is shot on the widescreen format, it is also possible to produce standard-definition programming on a widescreen format as well. The most common standards are:

- 480i
- 480p
- 720p
- 1080i
- 1080p

You will notice first that each standard has a number and then a letter. The letter indicates an interlaced signal (i) or a progressive scan signal (p).

Interlaced Video

Interlaced video scans every other line when producing a video image. These lines are often referred to as "fields." It appears as though the image is being shown frame by frame, but in reality it is being displayed half frame by half frame.

First, your television will display the odd field; then, 1/60th of a second later, the even field will be displayed. This originally came about because televisions were too slow to scan the full 480 lines of resolution at a time, so by breaking the image up and firing half the image every 1/60th of a second, they could make what appeared to the human eye to be a solid image.

Because of the way the human brain interpolates information, interlaced video works. However, sometimes there are artifacts in the image and it has a tendency

to flicker. If you have ever paused an interlaced signal or played it in slow motion, you will notice significant artifacting (often called "combing") in the image.

We see interlaced video once again rear its head in high definition for similar reasons. Many consumer-based electronics simply can't process full 1080p HD video fast enough to keep up. Therefore, the industry decided to go with a less stable interlaced option (again, firing half the image at once) to provide for more resolution as a whole. The result, while technically higher in resolution, is usually a less clear picture due to the artifacting of interlacing the video.

Progressive Video

Progressive scan still scans the entire frame, from side to side at one time. This yields a smoother, more reliable image that doesn't flicker or artifact. However, it takes a fair amount of processing to handle this much information at once. When we get into higher definition resolutions (like 1080p), it becomes difficult for less powerful equipment to handle that much information at once.

Most people will agree that progressive scan is a more favorable delivery standard. The image detail is better, the artifacting is less, and the stability is greatly improved.

RESOLUTIONS

Now that we've discussed the letters, let's look at the numbers. Basically, the numbers are shorthand to indicate the native resolution of the format.

480p and 480i refer to 480 lines of resolution. The 480p is 480 lines scanned all at once, and the 480i is 240 lines scanned in an odd/even pattern every 1/60th of a second.

720p refers to a high-definition standard of 1280 × 720 pixels. Likewise, 1080i or 1080p refers to the high-definition standard of 1920 × 1080 pixels (regardless of progressive or interlaced, the resolution is the same). Of course, with interlaced delivery, your resolution is not fully delivered since it's appearing on opposite fields at a time.

VIDEO
207

720p	1280 × 720 pixels
1080i or 1080p	1920 × 1080 pixels

As a comparison, standard-definition video is 640 × 480 pixels!

INFRASTRUCTURE IS IMPORTANT

Just like every other aspect of technology, your video will only be as good as its weakest component. Cable quality is very important for video playback and recording systems. Too many people try to make budget cuts with cable – this is the worst place you can cut money. A piece of equipment can be sold and upgraded with few headaches, but cable and connections are infrastructure that cost far more to replace down the road and are always going to present road-blocks to quality.

When wiring a system, think about the future. In respect to an entire system, running an extra set of cables or using an upgraded cable that exceeds your current needs will be a huge investment when it comes to future upgrades. Likewise, it is always smart to run Cat6 cable with new cable runs – video is moving more toward network-based devices. Similarly, more and more content is becoming available on demand via the Internet.

Forward thinking will serve you well in the years to come. If you have to make budget cuts, do it for equipment that you can easily change and upgrade in the future.

CHAPTER 22

Front Projections vs. Rear Projection

When projecting video, you ultimately have two choices on how to do it – front projection or rear projection. Both present their own positive and negative points. In general, a House of Worship that can do rear projection is usually better served to do so.

REAR PROJECTION

Rear projection offers the neatest install option. The projectors are located behind the screen and out of sight. The screen has a magical "flat panel" look and is often built into the décor of the facility. This cohesive design offers a full compliment to the room.

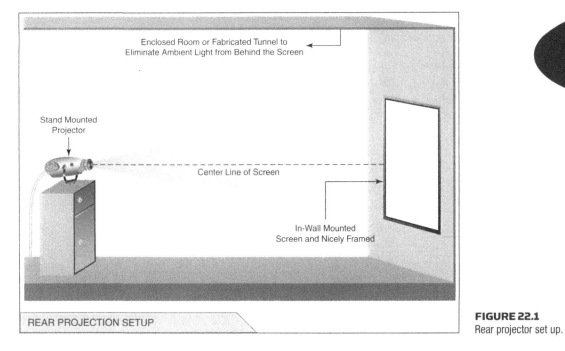

REAR PROJECTION SETUP

Enclosed Room or Fabricated Tunnel to Eliminate Ambient Light from Behind the Screen

Stand Mounted Projector

Center Line of Screen

In-Wall Mounted Screen and Nicely Framed

FIGURE 22.1
Rear projector set up.

Rear projection also needs fewer lumens than front projection. The reason is because the projector is facing the viewers; they are staring into a light source that is emanating through a screen and continuing beyond. There are no issues with reflection and fewer problems with ambient light because the intensity is being projected through the screen material.

Another advantage is that the projector is usually easier to get to. This makes general maintenance and lamp replacement far easier. It also makes trouble-shooting the system easier as you are not usually working at great heights and uncomfortable angles to manipulate the projector. Should a projector fail, it's also usually easier to get a temporary replacement on the stand and pointed at the screen.

One great advantage to rear projection is that you can stand in front of it and not cast a shadow. This is great for large screens at low elevations because it allows you to do a digital set or project talking points behind the speaker while he or she walks in front of and even interacts with the image. This can be a great way to break down walls of communication and pull the audience into the message.

However, rear projection has some downfalls. First, there is usually a noticeable hot spot in the image where the concentration of the lens energy can be seen. Another drawback for rear projection is that it takes an enormous amount of space. While one can incorporate extensive mirror bouncing to help limit the physical distance from the screen, the truth of the matter is that you are going to need to eat up some serious real estate to utilize rear screen projection. The larger your screen, the more real estate you are going to have to surrender. For many Houses of Worship, this alone is a deal breaker.

Rear projection requires that you have no other light spill from behind the projector. In outdoor venues, rear projection utilizes something called "tunneling." The idea is to build a completely masked area from the projector location to the screen so that no ambient light can spill onto the screen from behind. When ambient light is introduced from behind the screen, it competes with the projector and washes the image out. Likewise, inside installations must make sure the lights are out in the projection room and the door is shut. Should someone open the door with a light on in the other room, it will be very noticeable on the screen.

Generally speaking, the cost of building out a rear projection screen is more than a front projection solution.

Another negative aspect to rear projection is that the real estate you eat up cannot be used for storage or anything else (including speakers). The projection room has to be a large dedicated area of dead space. The beam of light cannot be interrupted by any physical object. You will have an entire room (or sometimes two or three) used for nothing other than projection. With construction costs and limited land available, this can sometimes be a hard pill to swallow.

While there appear to be more negative points than positive ones, rear projection is still an overall better projection solution if you have the space to utilize it. You'll need a less powerful and less expensive projector and you'll have a much more finished installation.

FRONT PROJECTION

Front projection appeals to many modern day Houses of Worship. It's much easier to implement (especially into an existing structure) than rear projection. The screen can be flush mounted to a wall and the projector hung from the ceiling or placed on a shelf on the back wall. The amount of "empty space" needed for projection is already empty because it's high up in the air in an open area that can't be utilized anyway.

Front projection systems offer more flexibility in the location of the projector related to the screen. Front projection is sometimes easier to do by a group of well-meaning volunteers who buy a projector on eBay. There is no complicated build out, no waste of space, no difficult trim work, no precise angles, and mirror bounces. By and large, you hang a screen, mount a projector, point it, size it to fit the screen, focus it, and play your content. This is appealing to many churches – so

VIDEO

211

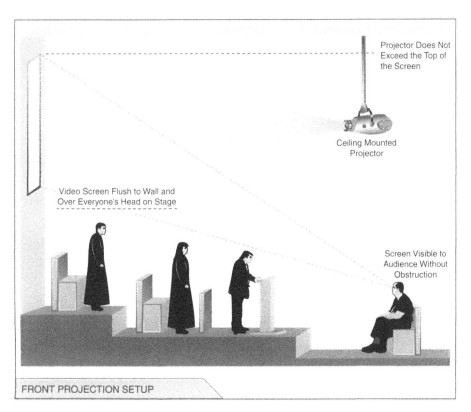

FRONT PROJECTION SETUP

FIGURE 22.2
Front projection system.

appealing that they choose to ignore the big ugly projector hanging from a stick in the middle of the room (or on an oddly placed shelf on the back wall).

However, front projection requires a little more "oomph." The image is not being shone into the audience through a screen; instead, it is being bounced off a screen and reflected. Sheer laws of physics will demand that some of that light is absorbed, while some of it is refracted and the remaining bit is reflected. Much of the lamp energy is wasted via the reflective screen, thus requiring more energy in order to be bright enough for the audience.

Likewise, if the screen is too low, or if anything gets in the way of the projector (for example, a person carrying a worship banner), you are going to experience terrible shadows on the screen. Unless you are doing shadow puppets, this is not an ideal situation.

Another downfall for front projection is the unsightliness of the installation. Like it or not, the projector is going to be in the room, cables are going to connect to it (although this can and should be done neatly), and it's very possible that fan noise is going to be heard by those near it.

General maintenance and lamp replacement is much more difficult. The projectors often require a lift, a large ladder, or scaffolding to reach. This can be time intensive, expensive, and more dangerous for the person maintaining the projector.

However, at the end of the day, front projection is usually a cheaper alternative. Between the cost savings and the space savings, many churches choose to utilize front projection, especially when installed in existing structures.

CHOOSING WHAT'S RIGHT FOR YOUR CHURCH

How do you choose what's right for your church? Many things will help you decide this.

The first thing to consider is your budget. Can you afford the build-out cost of rear projection, and then, can you give up the space needed (do you even have the space needed)?

After that, it comes down to practicality. How long will you be in the space before moving into something larger? If you are only going to be in the facility for a couple of years, the overall cost and manpower to do rear projection might not be worth it.

Are you interested in having an image behind the speaker and then giving the presenter the option of interacting with the image? Are you interested in using video as a scenic backdrop?

What is your primary goal for using video projection, and does this goal mandate or require rear projection?

EDGE BLENDING

One relatively newer technology (especially for the House of Worship) is the idea of edge blending. Edge blending allows you to use multiple projectors side by side to create one large image. There are software solutions that allow any projector to edge blend, as well as projectors with edge blending built in. Sometimes you might find yourself better off using an external processor that will do the edge blending, scaling, and image assembly for you. Every application is a little different, but there are a lot of tools available to help you accomplish this edge-blending effect.

By carefully aligning the projectors and utilizing a video distribution matrix, you can achieve one super-large image on a single screen. This is much like the idea of using multiple monitors on your computer, except there is no boundary – the two screens would literally appear as one.

> **TIP**
> Remember, when using multiple projectors, it's important that the images match in color, brightness, and focus. Some churches might try to save money by purchasing used projectors at low-market values. If you do this, you should purchase the same projector for both screens to increase your chances of matching them visually!

> **TIP**
> When using edge blending, you must keep in mind your aspect ratio. If you make a screen with an odd ratio size, the image and/or video is either going to have to be custom-made for your screen or it will be oddly distorted or cropped.

STACKING

Stacking has been around forever. Imagine you are doing an outdoor festival, and due to such factors as sunlight, you need 15,000 lumens. You have a choice – one heck of a rental bill or stacking three identical 5000-lumen projectors. Stacking requires precision aiming and usually utilizing test patterns to get it right.

If the projectors are not aimed correctly, your image will be filled with ghosting and have an appearance of being doubled. Any hope of clarity will be lost, and the overall result will be dismal.

VIDEO AS LIGHTING

Another interesting twist to conventional video is using a projector as a light source to create a stage wash on your set and performers. Video as lighting is a fairly unused lighting form to many people, and that's a real shame. With a good computer playback source and a basic switcher (for dimming and dousing control), a projector can cast an unlimited amount of textures and shapes to the stage floor.

Imagine using a moving background that you have created or purchased from any number of websites. These sparkling images with majestic motion could scroll over your entire set in ways a simple spinning pattern never could.

VIDEO
213

> **TIP**
> When using a projector as a light source, it is necessary to create a mechanical douser in front of the lens; otherwise, the contrast ratio of the projector will cause a gray light over the stage at all times. A douser is a simple piece of opaque material (such as heavy cardboard) that can be moved in front of the lens to physically block the light.

Likewise, you can shoot color washes out of the projector and wash them over the stage as well! As with regular stage lights, you can adjust the focus for your specific needs.

When you stop thinking of video projection as simply video images on a screen, a whole creative world opens up to you. Imagine using a multiple display projection system and projecting words and backgrounds on your side screens, but projecting only the moving background on your set (without the words). This would automatically bring a cohesive look to your lighting and video designs!

CREATING DYNAMIC LOOKS WITH VIDEO

Remember when we were discussing the idea of standing in front of rear projection? This can also be achieved via flat panel arrays and video walls. When you have such a background with motion and color behind your band, it creates a breathtaking effect. This can really push your visual limits without your having to use a lot of static and intelligent lighting.

The motion from the rear screen with the people and instruments standing in front of it will really add to your visual excitement in worship.

FIGURE 22.3
Rear screen.
Photo Courtesy of
Renewed Vision. All
rights reserved.

You are only limited by your imagination. Even budget constraints can be overcome with creative thinking.

CHAPTER 23

A Closer Look at the Video Screen

Video screens come in a variety of sizes, shapes, and materials. You can also purchase screen material in raw form and stretch it to your own frame in any shape you like. Projection screen material stretches in a similar way to canvas. It's fairly easy to make your own frame using simple carpentry techniques and projection screen material. This can give you a lot of flexibility in how you encompass video design into scenic design.

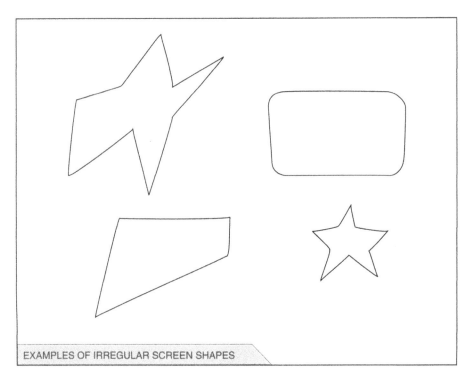

EXAMPLES OF IRREGULAR SCREEN SHAPES

FIGURE 23.1
Shapes for video screen
in scenic elements.

ODD SHAPES FOR INTERESTING EFFECT

If your projection screen is embedded into a set with walls on either side, the excess video image simply spills onto the back of the set and is never seen by the audience. If, however, the screen is suspended in the air or is in a space by itself, you must build a mask that will match the screen to place in front of the projector lens – thus eliminating video overspill and matching your image (Figure 23.2). This mask can be made out of cardboard, poster board, or aluminum materials fairly easily. For a more permanent solution, you could determine the exact shape using poster board and then translate that as a stencil onto aluminum for cutting.

FRONT AND REAR PROJECTION SCREENS

Projection screen material comes in two primary types – front screen and rear screen.

Front projection screen material can only be used for front projection. The back of the screen is lined in a heavy black material that will not allow light to pass through it and helps ensure the majority of light is reflected back to the audience.

A rear projection screen is designed for the projector to shine through the translucent material and help the light source blend through the material at a consistent rate to produce an image on the backside. Rear projection material can be projected on from the front as well. However, the screen is not designed for reflection, so the image will be much dimmer than if projected on a front projection screen.

The rear projection screen comes in different densities that are identifiable by their color.

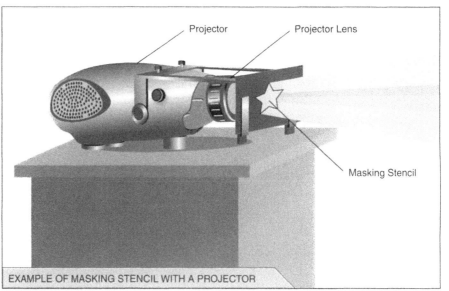

EXAMPLE OF MASKING STENCIL WITH A PROJECTOR

FIGURE 23.2
Video Screen/Stencil
Mask/Projector.

Many home theaters use a dark black projection screen. This dark color helps to saturate the blacks in the image and enhances the contrast ratio. However, the image appears to be much darker because the transmission rate of the material is very low. This requires a higher lumen lamp for proper penetration. The dark screen also has a smaller viewing cone (this affects how people on the extreme sides can see the image). The viewing cone for a dark rear screen like this is often as low as 60 degrees. This means that unless you are practically in front of the screen, you will have a hard time viewing the images.

Perhaps the most common rear projection screen is the darker gray color. While not as effective at controlling the blacks, it has a much larger viewing cone (usually around 120 degrees) and requires fewer overall lumens to punch through since the material is more translucent.

The third type of rear projection screen is a very light gray. This is very translucent and is often used in high-ambient lighting conditions. However, because of its super-translucent nature, the hot spot of the projector image is more pronounced.

Most Houses of Worship utilizing a rear projection system would likely use the darker gray-colored screen for the overall advantages of image display and viewing cone.

PERFORATED SCREEN

It's also possible to order a perforated video screen. While not noticeable to the human eye at a distance, these screens are designed to allow sound waves to pass through them. Perforated screens are often used in movie theaters, where the speakers can be mounted behind the screen, thus creating the effect of the sound literally coming from the visual source on the screen.

Now, at this point you might be thinking, "I thought rear projection screens had to be unobstructed." Well, they do. But think about how the projector emits light. It starts at the lens and expands until it hits the screen.

As long as the beam of light is not interrupted by the speakers (or other object), it's fine. So in this case, the projector sits higher to be in the center of the screen, and the speakers are located closer to the projector but under the beam – therefore not in the way (Figure 23.3).

Perforated screens can be very useful for Houses of Worship. Depending on the screen location, it can be possible to have side-fill speakers, subwoofers, or even some organ speakers in the projection room.

SCREEN GAIN

Screen gain is another option you will want to investigate when purchasing your screen. A screen gain of one is normal. As your gain increases, the screen will have the appearance of a brighter image. However, remember: When something

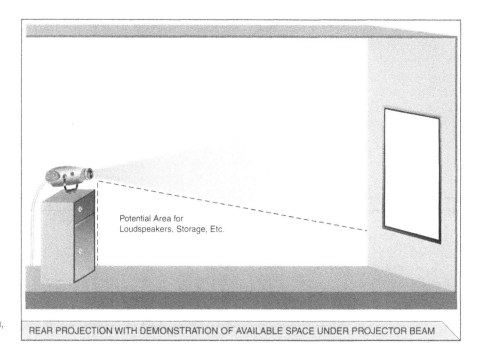

REAR PROJECTION WITH DEMONSTRATION OF AVAILABLE SPACE UNDER PROJECTOR BEAM

FIGURE 23.3
Projector beam, screen, and speakers.

seems too good to be true, it usually is. There are trade-offs with using higher screen gain. For instance, the image quality can appear less smooth (sort of pixilated) to some viewers because of the way the screen reflects light.

Typically, as screen gain increases, the red, green, and blue colors will reflect differently, resulting in a color shift of the image depending on your point of view. Likewise, the higher the screen gain, the lower the viewing angle. So, as your screen gain goes up, your available viewing angles go down; this is typically not good for most Houses of Worship.

As a screen gain increases dramatically (over 1.4), there will tend to be a noticeable hot spot in the image. This hot spot will appear in different screen locations, depending on where one is sitting.

However, a higher screen gain will result in a brighter image as more light is being reflected. There are some instances (primarily where the viewing angle is mostly straight on and a large amount of ambient light is present) where a high gain screen can be very effective.

By and large, I would urge most Houses of Worship to work with a 1.0 gain screen whenever possible and purchase the right projector for the job.

MOTORIZED VS. PERMANENT

Another big question a House of Worship must face is whether they should use a motorized screen that can be remotely raised and lowered or utilize a permanently framed screen that always stays in position.

The answer to this will ultimately be up to you and the confines you have to work with. In some cases (especially in retrofits), there is simply no way around a motorized screen.

In general, I find motorized screens in Houses of Worship to be a huge distraction. They tend to be clumsy and noisy at best. The transition of the screen is rarely well concealed, and I believe it detracts from the seamless communication we should seek. Anything that can be a distraction has no place in the House of Worship. We should be about helping people to focus on God and engage in corporate worship. Distractions of any kind make this difficult.

If you are considering a motorized screen, you should weigh all your options. If you are installing a screen in new construction, you should carefully design your building for all of your A/V systems – including video and screen location. I would always advise a church, whenever possible, to use a permanently framed screen and avoid a motorized screen for the worship center.

HOW BIG IS BIG ENOUGH?

Many Houses of Worship are tempted to use flat panel displays in their worship center, but generally we find that they are not large enough. This prompts the question, "How big should my screen be?"

THX cinema standard states that the furthest seat should have no less than a 36-degree horizontal viewing angle and that every seat should be unimpaired visually (www.THX.com/cinema/builtTHX/screen.html). While this is a cinema standard, we can derive some useful information for our House of Worship.

Ultimately, viewing size is up to the user, and the definitions set by THX for cinema don't really apply to the House of Worship since the screen is not the "feature presentation." However, it is important to have a screen that is easily viewed. The audience shouldn't have to crane their necks to see the screen. People should be able to see the screen without obstruction, and likewise, it's important that the person on the back row is able to easily read the screen. After all, this is the point – to communicate with people via the display of choice. So, it stands to reason that if everyone in your congregation can't read the screen, it's too small.

Also, I prefer to set up video screens where the viewer is looking across the stage to see the screen. This way the worship leader and other activities on the stage area are always in the line of sight. Otherwise, the audience members must look away from the screen to see words and videos. This is not an ideal situation. Ideally, you want people engaged in what's happening on the stage. The lyrics and other video content should add to what's happening on the stage.

Sometimes, when screens are mounted so the people in the back can see, they can be mounted too high or too much out of the way for your congregants closer to the alter or stage area. A common solution is to place smaller flat panel displays along the front edge of the stage for this group of people.

WHERE SHOULD IT GO?

Perhaps the next big obstacle is determining where the screen should go. This is most easily determined by ruling out where it can't go. Many traditional churches have a high apex in the center of the auditorium, so it may seem to make sense that a center screen be mounted on this section of the wall. Unfortunately, however, there is almost always a religious icon of some sort at this location, which the screen covers, and that's a sad thing – to cover an icon with a video screen. Likewise, many protestant Houses of Worship have baptism pools in this area of the facility, forcing the issue of a motorized screen and awkward transitions.

Oftentimes, the real answer is to utilize multiple screens, but this solution is often resisted due to cost. Sometimes, there is no alternative but to place a screen in a less than ideal location.

Here are some important things to keep in mind in regards to screen location:

- Are you covering up something important to your fellowship?
- Can everyone clearly see the screen?
- Does it affect your stage lighting (and can you focus your stage lighting so it doesn't wash out the screen)?
- Is it comfortable to view for an extended period (both while congregants are sitting and standing)?
- Is it stable (not moving with air currents, flapping, etc.)?
- Does the placement encourage uninhibited worship?

As many Houses of Worship add video to their services, they also add screens and displays for the worship leader, praise team, band, and choir. This can be a simple duplicate of what the congregation is being shown or a specific feed that is sent via another operator especially for the people leading worship.

To assist the worship leaders, televisions and flat panels can go neatly in front of the stage area or in front of the choir on the stage, while projected screens are normally projected on a screen on the back wall. You want to pay attention to not creating a distraction to the congregation; it's intended to be a worship aid to the leadership, but it should not be a barrier to the congregation for worship. It can become a distraction to the congregation if the image is visible to the congregation and flashing a different feed out of sync with the ones being provided for the congregational worship.

CHAPTER 24

Cameras and Tripods

There was a time when the only real camera solution that had any quality to it at all carried a price tag of over $60,000 per camera. Thankfully, those days are by and large over. Don't get me wrong – there are still many high-quality cameras at this price point (and well beyond), but the modern-day House of Worship has many other choices for cameras at lower prices.

When it comes to cameras, the House of Worship really has one of two categories to choose from – the smaller format "pro-sumer" and the full-format "ENG" size cameras.

Both types of cameras have huge advantages and disadvantages to ministry.

CAMERA OVERVIEWS

Charge-coupled device (CCD) technology is how most digital cameras process images. Generally speaking, the larger the CCD chip, the better the image. Also, the larger the chip, the better the camera tends to work in low-light applications (larger lens openings also create better low-light images).

High-end video cameras, like the ones you want to use in ministry, will be three-chip cameras. While you can purchase single-chip cameras, they are often of inferior quality and not usable for any type of broadcast application (including IMAG and service archives). A single-chip camera must capture all luminance

FIGURE 24.1
Panasonic AG-HPX500
and Panasonic
AG-HPX170.
Photo by Brad Herring.

and color information on one chip. A three-chip camera utilizes a separate chip for each color (red, green, and blue), thus allowing a higher-quality image.

Cameras can also trick you with claims of "high definition." Sure, they can capture the high-definition signal, but often lower-priced cameras are very limited by bandwidth. Anything less than 25 Mbs (megabits per second) is possibly going to result in artifacting when used for recording. Many would argue that anything less than 100 Mbs is inadequate for broadcast needs. Side by side, all the cameras look wonderful. Every camera and every format is different. To get a true comparison of cameras, you need to look at playback from their recordings. This will reveal far more to you than simply looking at a monitor of it shooting live. You may ask yourself why you should spend so much money for the expensive camera. The answer lies in features and bandwidth.

There was a time when smaller cameras offered few features that would be desirable for a broadcast ministry (they lacked XLR inputs for audio, had poor – if any – meters, etc.). That is not so much the case anymore. Granted, there will most likely always be more features packed into a bigger camera (sheer size alone would indicate that), but increasingly the smaller cameras are becoming packed with high-end professional features.

Likewise, a camera is often defined by the quality of its optics (the lens). It is often quite helpful to be able to interchange lenses based on your needs. It is also true that a larger piece of glass in the lens will often lead to a better image (particularly in low-light applications). Many pro-sumer cameras do not offer you the opportunity to change the lens. Most will have some sort of adapter you can use for add-ons, but they never really compare with a full-size interchangeable lens; it's part of the compromise you make in purchasing a less-expensive camera.

A camera should be evaluated for its entire package. Consider the available accessories, power requirements, battery life, optics, outputs, and weight. Each of these aspects will be important to you when you consider a camera purchase or rental.

PRO-SUMER CAMERAS – THE GOOD, THE BAD, AND THE UGLY

Pro-sumer cameras are recognizable because they are barely larger than a personal camcorder and almost exclusively have a fixed lens that cannot be interchanged. Another giveaway is the sub-$6000 price tag that most of them carry.

These cameras are great for a lot of ministry applications. They usually utilize small lithium-ion batteries that are not expensive and last several hours per charge. They are great for youth ministries, man-on-the-street interviews, baptism videos, and general video shooting. With proper lighting, they can also be used for main-service cameras. However, if you are working in dim lighting, they might not always yield the result you hope for.

If you are planning to use a pro-sumer camera in a multicamera shoot for live switching, the biggest drawback might be the lack of camera control unit

(CCU) operation. One of the main advantages to using a CCU is shot consistency. We'll talk about CCUs in more depth when we complete our camera comparison.

Smaller cameras are often very lightweight (commonly weighing in at under 5 pounds). However, this can be a detriment as well because they are sometimes hard to hold still for long amounts of time. The cameras are typically handheld, although some companies offer attachments than can modify the camera to a shoulder-mount camera. The lightweight nature can be cause for more jerky pans and tilts – especially at the beginning and end of a movement.

These smaller pro-sumer cameras often cheap out with the electronics. Many of them utilize a $\frac{1}{8}$-inch connection for sound input and a similar connection for headphones. Some companies offer a conversion box that will accept XLR and adapt the signal to the $\frac{1}{8}$-inch jack on the camera. While this is helpful, the quality is still not usually as good as a real, built-in, balanced XLR connection.

Pro-sumer cameras often provide iris controls and zoom controls via electronic connections. Sometimes there is a ring on the lens that allows for true manual operation, but more often at least some of these controls are via nondirect controls. This sometimes limits their smoothness and effectiveness.

FULL-SIZE (ENG AND STUDIO) CAMERAS

A full-size camera offers a ton of features and image control that easily surpass the pro-sumer camera. This should be evident by the huge price increase. In all fairness, every day this gap narrows, but in reality there are still many features found on a full-size Electronic News Gathering (ENG) or studio camera that make it worth its weight in gold (and by the prices, you might sometimes think that is literal).

As you have probably already figured out, full-size cameras often allow for CCU control – a huge advantage to multicamera shoots in the House of Worship. This is the easiest way to balance all the cameras and keep the shots consistent. Many full-size cameras use TRIAX-compatible connections – this allows CCU connectivity as well as communication systems, tally light control, video preview, and a host of other features. TRIAX allows video to be sent up to 500 meters without degradation. TRIAX cable will also provide power to the camera, so it really is one connection for all needs. This makes for a quick setup and neat installation. However, TRIAX comes with a price; not only are the cameras that utilize the technology more expensive, but the cable itself is expensive as well. Nonetheless, this is a true broadcast solution, and one that will pay for itself in shot consistency and control.

Full-size cameras are typically heavier (some weighing over 15 pounds). However, this weight adds to the stability of the camera and allows for smoother pans and tilts. Being shoulder mounted, the camera is supported by the entire body and with a little practice can yield a very steady shot even without a tripod.

Full-size cameras often offer zoom and focus remotes – these are true remotes that connect to and manipulate the lens itself (not some digital knockoff trying to

electronically move controls). This allows operators to have full pan, tilt, zoom, and focus on the handles so they can manipulate the cameras and achieve the best shot without having to reach to several different places.

On a full-size camera, the zoom, iris, focus, and back focus are all true lens controls and as such are mounted on the lens itself. This gives you a very smooth movement on the actual optics of the lens. Smaller-bodied cameras usually control this via rotary wheels and buttons, and the adjustment is often stepped (i.e., noticeable). Typically, these are electronic controls and not actual optical controls. Having the luxury of true optic control is yet another advantage to the full-size camera and will provide a better quality picture.

The CCD sensors on full-size cameras are often larger than the pro-sumer units. Typically, these cameras will have three CCD chips at least half an inch in size (as opposed to the smaller $1/3$-inch chips commonly found in pro-sumer cameras). This larger CCD will yield a better image and decrease your depth of field.

One of the primary perks to a full-size professional camera is the lens. Lenses on professional cameras contain a larger, higher quality glass. This automatically makes them better in low-light conditions. As with any camera, the image is only as good as the optics. Clearly, with better glass (the lens) you will achieve a better image. Being able to interchange lenses is a huge advantage as well. For instance, if the shot is close up, you might want a wide angle lens, but if the shot is back from the balcony, you are going to want a lens with more zoom. Now you can match the ideal lens to the shot desired. By matching the optics to the shot, you will continue to achieve a better quality picture. Likewise, you can opt for high-end lenses that will give you better depth of field.

Depth of Field

Simply put, depth of field allows the image to separate the background from the foreground with more intensity by causing one or the other to be in focus while the rest of the image is out of focus. You see this in film all the time – the foreground is in focus, while the background is very blurry; then, there is often a shift as the background object comes into focus and the foreground blurs out (this is called a "rack focus").

A "short" depth of field will give you an object that is distinctly in focus while the rest of the image is out of focus, whereas a "large" depth of field will tend to make everything in focus. Wide-angle lenses will give you more of a long depth of field, while telescopic lenses will give you more of a short depth of field; hence the advantage that can be achieved by interchangeable lenses.

Depth of field is truly one of the most noticeable differences between video and film. A film camera will typically have a very short depth of field, while most video cameras will tend to have a larger depth of field. Depth of field with video comes down to image sensor size, lens length, and aperture

TIP

"Depth of field" by definition is the distance range from the camera in which the subject will appear to be in focus.

setting. You can do a lot with video, but the fact of the matter is that film still offers an overall better depth of field as well as a warmer, less sterile look.

There are several other factors that determine depth of field – iris, the distance of the subject from the lens, lighting, and shutter speed all play a factor in determining your depth of field. Generally speaking, a more open iris will result in shorter depth of field, but your lighting has to be lowered to keep the image from overexposing. Another option for digital cameras is to use neutral density filters, which limit the amount of light coming into the camera without shifting the color. This will allow you to use a larger aperture at a given level of light, thus limiting your depth of field.

CAMERA CONTROL UNIT

A CCU will allow a single person to operate the iris for each camera. This is commonly called "shading." This means your camera operator simply has to point, zoom, and focus the camera. When the director calls up the shot, the CCU operator will make sure the iris is consistent with the other cameras and playback devices being utilized.

A CCU can also control color balances, shutter speed, black levels, and camera gain as well as a variety of other camera controls. Utilizing CCU systems, you can also activate talent lights on the active camera, send signals to the camera operator, and allow each camera operator to see the currently used shot at a flick of a button.

Mostly, only the large ENG and studio cameras offer CCU control (Figure 24.2).

PTZ Camera Control

Newer technology allows for full pan, tilt, and zoom control. These are often referred to as "robotic cameras" and are a great choice for many Houses of Worship. One common problem all Houses of Worship face (as we have mentioned several times) is avoiding distraction. It's hard to be inconspicuous with three camera operators, on camera stands, running cameras.

PTZ cameras allow you to mount the camera on a wall, under a balcony, behind the choir, or anywhere else your heart desires. Now, from a remote room one person can control all aspects of the camera. On many units, you

VIDEO
225

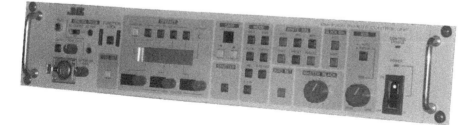

FIGURE 24.2
CCU.
Photo by Brad Herring.

FIGURE 24.3
Remote camera on a
pan/tilt camera system
with controller.
Photo by Brad Herring.

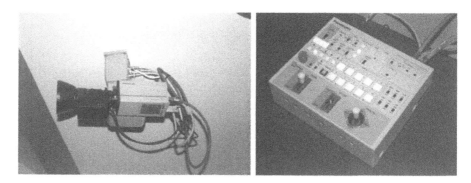

can program common movement paths (complete with speed of panning and tilting) and save these as presets. Then you can call up that movement preset, switch to it, and switch off it before it completes. These cameras can be real lifesavers for worship! They also free you up from having one more operator to book for every service. On the other hand, it's very difficult to follow a speaker or other talent on the stage smoothly with a PTZ camera, so these are best used for static or preprogrammed pan/tilt/zoom shots.

Camera Summary

Deciding upon a camera will ultimately be up to your budget. If you are doing broadcast or archive recordings for worship (including IMAG), you should try to find a full-size camera that falls within your budget, if possible. You should also base your purchase on a plan for the future.

Utilizing TRIAX is ideal if the budget permits, but not necessary if you have to cut costs. Having a full-size camera without TRIAX is better than nothing at all. The TRIAX simply makes the production better.

For portable shoots, location shoots, and man-on-the street interviews, a pro-sumer camera is often preferred because of cost, battery life, and weight.

One other thought: If you are planning to do green screen shoots and key-in backgrounds, you will usually find a bigger camera works better. The larger chips inside the camera often capture more detail, allowing for a better key. That being said, people key pro-sumer cameras all the time, but the results are typically better with full-size cameras. When you think about it, if the larger cameras didn't offer better solutions, don't you think the large studios would use the cheaper cameras?

Ultimately, it's like everything else – you get what you pay for. However, when you start to count ministry dollars, you have to realize you don't always need a Prevost motor coach when the old school bus works just as well.

TRIPODS

A $1200 tripod is a deal – not highway robbery. Many people start looking at camera tripods and have to pick themselves up off the floor when they start to see

FIGURE 24.4
Tripod.

prices. When it comes to high-end video, your tripod makes all the difference.

You need a professional-grade tripod with some substance to it. The legs should securely lock and, ideally, it should have spreaders at the bottom.

The key to tripod success is buying a fully floating head that matches your camera weight. Likewise, the head should be matched to the camera for size and weight.

Less-expensive tripods are generally lighter weight with a semi-fluid or non-fluid head. This is unacceptable for broadcast (or IMAG). If you intend to lock down one shot and never pan or tilt, then maybe you can get away without a fluid head.

A fluid head is a fluid-filled, balanced tripod head that allows smooth and fluid panning and tilting from start to finish. With a fluid head, there is no jerking motion at the start or end of the motion, and during the pan or tilt everything is nice and smooth. Smooth camera movement is a primary component of high production standards.

Cheaper tripods will also result in a shakier shot because they are made out of lighter-duty materials. It's vital that your shot be solid and your movements be smooth. This can only be accomplished by utilizing a professional-grade tripod and head.

Tripod Platforms

It's also important that your shooting platform be elevated when and where it makes sense. You can do this with custom-built platforms, seating risers, or specific platforms designed for cameras. Ideally, the camera is on one platform and the operator is on another. This will keep the tripod and camera from shaking when the operator moves around or shifts weight. If you are on a permanent structure, this is not as pertinent.

CHAPTER 25

Worship Presentation Software

If your ministry is still using PowerPoint or other similar static presentation software designed for the boardroom (some would argue that should be spelled "bored room"), do yourself and your ministry a huge favor and STOP. As worship has become more A/V supported, new companies have emerged that bring custom worship presentation software to our door.

These software packages offer huge advantages to the House of Worship. Typical features include:

- Song libraries
- On-the-fly changes
- Operator screens that allow for easy changes in workflow
- Integrated scripture (often in multiple translations)
- Controlled CCLI (Christian Copyright License International)
- Motion graphics behind text
- Full DVD playback (on computers that support DVD drives)
- Full video playback
- Dynamic messaging (like nursery calls)
- Excellent character generation for external keying
- And much more!

VIDEO
229

Almost all of the titles available at the time of this writing are similar in cost and, for the most part, similar in features. All of these companies offer free downloads on their sites so you can try before you buy.

While they all do the same basic things, each of them has its particular way of doing them. For instance, some titles will play back a PowerPoint presentation as if it were being played out of PowerPoint (complete with transitions and animations), while others will take a final image of each slide and present that slide (without the animations and transitions).

Some handle the DVD playback better than others. Certain titles tend to have crisper text that can be keyed more easily than other titles. Some of the software packages offer outstanding graphic flexibility but limited scripture lookup.

Some are easier to use than others, while others give you more flexibility and design choices.

So, it really is worth downloading the free trial software and seeing which works best for you.

As of the time of this writing, the most popular software packages are:

- EasyWorship (www.easyworship.com)
- MediaShout (www.mediashout.com)
- SundayPlus (www.sundayplus.com)
- ProPresenter (www.renewedvision.com)*
- LiveWorship (www.liveworship.com)*

Worship presentation software should be used in any House of Worship utilizing video for worship. The mere fact of song libraries alone is enough to justify the expense. If the songs you use are not already in the program, you can download them from CCLI and other third-party sources or type them in yourself. Once you've done this, the title is there in the database for future use. Should the worship leader choose a song off the playlist, it's a simple matter of grabbing the song from the database and projecting it on the display. Literally, seconds later the song is up and running. The songs are divided by verse, chorus, and bridge, making it easy to navigate during worship. You are not limited to a linear slide design – you can go from any slide to any slide at the click of a mouse.

WORD PHRASES

VIDEO
230

One often-overlooked detail by many churches starting out with video projection is how the words will appear on the screen. Oftentimes, the operator will cram as many words as he or she can fit on a page, and then start the next. This does not help worship flow smoothly.

Instead, each page should have a logical phrase on it. This should follow the song break musically or the thought that is being portrayed. Fewer words are good for the people following along, although it means a little more work for the operator.

VIDEO MOTION CONTROL

When video projection in churches first began, it was primarily managed by PowerPoint. We had a static background (usually something fairly unimpressive) and large text. If we were lucky, there was some form of color coordination.

* ProPresenter (as of the time of this writing) is a Mac-only application and LiveWorship is a Mac and PC application, while the others are PC only. There has been a lot of talk in the industry that some of the other titles are considering a Mac solution. EasyWorship has just announced it is coming out with a Mac version but has not made an official release date.

As we began to advance, we saw the development of worship presentation software. In the beginning, it was PowerPoint on steroids – still utilizing static backgrounds, but starting to use features like song libraries, scripture look-ups, and dynamic control.

Generation two software integrated motion graphics behind the words. Suddenly we could play looping backgrounds of video images and digital images to add a dynamic impact to the words that were on the screen. As computers and displays became more advanced, so did the ability to play back various forms of media on the screen.

Today we have full-out motion control capability. Now clips can be called up and played real time. They can be played forward and backward, regular speed, slow motion, or accelerated. Color hues can be changed, and image masks can be added and played on individual screens or spanned across multiple screens.

With video motion control, we can do with video what for years was only dreamt of with lighting. Now, one person sitting behind a video playback station can literally tell a story with video. As the songs progress, so does the video. Clip after clip can be strung along to create a masterpiece of imagery that is complimented by powerful lyrics and hundreds of voices.

Perhaps one of the first manufacturers to offer equipment specifically for this purpose was Edirol when they introduced Video Canvas. Shortly afterward, Renewed Vision introduced Pro-Video Player. Video Canvas is more of a proprietary hardware solution, while Pro-Video Player is software based and utilizes the Mac. Both work well in a House of Worship.

With a creative person on board, these tools can be used to craft an amazing visual story that will go hand in hand with worship. Compliment the video motion control with your lighting and you will have one stunning visual display.

VIDEO
231

These devices can play multiformat clips (anything from still images to SD formats to HD formats as well). There are many websites that sell footage specifically for worship applications. Be it short visual clips, mini movies, or man-on-the-street interviews, you now have unlimited choices on how you communicate with your audience. You can even produce your own clips and use them.

NETWORKS IN WORSHIP

Based on CCLI look-ups, video and still clip downloads, and other Internet functionalities that are built into many of these programs, it's a wise idea to have a network drop in the booth. Not only will this allow you to access files online, it will also allow you to easily swap data from a central server. This can be a huge time saver and increase workflow efficiency.

CHAPTER 26

Conclusion of Video Systems for Worship

A video system can truly complement our attempts to communicate with people. It adds the visual component of learning and increases the chances that people will walk away with what you are trying to teach them.

Through video clips, we can tell stories and take those in attendance to foreign places. We can introduce them to the community, walk them down the street, and see what people really think. We find that people are very revealing when they talk to a video camera. They will say things that they wouldn't say in normal conversation. It's odd, but it's true: People become very open when talking to a camera. This openness can allow you to express reality to your audience in ways otherwise not possible.

Utilizing words on the screen helps to lift the faces of those engaged in worship. This gets them in good singing posture and promotes corporate worship. Their faces are pointed toward the altar where the ones leading in worship are often standing. Everything about video helps to encourage corporate worship.

By using purchasable video clips and combining them with making your own clips, you are unlimited in how you can effectively touch people. Video uses strong imagery to speak directly to a person's soul.

Some churches make a conscious choice not to use video at all, while others make it a central part of worship. Ultimately the choice is up to the individual House of Worship and how you choose to communicate with people. If you do choose to use the video medium, please realize that it is not a stand-alone system. In order for the video playback system to truly be successful, it must be used in tight concert with the sound and lighting aspects of worship. Together, the three systems combine to communicate your message to the masses in a way that will remain with them well past the next meal.

CONCLUSION

Conclusion of Book

PUTTING IT ALL TOGETHER AND MAKING IT SYNC

If I had a penny for every pastor who has complained to me about the words being wrong on the screen, I could retire in the tropics. Add to this the number of missed microphone cues, poorly cued CD's, unintentional blackouts, wrong video switches, and so forth, and we could all retire in the Tropics.

Churches often feel at a loss as to how to make it better and get things right. There are many things that can be done to help this.

The Playbook

While it requires more planning on behalf of the worship leader, the only way to guarantee the words are right on the screen is to create a playbook each Sunday. This playbook is more than a simple "order of service." It is the entire service skeleton. Take a look at this imaginary sample playbook:

Time	Description	LX	FX	VID	STAGE
10:55 AM	Begin service count down on screen.	Preset 1	Preshow music	CPR fall countdown #4—all screens	—
10:58 AM	Call worship team to places.	—	—	—	Vocals stage left, band stage right
10:59 AM	Send the band and worship team out on stage.	Preset 2	—	—	Everyone on stage

237

(*Continued*)

CONCLUSION

Time	Description	LX	FX	VID	STAGE
11:00 AM	Worship band starts playing at 0:00 on the timer.	Preset 4	Preshow out/band and vocals up	IMAG — Worship Leader	—
11:01 AM	Song 1 (insert title here)	Yellow backlight/ spot on Worship Leader	—	Words with motion graphic swirls V1, C, V2, C, V1, B, V3, C	
11:08 AM	Song 2 (insert title here)	Purple backlight/ hazer on for 20 second burst	Solo on mic 3 at V2 Solo on mic 1 at V3	Words with background of rivers #5 V1, V2, V3, C, V1	Prepare for pastor; podium and stage set up for drama.
11:09 AM	Call actors to places stage right — prep props that will come on in blackout.	—	—	—	Call to places and prep.
11:17 AM	Actors on stage	Black out until set, then up on preset 7	Head-worn mics 5, 6 and 8 up, band and vocals out	BLACK OUT	Actors go stage right — props on from stage left.

The playbook indicates the ideal time that the event will happen. Obviously, this will slide back and forth, but it gives a good frame of reference – both to the person planning worship and to the people executing it.

You will notice that each event is listed (even preparation events) and each category is listed along with instructions of what should be done. This example has been scaled down for simplicity, but in the real world you could have as much detail here as you want. Notice that under the video tab detailed instructions are given – INCLUDING SONG ORDER. This way there are fewer surprises. Obviously, worship has a level of dynamics to it, but at least this is the plan.

If you ever watch the news on a regular broadcast, you'll notice everything is fairly smooth and well timed. The newscasters are working from a playbook.

However, when they break in with a big story, if you pay attention, you'll notice things go downhill really fast. People start stumbling on words, text and graphics tend to come up late (and sometimes wrong), cues get dropped, microphones don't work – it starts to feel like many of our church services. Why? Now the newscasters are reacting to a situation and not following the plan.

Unfortunately, we tend to run all of our services like this – reacting to the events unfolding on the stage instead of knowing ahead of time what should happen and acting appropriately.

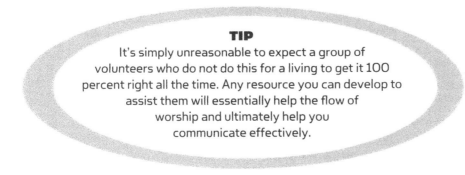

TIP
It's simply unreasonable to expect a group of volunteers who do not do this for a living to get it 100 percent right all the time. Any resource you can develop to assist them will essentially help the flow of worship and ultimately help you communicate effectively.

Volunteer and Staff Buy-in

Another thing that is important is volunteer buy-in. The people executing the service have to understand that they are a critical part of worship – a critical part of communicating the Gospel message. If they are zoning out, goofing off, and missing cues, the message is being dropped.

Once you have a solid buy-in, people will start to genuinely care about their ministry. They will want to excel in it. With buy-in, you can start to get people more involved in rehearsals and other practice times. You can start building a team that truly works together and is heading in the same general direction.

Without buy-in, you get people who show up late, cancel at the last minute, or simply don't show up at all. They half-heartedly attend to their tasks and fail to realize the critical nature of the work they are doing. You cannot build a dynamic A/V ministry like this – much less have accurate words on the screen.

Service Producer

Having a Service Producer is the big answer. Aside from perhaps the smallest of community theaters, no production in the world would ever think of running without a stage manager – the one person who is in charge of the complete execution of the service. Yet, as media savvy as we are, most Houses of Worship run reckless during worship. We hand hundreds of thousands of dollars worth of equipment to men and women who, as a rule, come from very diverse backgrounds, often not technical in nature.

We expect these people not to only master their area of ministry (often with very little hands-on time to gain experience and little, if any, training), but also to be able to make critical decisions, work under pressure, and catch every cue. It's mad!

The utilization of a Service Producer will make many of your woes go away. A Service Producer should be someone who is organized and good at administrative tasks. Service producers should be able to think on their feet, think outside the box, and – most of all – be team players. This person doesn't necessarily have to have technical expertise, but he or she should have at least a working knowledge of each of the systems you employ, as well as a reasonable idea of how long a request will take and how much work is involved.

The Service Producer needs to be a good communicator. He or she should be able to talk to the tech team in a way that is well received and welcomed while at the same time, be able to talk to the pastoral team in a way that they can understand. The Service Producer bridges the gap between technical and non-technical. This person also has the overall vision of where the ministry is going.

In an ideal world, the Service Producer is *only* a Service Producer. He or she spends time with the worship team as well as the pastoral team and should have not only the vision, but also a keen sense of where the service is going. For instance, if the Worship Leader deviates from the plan and starts into an intense worship song, the Service Producer would be close enough to all the people involved to know what is happening. He or she would in turn call for the video screens to go to black (or perhaps to a certain video clip to complement the song) or might call for the lighting to dim in the house or on certain areas of the stage, and this person would, most of all, be the reassuring voice of calm to the rest of the team.

The Service Producer – one person, in control, making decisions, and helping everyone to stay on task: Doesn't that one description alone give you hope?

Now the sound engineer can be freed up to concentrate on the mix; the lighting person can be focused on the lighting *quality* – not worrying about when his or her next cue is coming up; the stage managers have a central person helping keep them on track; and everything is running smoothly. Most of all, when the service goes off book (and it will), you have one person who's just as entrenched in the spirit of worship as the Worship Leader. This person can quickly make the decisions to follow the action on stage and confidently lead the team.

This also gives the Worship Leader a single point of contact. Now, the Service Producer deals with all scheduling and personnel issues. If a cue is missed, the leaders come to the Service Producer, who handles it on the technical level with the person who needs the information. Ideally, the Service Producer is one who can, in his or her own way, develop relationships with the tech team (perhaps even form a small group with them) and begin to transition your A/V team into something far more than a group of people who meet for worship services to run the service.

The Service Producer then produces the service. Here is the ideal worship team structure:

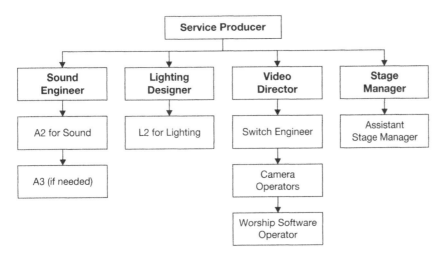

So, in the example above, the Service Producer would communicate directly with each department head. In the actual running of the service, the only exception would be for audio; the Service Producer would be on headset with the A2 so the sound engineer can still receive cues but isn't confined to a headset, so he or she can mix the service.

All the various department heads have the people under them that they are responsible for. The A2 would normally sit at the sound console with the main mix engineer. He or she takes cues, helps cue tracks, and is a second set of eyes for the engineer who is spotting people about to speak in a microphone. The A3 would, in most cases, be on the floor somewhere near the stage.

The lighting designer would control the light desk and be on headset with the producer to make sure the lights were doing what was needed. The L2 would be available for refocuses, gel replacement, troubleshooting, and so on. In many Houses of Worship, the L2 would be omitted except for in large productions.

The video director would be calling video cues. The director usually has his or her hands full and would not be on headset all the time, but would have an open line in order to hear the producer during the service. Oftentimes, the video director will also control all video playback for the service, as well as the lyrics and motion video happening on the screen – so it's critical that this person is in the communication loop.

Finally, the stage manager is on the floor ready to handle emergencies and cue people on timing. He or she might be changing batteries, exchanging microphones, resetting staging or props, handling transition times, and making sure all people are where they need to be when they need to be there. Commonly the stage

manager would be on one side of the stage and the assistant stage manager would be on the other; this way both sides are covered in the event of an emergency.

In short, utilization of a Service Producer will solve many problems that the average House of Worship faces.

TRAINING

Continued training is imperative for the House of Worship technician. Today, more than ever, opportunities exist for Houses of Worship of any size and any budget. I'd say that 90 percent of the Houses of Worship I work with could improve their A/V systems tenfold by simply getting the right training. We see a full turnaround in quality, morale, and performance simply by investing one or two weeks in training people how to be empowered in the area of ministry they serve.

The church has several training methods available to it.

Conferences

There are several major conferences and hundreds of smaller ones that you can send your people to every year. These conferences give your people an opportunity to catch vision as they see all the equipment available and the new things happening in the industry. They also get to spend time with other people just like them and learn from their experiences. This alone can be a huge source of encouragement, not to mention a source for the skills that are learned.

Many of the top consultants and training experts in the Houses of Worship field show up to share their knowledge with the technicians that attend. It's a great time to receive instruction, ask questions, and make new contacts for people who can help you in the future.

The top three national conferences are National Association of Broadcasters (NAB), Lighting Dimensions International (LDI), and InfoComm. These conferences are for the A/V and broadcast industry at large, but within the past few years there has been a large, growing House of Worship sector at these shows, spearheaded by *Technologies for Worship* magazine and their Worship Pavilion.

The Worship Pavilion offers free hands-on classes, showcases the newest equipment, and offers the chance to chat one-on-one with many of the instructors and editors for the magazine.

WFX is another conference that is well attended. Hosted by *Church Production* magazine, these conferences are self-contained and cater specifically to the House of Worship. They too provide some of the best experts and instructors available to teach in-depth classes to attending technicians while also providing a show floor with exhibitors from many major companies.

The WFX shows are smaller than the huge industry shows (like LDI, NAB, and InfoComm), but they are targeted specifically to the House of Worship.

Willow Creek Association is another excellent conference-type solution for the House of Worship. Hosted by Willow Creek Church, this conference is all about using media and technology and thinking outside the box. The reputation of Willow Creek inbues their church conferences.

There are also a ton of smaller regional conferences that are hosted by private companies, churches, and associations. These conferences are also advantageous to consider. They often require fewer travel expenses and sometimes, depending on the conference, can be a real value to your team.

DVD Training

One of the ways we primarily equip churches is via DVD training materials. This lets the church make a one-time purchase that can be used over and over again. The benefits are that the training is consistent, the graphics and illustrations really help stress the lesson, and each viewer is able to get a general survey of what is being covered. Viewers can go back and review at their leisure. Most of our DVD's also come with PDF manuals for classroom support.

The drawbacks are that the information is not tailored to your specific equipment and you cannot stop and ask questions. However, the cost is far less than a single trip, and the benefits can last a ministry a lifetime.

When looking for DVD training, make sure the training covers the area you want to learn (i.e., live sound, recorded sound, intelligent lighting, video switching, etc.). Many DVD's are simply remasked from other markets, while others are specific for the House of Worship. Each has its place in training, but church-targeted materials are a good place to start.

DVD training is a great way to educate your people without spending large amounts of money doing so. It's also a great way to get everyone on the same page. If you experience people on your team that need training (but they don't think they do), it's a nonthreatening way to do a group training exercise without arguing the fact.

Internet Based Training

One of the newest ways to train Houses of Worship is via low-cost, downloadable, on-demand training over the Internet. These videos can be purchased without having to incur the expense of packaging and shipping, there is no delay in receiving the materials, and you can start right away!

There are several models on the Internet. Some involve monthly fees, some are pay-per-view, and others are one-time purchases. Training is available on everything from changing a lamp in a fixture to programming a console to using Photoshop™.

Some websites worth looking at are:

- www.lynda.com
- www.churchproductionresources.com
- www.digitalcontentproducer.com

CONCLUSION

On-Site Training

The final training option that is commonly available is on-site training. These sessions offer a lot for Houses of Worship in that the expert can come directly to your facility, teach on your equipment, and tailor the training specifically to your needs and questions.

While sometimes a costly option, on-site training offers a level of detail that is unobtainable with any other method.

We find many Houses of Worship will often purchase a set of DVD's for the basics, then at a later date will schedule us to come out and follow up with on-site training.

Magazines

There are several magazines available, both in print and electronic formats. These magazines offer a monthly, bi-monthly or quarterly opportunity for your team to see what other churches are doing and catch up on the newest trends and equipment offerings. Many of the articles are insightful and offer excellent training.

Some magazines you might want to search for include:

- *Technologies for Worship*
- *Church Production*
- *Rev*
- *Worship Leader*
- *Worship Arts & Technology*

Books and Blogs

There are a myriad of books on various media technology subjects as well. While they might not be "worship oriented," as this one is, the information is unbeatable. There are books dedicated to specific topics, with hundreds of pages of information. For instance, Richard Cadena's Automated Lighting (9780240807034) and Steve Shelley's A Practical Guide to Stage Lighting, Second Edition (9780240811413), are all excellent books to read to further your study on specific areas of interest.

Likewise, the Internet is full of blogs and websites on subjects relating to media ministry. Some excellent ones to check out are:

- www.churchtecharts.org/Blog
- www.churchmedia.net

However you choose to get the training, it is a necessary part of technical ministry. Likewise, it's important to keep track of your team on a personal and spiritual level. The enemy chooses to attack us all in various ways – only together can we stand firm.

In the midst of the chaos that we call "service production," don't lose sight of the people in the equation. While our ministry might involve a lot of technology, all ministry is ultimately about people, and that should never get lost in the fray.

APPENDIXES

APPENDIX A
Working with Contractors and Having a Christian Witness

The House of Worship has a bad reputation in the world of technology contractors, and that's a sad statement. However, it's true. Many manufacturers have opened up entire divisions of their companies to tailor to the House of Worship, but in many cases that's simply a financial move. It's a true statement that the House of Worship out-buys many theatrical and touring markets. Every day the House of Worship becomes more vested in technology and the fruits that it can bring.

However, the actual contractor working with the House of Worship often has a very negative impression of the church. The reputation is so bad that several industry books that target the contractor as an audience warn them about the hazards, and several books aimed toward the House of Worship warn of the industry's impression.

Many times Houses of Worship can be difficult to deal with. Odds are, you are nodding your head as you read this. Many times the House of Worship is committee driven, often by people who are very well meaning but have no idea what reality is – especially with high-tech equipment.

Budgets are tight for everyone and, as we've mentioned in this book already, one ministry dollar spent on technology is a ministry dollar that can't be spent elsewhere. So it pays to be cautious and to try to stretch your budget as far as you can, but not at the expense of your testimony.

I've heard contractor after contractor tell stories of churches inviting them in to bid a job only to take the bid and use the information to do the job themselves. Providing information of that kind is called consulting, and these contractors usually charge for that service. If a contractor is offering design information as a part of the quote for the job, recognize that for what it is and don't take advantage of it. Either pay for the design or pay for the install, but don't ask a contractor how to do something and then just do it yourself. First, it's unfair; second, it makes the contractor feel used – a feeling we'd never want to purposely inflict on someone.

Likewise, be honorable in how you deal with your contractors financially. Keep everything in writing. Oftentimes, my company, as well as others like mine, will operate as an on-site consultant for a job. This way, the church is not in an awkward situation – it does not pay the contractor until the consultant signs off, approving the work. This arrangement makes the consultant the "bad guy" and protects the reputation of the pastoral staff and the church in the process.

Put everything in writing. This way, everyone knows what they are getting and there are no assumptions on either party's part.

Handle the contractor with love. Remember, a lot of these guys are not believers. Their business model drives them to the House of Worship because such institutions are a large target for A/V business. The way that they are treated, both as a person and as a business, might be the only opportunity the House of Worship has to leave a lasting impression.

When contractors make a visit to your facility, they are taking time from their day. That time is worth a lot. Be aware of this when you bring them out. Likewise, check their references thoroughly. This will help you avoid a bad situation.

Finally, don't expect everything for free or everything at a discount. Be honorable. If a price is too high, simply tell the contractor that it's out of your budget, and either continue shopping around for a better price or start saving toward the project. The House of Worship is nonprofit, but contract companies are not. Their employees have to make money and put food on the table just like everyone else. We should not expect everything for a discount or for free. Remember, a worker is worth his or her wages.

Awkward emotional situations can arise when you ask for a discount or a "freebie." On one hand, contractors recognize that Houses of Worship are nonprofit; but on the other hand, they need to make a profit. Don't guilt-trip contractors or make them feel like they owe you something. If you can't afford the work, move on until you can.

Above all, always act in a manner above reproach – not only with contractors, but with everyone you meet.

Many churches hire in temporary help for the main worship services. These people are often contractors as well, from all different walks of life; however, they are skilled in the A/V area and they pick up extra work with various churches. All too often people (including pastors) assume these people are either a part of the church or are believers. Many times, this is not the case, and unfortunately, they are exposed to the inner workings of the House of Worship, which can sometimes be unseemly. After all, we are all people and we all have our shortcomings. However, always assume the people you hire are not believers until you know otherwise. Treat them with love and respect, and provide a good testimony for them at all times. After all, this is what we should always be doing – not just when we think nonbelievers are watching.

APPENDIX B

Building Teams and Finding Volunteers

Perhaps one of the most frequently asked questions is "How do I find volunteers for my A/V ministry?"

The key to getting volunteers starts with having a good team philosophy. People often watch for a while before getting involved in something. For instance, if they see the pastor chastise the sound engineer from the pulpit, odds are they are not going to want to put themselves in that same position. This will make it difficult to get people in the "hot seat." If they see that people are working around the clock, time after time, and are always at the church, odds are they will not want to beat your door down to volunteer. Likewise, the spirit and attitude of your team will be another key factor in people's willingness to volunteer.

Many people become involved because they want to challenge themselves and learn a new skill. Do you have systems put in place to train and empower people to get better at their technical ministry? Or will they be thrown into a duty that they don't know how to master and will ultimately fail and become frustrated? This too does not make a healthy environment that encourages people to volunteer.

Many pastors become so desperate to get someone behind the sound, lighting, and video consoles that they will take anyone who walks near the equipment and shows even a basic curiosity. However, this is a critical area of ministry, and the people working in it should have the spiritual gifts to best match the work. You should look for people who have a good spirit about themselves. Your leaders in the A/V ministry should be spiritually mature; after all, the ones who work for them will look to them for leadership. Ideally, the people in your A/V ministry will be creative. For instance, it is much easier to teach a musical person how to mix than to teach a technical person how to have an ear for the mix. It's easier to teach a graphics person how to use presentation software than it is to teach an IT person how to choose complementary colors.

BUILDING GOOD TEAM DYNAMICS

Your team should have a good dynamic. If your team has healthy relationships, both with each other and the pastoral staff, you will find people more willing to get involved. If your team has a healthy dynamic, you will also find very little "kingdom building" going on and the drama will be left to the stage. This too will encourage people to become involved. Ideally, the A/V ministry forms a small group who hold each other accountable and live life together. Independent of what your outreach and discipleship strategy is, having the A/V group function as a small group is a huge plus.

We must also be careful not to burn out our volunteers. This happens easily in media ministry. These men and women are working countless hours during the week to pull things together. Add to this a huge production and you will quickly find people at the church until 1 AM and later. Many of them work a full 8- to 10-hour day, then forgo their families to get the media systems ready for production, often going one or two weeks nonstop. This can be burdensome and can cause a high burnout rate. It is something to avoid at all cost.

If you can work spouse support into your ministry, you will not be disappointed. Spouses are supposed to be helpmates to each other, and sometimes working in the area of media ministry pulls people away from their families. This can cause bitterness or resentment between the husband and wife; it can also cause an opportunity for the enemy to do work in the relationship. Obviously, this is counterproductive to everything we are trying to do. So again, it pays to have a healthy environment in which everyone serves. Consider having group socials or perhaps a fun work call that the spouses can help with! Perhaps it's labeling storage bins, sorting connectors, coiling cable, sorting gel, labeling video tapes, or duplicating CD's and DVD's. At least once a quarter, think of a way to involve spouses and once again bring everyone together as a group.

Likewise, I believe it's important for the leader to have quarterly fellowships, at a minimum. Something casual and away from the "technology" is always a good idea. Perhaps it's a backyard barbecue or a day out at a local lake – but whatever it is, make it about the PEOPLE.

TIP
Remember, our work is about people. Not what they can do for us or how much work we can get out of them, but about the relationship we can have with them and the opportunity to disciple them to walk more closely with God in their own individual lives.

Once you start to build these dynamics, you will see a healthier overall approach to media ministry. Now you have created an atmosphere that people feel good about being a part of. This will make your search for new volunteers much easier. People on the outside will see this and will have a much more positive outlook on the work that is happening.

FINDING PEOPLE

The first thing you can do to find people is to watch and listen.

Try not to jump on the "come work for us" bandwagon immediately. This is especially true if you find that someone within your fellowship does A/V by trade. It's really tempting to get the professional in place fast, but the reality may be that God has that person there for another reason. It can be quite draining to do A/V full time as a living and then come to church and do it some more.

Build relationships first. See where the person is with God and where he or she is in life. If this person is meant to work in the A/V ministry, God will bring it to pass. Get to know the person and begin to live life together.

The true "gold mine" in finding people is connecting with the inquisitive person who keeps looking at the soundboard and starts to ask questions. This is always an opening to talk to him or her further about being on the A/V team. Clearly, there is an interest; now take it to the next level by getting to know the person and identifying his or her strengths and spiritual giftings.

You will find that when you get people working within their area of gifting, they will be happy and tend to work hard.

If you need help, ask. Use the tools that you use best to drive home the point. For instance, turn it into a sketch. When you get ready to ask for help, turn all the lights off, turn all the sound off, turn all the video screens off. Then, announce acoustically from the stage, "Our media team works hard to pull off the things you see and hear. But we need help. Without help, this is what we have." Then bring everything back up. Media is often taken for granted. Look for ways to point out everything that happens, and then ask people to get involved.

Many times, people think that the media ministry is working fine and you don't need anyone else. So they don't get involved. You have to make your needs known.

People are also intimidated. What we do is fairly complex. They need to know that they will not get thrown in the middle of it and have to sink or swim. That's scary. Instead, make sure they know that there are systems in place where they will learn the skills they need and be gradually placed in an area of ministry. **HAVE THESE SYSTEMS IN PLACE**. Training is critical – not only for good service execution, but for bringing new people into the work as well.

Offer people the chance to sit backstage and just watch. This way they can see what happens and decide if they want to be a part of it or not. This is where team dynamics are critical. If potential volunteers walk into chaos and people yelling at each other or making disgruntled remarks about the pastor (no, that never happens), they are not only not going to want to be a part of your team, but they might question why they should be a part of the church at all! There could be more harm done than good – so good team dynamics are critical to finding new people.

Make "Help Wanted" signs and hang them around the tech area. It's funny, creative, and gets people's attention. Add a link on your web site where people

can sign up for more information on the media teams. Use all of your available outlets to communicate the need.

Invite prospects to your socials. This will help break the ice in a casual atmosphere and help them to form relationships with the people they would be working with. Do you see a common theme here? I believe if you make everything about relationships, the rest will fall into place.

Build in a way for people to slowly work their way into the media ministry. For instance, a new person would make an excellent A2 (the main engineer's assistant during the service) – that is, a person not actually mixing, but helping with setup and spotting cues during the service. Then you could slowly move this person into mixing a sound check or an evening/midweek Bible study. Next, you could let him or her mix the pastor's message during the service (this way he or she starts to get used to being behind the console in the actual setting but isn't really doing very much). Then let your volunteer mix some of the songs for worship and eventually turn him or her loose on an entire service (with someone assisting for a couple of services until the volunteer feels confident). Do you see how this is a much more inviting method than throwing a new person behind the console to sink or swim in the first week out of the gate?

If you adopt methods like this, the people on your team will become allies for finding new people. They will say, "Oh, it's easy to get involved – you can start by watching," and it will progress from there. This makes a scenario in which it is a lot more likely for someone to say, "Sure, I'll come in and watch" than by saying, "Hey! We need someone to mix the next service – you can figure it out!"

Another great source for volunteers is your musician pool. It's hard sometimes to let a guitar player mix the service because you don't want to lose the guitar player, but if you have two or three people that can play guitar, try letting the musician moonlight one or two weeks a month at the soundboard. This will not only get a musical person mixing, it will help bridge the gap between the technical and the musical. It will also let your technical people see and hear a new perspective on mixing.

Remember – it shouldn't be media team and worship team. We might talk about them that way to identify what we are talking about, but at the end of the day there is only one Worship Team. Everyone makes it happen in his or her own unique way.

AVOID BURNOUT

This is hard for many Houses of Worship. Let's face it, most of us have one person who does media ministry day in and day out. Maybe there are two or three people, but they are always there at the church working away. They are at every rehearsal, every service. This can wear on the volunteer.

However, media ministries are hard. If people don't do it on a fairly regular basis, they will never develop their skills to the point of excellence. They will always be a little timid and you will never truly get the person to his or her fullest potential.

So, you must find a way to rotate your people, but at the same time offer them enough hands-on time to stay proficient.

Many Houses of Worship have their own way of doing this. Sometimes one person mixes worship while another mixes the teaching time. Some will use one person for one service a day, for a month at a time, and then give this person a week or two off. Others rotate in weekly schedules or have one person mix Sunday, then skip the next Sunday but mix the midweek service, rotating back and forth.

Whatever you do, it's important to realize two things about your technical servants:

It's easy to hide in the technical realm. God wants to develop and grow everyone in the church. While working with technology, it's easy not to "hear" the message because you are "listening for the cue." It's sometimes difficult for God to do a work in someone because the person is so busy working for the Kingdom. It's important that your people have time for spiritual growth. If they are always behind a piece of technology, it's hard for this to happen (another reason the media small-group idea is so important).

The media team needs time to truly worship and get away from the crazy pace of technology support every once in a while.

Utilizing the idea of a small group outing is really helpful for reducing burnout. We have mentioned some ideas for this already, but others might be teamwork exercises, rope courses, paintball challenges, a day at the park – you get the idea. When you help encourage the group to live life together, the work they do becomes fun – not burdensome. This is the key to reducing burnout.

You should also find ways to make your training sessions fun. Include food – that always works. Think about something you could do as a group, and then incorporate training around it. I tell people who use our DVD training to do it as a group. Invite everyone over to the house one night, order in some pizza or make lasagna, enjoy the fellowship, and then watch a session on TV. Discuss it as a group and try it later at the church. Or perhaps watch it at the church and follow along, but go out afterward and play miniature golf or do something silly as a group.

Build relationships with your people. Make lifelong bonds that stand the test of time. The more the team understands each other and the church leadership, the easier it will be for them to execute good decision making during worship and help the entire team to reach their ultimate goal.

UTILIZE A SERVICE PRODUCER

We've discussed the idea of a service producer, but we haven't talked about how it helps you find people. One of the biggest turnoffs to working in media

ministry is the amount of responsibility someone has in making the right choice and the fear of making a wrong one.

With a Service Producer calling the shots, people are asked to do just their task. They can now make the lighting look good, make the sound balanced and well mixed, utilize a piece of software to get the words on the screen when they are told to do so, and so on. Now people don't have to worry about making a decision that's going to be very noticeable if they are wrong. With this fear eliminated, it's easier to find people to step in and run different systems.

Not everyone is cut out to be a leader or a decision maker. So if you can create an atmosphere where you have one or two solid leaders and decision makers, you make it much easier to find people who can do the other stuff.

BE CAREFUL HOW YOU CORRECT BEHAVIOR

This is probably one of the biggest things you can do to find new people – don't beat your current people up in front of everyone. For that matter, don't beat your current people up at all.

For instance, when there is a 95-dB squealing feedback in the house, the sound person knows he or she has messed up. There's no need to run back there and make a big deal out of it.

Let me give you an example by relating a story of one time when I was working with a church on a weeklong training course. It was Sunday and we were head-long into the service. The first service was executed by the main sound engineer and it went very well. We were now in the second service, and it was being mixed by one of the newer engineers. The church had a digital console, so the engineer was behind the console and I was downstairs watching the mix console from my computer. I was doing two things: First, I was trying to tweak an EQ issue we were having, and second I was trying to let the engineer feel some confidence by not hanging directly over his shoulder (although I had full control of the console via my laptop, should I need to adjust anything).

Suddenly, I heard a thump that was out of the ordinary for the mix. There was one person on the stage, but clear as day you heard "boom, boom, boom." At first I thought it was a passing car outside, and I started flipping through the layers on my laptop looking at all the channels. Then I saw it – the aux channel input was open and signal was pushing through. About the time I got the mouse to kill the aux, the engineer caught it and removed the aux send from the channel, and the thumping went away.

I knew what had happened. The engineer had left a channel open and tried to cue an upcoming video. The channel was muted, but it was pre-fade to the subwoofer. I didn't move. I didn't go running up to the sound console and talk to him about it. About a minute later, I noticed a laser pointer dancing over my laptop. I looked up and the sound engineer was looking at me with a sheepish look on his face and motioning me to come up there. So I did. Once I arrived,

he leaned over and said, "That thumping you heard was me." It was hard not to chuckle. Of course it was him. I knew it, he knew it – the entire church fellowship knew it.

I simply patted him on the shoulder and told him the mix sounded good. He didn't need to be scolded. We didn't need to have a lesson in auxiliary sends. It was a simple oversight. Instead, he needed to be encouraged – the mix did sound good.

When trying to improve the quality of your technical ministry, always focus on the positives. Have more positive than negative comments. For instance, if there is something wrong, address everything that is right or that has been improved, then talk about the one thing that needs work. Ideally, finish on another positive point. This is just good leadership. People have enough stress and failure in their lives without everything being negative. Praise them for the good they do, and then gently instruct on the things that need improving.

If you find that there are more things needing to be improved than to be praised, let go of some of the items that need improvement. Focus on the positive, then talk about the one or two glaring things that need to be worked on. Then next week, if there is improvement in those areas, say so, and then start to work on something else. Try to keep a positive outlook on the process and encourage the people doing it.

Sometimes, this is not possible. For instance, you might be under a production deadline and everything is falling apart. Sure, there are times you have to encourage your people to "put their big boy pants on" and fix some problems. But even then, you can do so in a way that fosters teamwork. Remember, ministry is about people. I can't stress it enough. When we lose sight of that, we are treading in dangerous waters.

TIP
Most of all – pray. Pray as a team, pray as an individual, and encourage prayer. Prayer is the answer, even to the most technical problems. As you pray with your team, seeking God in the good and bad times, the attitude will be one focused on Him and the result will always be a better one.

APPENDIX C
Checklists and Procedures

SOUND SYSTEM POWER UP/OFF SEQUENCE

Power-Up Sequence:

Console
Accessories (CD players, mini-discs, etc.)
Equalizers, compressors, and other processing equipment
Amplifiers

Power-Off Sequence:

Amplifiers
Equalizers, compressors, and other processing equipment
Accessories (CD players, mini-discs, etc.)
Console

TIP
It is important to turn the amplifiers on LAST
and to turn them off FIRST. This will reduce the chance
of getting speaker pops and thumps that can damage your
equipment. Ideally, you should use a power sequencer
that will allow you to turn your components on
and off with a throw of a switch.

LAMP CHANGE SEQUENCE

While it may seem like common sense, you would be surprised how many
people forget to unplug a device prior to working on it. This can result in
burns, electrical shock and potential glass rupture. For safety, always follow the
following sequence prior to changing a lamp:

- Unplug the fixture.
- Remove the lamp housing from the fixture.

TIP
NEVER TOUCH A LAMP WITH YOUR BARE FINGERS. Doing so will cause the lamp to prematurely blow as a result of the oil on your fingers. Should you accidentally touch the lamp itself, wash it thoroughly with alcohol and allow it to dry before using it.

- Check for bad wiring, cut wires, or other damage.
- Remove the lamp from the fixture.
- Check the base for excessive corrosion, looseness, or other potential problems.
- Firmly grasp the new lamp by holding the base and reinsert it into the fixture.
- Replace the lamp housing on the fixture.
- Plug in the fixture.
- Test.

BASIC SOUND CHECKLIST PRIOR TO SERVICE

- Arrive early and anticipate problems.
- Turn on the sound system.
- Play a CD and make sure each main speaker is functioning (by isolating each zone).
- Continue using the CD that is playing to check each monitor speaker for proper function.
- Ensure that all microphones are plugged into the correct channels.
- Do a "line check." Using a partner, speak into each individual microphone while the primary sound engineer brings up each individual channel (only one up at a time). If a channel doesn't work, troubleshoot and repair.
- Replace all batteries. Batteries are too cheap to try to "get by with" one that may be old. Make sure each wireless microphone and in-ear receiver has fresh batteries.
- Double-check that all microphones are pointing in the right direction and in the proper place.
- Make sure all cables are neatly taped and out of the way so the stage area looks clean and uncluttered – this will also help in troubleshooting.

APP: C
260

TIP
Realize that sometimes even a brand new battery will fail! Sometimes an entire box will be bad. Unfortunately, it's just the nature of the beast. If you use rechargeable batteries, always make sure to have a box or two of regular batteries on the shelf for the rare time that someone forgets to charge your rechargeables!!

PRE-SERVICE LAMP CHECK PROCEDURE

Before each service, you should perform a lamp check and dimmer check for every fixture in the house. There are two steps here that I like to follow: First, I encourage you to bring every fixture in the house up to 10 percent. This way you (or your assistant) can stand on the stage and visually check that each lamp is working. By keeping the percentage low (10 percent), you can stare at the lights without being blinded, see what's working and what isn't, and, most importantly, you won't overload your dimming system.

If you see any fixtures not working, investigate. Check the lamp, the circuit breaker, the fixture, the cable – whatever it is – until you discover why it is not working.

Next, from the console I bring up each individual channel, one at a time. You are checking to make sure the patch is still the same, that fixtures come up correctly, and that the focus is accurate. If anything looks wrong, fix it before the service.

CUE TO CUE

After you know the dimming is working, the fixtures are working and the focus is correct, you should run through each cue for the service (in order). Make sure they all work as designed. Be sure to look for odd house light intensities and other oddities.

STOP USING DUCT TAPE

Duct tape is a terrible thing for your cables and your floors, and makes a mess of everything. It was intended for heating and air systems – let it stay there.

Use gaff tape for your stage and cables. Gaff tape (or gaffers tape) is available from any theatrical supply house. It costs more money, but it's a cloth-based tape. It tears well, adheres well to carpets (without residue), and won't leave sticky gunk on your cables.

Gaff tape has a ton of uses. You can use it on fabrics, to safely tape cables, to mark locations on stage, or for practically any other use you can think of. It's also available in many colors. Don't let initial sticker shock scare you away – gaff tape is a solution worth its weight in gold!

APP: C

261

LABEL YOUR CONSOLES

I am amazed at the number of Houses of Worship that don't label their consoles! It's madness! Use board tape or even white gaff tape and label your control surfaces.

This tape can be removed, taped over, and changed as needed, but everyone will know what's where. Labeling is probably one of the simplest but most important things you can do to improve the quality of your A/V department.

VIDEO SLIDES

Before each service, computer operators should familiarize themselves with the songs, scripture, and other slides that will be projected via the service. Each slide should be checked for accuracy and spelling.

Lyric slides should change when it makes sense – during natural phrasings of the song. The way the lyrics are displayed and changed will often make a big impact on the meaning of the song to the worshipper.

The operator should go through each slide and make sure they all play back correctly and that the computer is functioning correctly.

VIDEO SCREENS

Each video screen that will be used should be checked before each service. You should look for proper aiming, unusual light spill on the screens, color consistency between the projectors, and brightness consistency.

Take the time to make sure everything is set correctly. Once you begin a service, the video screens become a primary communication method with the congregants. Make sure you have the best look you can so it communicates without distraction.

ARRIVAL TIME AND MEETINGS

It's important that you arrive early. Always work on the principle that nothing is going to work and you are going to have to fix everything. Leave yourself enough time to do this. Hopefully, when you arrive, everything will work and you will have plenty of time to focus on the work you are about to do. However, if there are problems, you will have the appropriate amount of time to solve them without rushing and risking a failure during the service.

Once you get on site, be proactive. Make sure you are "prayed up." Have a good spirit about you and be in as good a mood as possible. You are often going to be one of the first personal encounters of the morning with the rest of the worship team. If you are grumpy or ill-tempered, that will tend to set the mood for everyone else. Be of good cheer and encourage those you are working with. It will become contagious and make things go a whole lot more smoothly.

Be proactive in asking if there is anything you can do – from setup to pre-service checks. Perhaps it's as simple as getting someone coffee. Think of yourself as a servant who gets the opportunity to participate in worship.

Recognize guest artists and other special guests that might be a part of the

TIP
It's always better to be calm before a service or production than to be scattered and stressed. Proper preparation is the key to being ready for a service.

service. Introduce yourself and make them feel welcome. A side bonus to being friendly is that if you are the sound engineer, this is a great time not only to get to know the people visiting your service, but also to listen to them speak. Hear the way their voices sound naturally and note this so that you can "eq" your microphones more quickly during the sound check.

I never will forget the lesson I learned on the first sound system I ever installed. I had a buzz in a single 70 V speaker and just couldn't figure it out. I was jumping all over the place trying to solve the problem, but nothing worked. This was one of the opportunities in my life for my father to pass on wisdom that taught me a valuable lesson.

On this particular day, my father taught me how to troubleshoot. I was having a conversation with him about the project, and I told him that I just couldn't make this speaker stop buzzing. He asked me what I had done, and as I explained it to him, he looked at me with a grin and said, "You need to learn how to troubleshoot."

My father was an electrical engineer with over 35 years of experience. So I sat back and let him talk. At this point, it dawned on me that troubleshooting is a process. Regardless of what type of system you are working on, the art of troubleshooting is a step-by-step linear process – not a shotgun approach.

Many people are scared away from pro-audio systems because of their complexity and the fact that they can't see anything. For instance, a hum could emanate from anywhere. It is not like lighting, where the light doesn't come on and you can track back two or three steps to identify the problem. However, when you think logically, even a complex sound system becomes reasonably simple to troubleshoot.

TIP

The key to troubleshooting any problem is to think logically.

BREAK IT DOWN

The first thing you should do when troubleshooting is to break down the systems. For instance, in a lighting system you primarily have a power system and a control system. Take the more likely of the two and work backward from the problem.

For example, you have a lighting fixture that doesn't work. Working backward, first check the lamp – is it blown? If yes, replace. If no, then check the power at the source – do you have power? If you don't have a tester, plug a light that you know works into the circuit where the failure is. If the light comes on, the problem is within the bad fixture. It could be bad wiring, a bad plug, a bad lamp base, or any of a few other problems. However, now you know the problem is in the fixture. If the good fixture doesn't light, you know the problem is in the circuit.

Now, you would work from the circuit to the dimmer. First, you should go to the dimmer to see if the circuit is tripped. If it is, identify why the circuit tripped (too much wattage on the circuit or direct short), fix the problem, and reset. If the circuit is not tripped, try swapping the dimmer. If the problem continues, you know the dimmer is not the issue. At this point, I'd make a mental note that it could be a wire that has come unlanded or a similar connection problem; however, in an installed system this is less probable.

So, at this point I'd turn to my control systems. I'd make sure the channel was really up and that it was patched correctly.

The idea is that you keep working backward on a single track until you find the problem. In the example above, if you were to try a new lamp, then try control, then look to the patch, then swap a dimmer, and so on, without following a reasonable sequence, you could easily miss something in the fray. Logically progressing from the problem backward is the only sensible way to find the problem.

In the heat of battle, it can be tempting to start solving by shotgun approach. It's always best to take a breath, think logically, and work the problem one step at a time.

If the problem were in the sound system, the approach would be the same. Let's say you have a buzzing speaker. You have two primary systems – power and signal. Buzzing is typically a result of a bad ground. Knowing that, I'd start with the power. Starting at the amplifier, I'd disconnect the input to the amplifier and see if the buzzing continues. If it does not, then the problem is occurring before the amplifier; if it does, the problem is at the amplifier or at a point past it. You see, at this time you've disconnected the signal from the amplifier. If the buzz continues, you have eliminated the signal portion coming into the amplifier, so you don't need to check there; you've identified that the problem is independent of the signal coming in. Hence the problem must be with the amplifier, the power, or a connection between the amplifier and the speaker. If the problem did go away, then you know that there is something upstream of the amplifier causing the problem. More than likely, it's a bad ground in a cable or some other signal problem. So you'd work backward, disconnecting source after source until the problem disappeared. In this way you eliminate systems one by one until you find the offending problem(s).

From this point, you could start working on the problem.

So, the first lesson in troubleshooting is to break it down into systems and work the systems until you identify which one is causing the problem, then work that system in a systematic way.

THINK LOGICALLY

As mysterious as the problem may seem, it's not just some random unexplainable problem. Thinking logically will always lead you to the source of the problem.

Problems are found by taking it one step at a time. You prove that something is working and move to the next step. Ultimately, you find something broken and repair it. If that solves the problem, you are done; if not, you keep working from that point, looking for the next problem.

DRAW IT OUT

Sometimes you can get lost in the details, especially in a complicated problem. So take a moment and draw out the system. As you go through the problem, you can mark off the areas you test one by one. This will help keep you from missing something, but it will also keep you on track. Sometimes as you get into the problem, you can find yourself lost in the systems. A drawing will help you visualize the problem and stay in touch with what you have and have not done.

DON'T GET RUSHED

Take your time in solving the problem. Even if it's a high-pressure situation, take a breath and work methodically and at a reasonable pace. If you allow yourself to get rushed, you'll make mistakes, overlook something, and simply get frustrated.

Try to remove emotion out of the mix and rely on logic. When troubleshooting, logic is the only thing that will get you a solution. So take the time it requires to find the problem and then fix it right. Too many times we patch something together in a "temporary" fix that winds up being a permanent fix (until the next time it breaks). As the expression goes, "Beware the longevity of the temporary."

Ultimately, if you take care of your systems, they will take care of you.

LEARN HOW TO TROUBLESHOOT

If you are going to be involved in media systems, learn how to troubleshoot effectively. It's a part of the territory. Once you learn how to troubleshoot, you will be a vital asset to your ministry team. You'll also be surprised to see how this skill set transfers to many other facets of life.

Index

273